Re ax and enjoy life

Relax and enjoy life

149 ultimate stress busters

Elisabeth Wilson

Acknowledgements

Infinite ideas would like to thank the following authors for their contributions to this book:

Rob Bevan, Janet Butwell, Dr Ruth Chambers, Peter Cross, Dr Sabina Dosani, Penny Ferguson, Lynn Huggins-Cooper, John Middleton, Natalia Marshall, Alexander Gordon Smith, Elisabeth Wilson and Tim Wright

First published in 2008 as Slow down
Paperback edition published 2009 by
Infinite Ideas Limited
36 St Giles
Oxford, OX1 3LD
United Kingdom
www.infideas.com

A CIP catalogue record for this book is available from the British Library

ISBN 978-1-906821-08-1

Brand and product names are trademarks or registered trademarks of their respective owners.

Designed and typeset by Baseline Arts Ltd, Oxford
Cover designed by Cylinder
Printed in India

Brilliant ideas

Life skills for the terminally busy

2. GOING DEEPER – PRIORITISE YOURSELF
Turn back the clock

Prioritise your peace of mind

3.   LOOK OUTWARD – FIND TIME FOR WHO AND WHAT IS IMPORTANT

Relax and relish your relationships

'There is more to life than increasing its speed.'
Ghandi

There are two simple ways to reduce stress: the first is to carve out more time for yourself. The second is to be ruthless in taking control of your own life so you don't waste precious time.

QUIZ: **What's your priority?**
Taking time for yourself or taking control?

There are two reasons usually why life gets frantic – we let other people hijack our life or we are constantly playing catch-up with all that we have to do. Which is your main problem?

1. ☐ When was the last time you spent a day doing exactly what you wanted to do that benefited noone else but you? *Can't remember? Score 1.*

2. ☐ Do you spend time looking for house keys? *Yes? Score 1.*

3. ☐ Do you ever take a nap, watch a movie or lie around reading the paper on Saturday afternoon? *Never? Score 1.*

4. ☐ How much money is in your bank account right now? *Don't know? Score 1.*

5. ☐ Do you sometimes feel you've crossed the line from 'energised' to 'stressed out'? *Yes? Score 1.*

6. ☐ What year does your passport run out? *Don't know? Score 1.*

7. ☐ Do you feel you spend enough time with good friends? *No? Score 1.*

8. ☐ Your home should be a sanctuary but does it feel that way? *No? Score 1.*

Score 2 or more on **odd questions** and your priority is to make time for yourself. Turn to *idea 1* and start reading.

Score 2 or more on **even questions** and your priority is to take control of your life. Turn to *idea 12* and start reading.

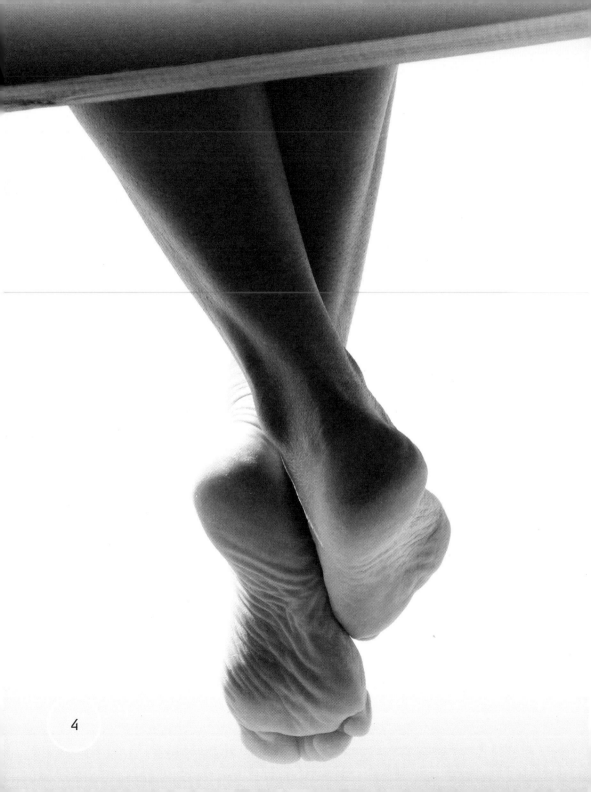

1

Part one

Relax and live your own life (only better)

You love your life – and it would be just great if only it were a mite less frantic. In the chapters in this section we have plenty of ideas on how to find more time to enjoy your life and how to get much more out of that time.

Mind willing but not sure you really can make the changes necessary? Tried to slow the pace of your life but always failed in the past? Take the quiz overleaf first – it can be a shock to realise just how pressurised our lives have got. And terrific motivation for doing something about it.

QUIZ: **How much do you need to relax?**
Give yourself a point for each ticked box.

1. *In the last week have you:*

Eaten a meal walking or standing up?

Repeatedly pressed the button for the lift even when you know it doesn't make any difference?

Walked up or down an escalator?

Eaten al desko (at your desk)?

Fallen asleep while commuting?

Broken the speed limit?

Packed most of your down time with activities you want to do/chores you have to do?

2. *In the last week, have you:*

Lifted the phone to a friend who has been on your mind?

Played with one of your children for longer than five minutes?

Stayed in bed after the alarm has rung?

Had a long bath?

Just sat, doing nothing very much with a quiet mind?

Deliberately switched off your mobile so you wouldn't be disturbed when you weren't doing anything else?

Found the time to chat to a stranger?

Compare your scores for the two sections.

If your score for the first part is three or more higher than your score for part 2 you're speeding through your life and it's time that you put your foot on the brake. Turn to *idea 1* immediately and then read *idea 10* for a wake-up call.

If your scores for parts 1 and 2 are within 1 or 2 points of each other you've got balance but still could benefit from relaxing. *Idea 6* will help complete the job.

If your part 2 score is higher than your part 1 score – fabulous. Time to start living. Turn to *ideas 95–104* for ideas on how to use all that time.

Find some time for you

QUIZ: **Why *are* you so busy?**

1. You're invited to an event that you think will be pretty dire. However, the person inviting you really wants you to go. You...
   a. Say 'yes' but feel irritated with yourself afterwards for not being able to say 'no'.
   b. Say 'yes' – You can arrive late, you don't have to stay long. There's always time to fit in something else.

2. You have friends coming for dinner but you have the day from hell and don't have time to cook. You...
   a. Spend a fortune buying food from a deli and all night apologising for not cooking from scratch.
   b. Send out for takeout – your friends know what you're like and half expect it.

3. You've had a busy day and a friend phones up for a good moan. You...
   a. Listen dutifully, you'd feel guilty if you didn't
   b. Listen for as long as you can but you haven't too long before you have to go out.

4. You often feel disappointed...
   - a. In yourself, that you don't get everything done that you'd like to.
   - b. That you don't have enough time to see all your friends regularly.

5. Your friends would say that you...
   - a. Are often harassed but always there for them.
   - b. Are often late but do your best to be there for them.

If you answered mostly 'a' you are busy because you have free-floating guilt and feel you have to do everything for everybody. Read *idea 2* for ways of saying 'no' nicely.

If you answered mostly 'b' you are busy because you pack so much into your time that there's no chance for you to slow down. See *idea 11* – it might bring enlightenment.

1. Find an hour a day to play

No, seriously is that too much to ask?

Shut your eyes. Breathe deeply. Picture what you'd do today if you had a whole hour each day to yourself to spend doing exactly what you wanted. 'Yeah, right', I hear you say. Like there's any chance of that.

SO HERE'S A QUESTION WORTH ASKING
I think that the 'desirable' things we'd like to spend an hour doing fall into two categories:

- The stuff we yearn to do because it's relaxing and fun.
- The stuff that's usually prefixed with a sense of 'ought to' because we know the rewards are worth it

In the first category is lying in bed watching a movie, in the second going for a run or quality time with the kids. We need to find the time for both. But both categories tend to get shunted to the sidelines of our life because of general business.

Exercise especially is one of the things that goes by the wayside when life gets stressful. How many times have you said 'I'd love to go to the gym – but I don't have the time.' So here's the useful question to ask yourself: how will I feel in five years' time if I don't?

Here's an idea for you...

On the move and stressed? Running cold water over your wrists for a minute cools you down on a hot day and it works to bring down your stress levels, too.

More to the point – how will you look?

Nothing in your life will change unless you take action. If you don't take the time to exercise, if you consistently allow family and work demands to be more important than your continuing good health, then at best you'll be more vulnerable to illness; at worst you'll be fat (and still more vulnerable to illness).

This goes for 'life dreams' that fall into the first category, like writing a novel or learning Russian. These have been called 'depth activities' because they add meaning to our lives. If I had a fiver for every time someone said to me 'I'd love to write a book but I don't have the time', I wouldn't be writing this one. Wannabe authors miss the point that in just an hour a day, you can make a start. Here's the big question: how will you feel in five years' time if you haven't at least tried?

People who spend at least a bit of their time doing the stuff that they want to do tend to feel that they're in control, and that's majorly destressing.

FIRST GET THE BIG PICTURE...

Get out your diary and write down everything you're expected to make happen in the next month. This could take some time. Include everything from work projects, organising baby-sitters, buying birthday

15

Defining idea...

'Life is what happens when we're busy doing something else.' – JOHN LENNON

presents, decorating the bathroom, taxing the car, medical appointments. OK, finished? Right, go through the list and mark the items that you can delegate to someone else. Be honest. What I said was the items you 'can' delegate, not the ones that no one else wants to do, or the ones that no one else will do as well as you. Don't worry. I'm not going to make you hand over all these tasks, just 10% of them.

In a spirit of solidarity, I've done this too. And guess what? On a list of thirteen things only two of them have to be done by me. Actually, only one – writing this book. (I could ask someone else to do it but the publishers might notice; or maybe they wouldn't, which is an even scarier thought.) The other one is to take my youngest for an injection and I could even delegate this if I wanted. But I don't. By actively thinking about it and deciding that it's something I want to do I've turned it into a positive – a choice rather than a chore. Big difference.

Now you've offloaded 10% of your work for the next month, think about dumping 10% of what you have to do every day. Jot down your 'tasks' for tomorrow. Quickly, without thinking too much, run through them marking each entry.

A – Must do   **B** – Should do   **C** – Could do

Now knock two of the Bs off the list and three of the Cs off and put down in their place an activity that you know would destress you or add depth to your life. Mark it with a whacking great 'A'. Soon, giddy with success, you'll be prioritising yourself all of the time. Well, at least for an hour a day. Life really is too short to wallow in the C-list – feeling busy but achieving nothing that matters.

2. Cure yourself of the disease to please'

Make 'just say no' your new mantra.

A huge amount of stress is caused by the inability to say 'no'. Result? We end up running to other people's agendas.

This is traditionally seen as a female problem. But I'm not so sure. On Saturday night I had dinner with a male friend who told me that for the first time in his ten-year marriage, he'd managed to get his wife to agree to going on holiday on their own without inviting at least two other families. Extreme? Yes. But I know many men whose entire domestic life is run to their partner's agenda and who feel that somehow they're being a bad dad or husband if they say no to the relentless socialising, child-centred activities and DIY set up for them by their driven other halves. I also know men who don't want to stay at work until 8.30 most nights, or go to the pub for an hour on the way home, but can't say no to the pervading culture of their workplace.

Now and then, all of us have to do things that don't benefit us much in order to feel that we're pulling our weight. But if it's a daily occurrence then we're going to get run down and ill. Worse, we're going to get seriously fed up.

Here's an idea for you...

If you just can't say no, try an intermediate stage. Next time some asks you to do something, say: 'I'm not sure, let me get back to you.' The breather is often enough to stiffen your resolve.

Try this quiz. Answer true or false to each of these questions:

I can't relax until I finish all the things I have to do ... *true or false?*

If I wasn't doing favours for other people most days, I wouldn't think much of myself ... *true or false?*

I seldom say no to a work colleague or family member who asks a favour of me ... *true or false?*

I often find myself changing my own plans or working day to fit in with other people's wants ... *true or false?*

I rarely, if ever, feel comfortable with what I've accomplished ... *true or false?*

I often feel I'm so exhausted that I don't have time for my own interests ... *true or false?*

I feel guilty relaxing ... *true or false?*

I find myself saying 'yes' to others when inside a voice is saying 'no, no, no' ... *true or false?*

I honestly believe that if I stop doing things for others they'd think less of me ... *true or false?*

I find it hard to ask other people to do things for me ... *true or false?*

Defining idea...

'I cannot give you the formula for success, but I can give you the formula for failure, which is: Try to please everybody.' – HERBERT BAYARD SWAPE, journalist

Add up the number of 'trues' you scored. If your score is between 7 and 10, you think it more important to please others than please yourself. If it's between 4 and 6, you should be careful. You're on the slippery slope to terminal niceness. If your score is 3 or less, you're good at saying no and keep your own needs in balance with others.

Aim for a score of under 3. Here are some ways to get there.

1. List your top 10 'no's', the things you want to eliminate from your life. Start each sentence 'I will no longer...'

2. Think of situations where you need to say no to improve your life. Imagine yourself in these situations saying no. Practise the exercise in front of a mirror if necessary. (This is brilliant. I tried it myself and the experience of actually saying no out loud, albeit in private, makes it much easier in real-life situations.)

3. Whenever you're asked to do anything, ask yourself: 'Do I really want to do this?' rather than 'Should I do this?' If the answer is no, then let someone else pick up the baton.

3. A zone of your own

Imagine a place with no phones, no noise, no hassles, no problems.

Peace is a state of mind, but it can also be a corner of a secluded garden, a cubby hole under the stairs, a bed that you share with no one else...or a garden shed.

My 'own' space is the garden shed and that's where I'm writing this. I live in a tiny, inner-city flat with three other people and it's impossible, short of locking myself in the bathroom, for me to be alone – and even then it won't be for long.

Mine is not one of those structures found in magazine articles where they interview people who work in 'sheds' at the bottom of their garden, and the shed turns out to be a fully equipped study, costing several arms and legs. Mine is quite literally a common or garden shed variety, so small that it wasn't even much good for storage, and so ugly that we nearly got rid of it when we moved in.

But since we gave it a makeover it looks great. Painted a soft white inside, with a wall shelved and devoted to my favourite research books, and room for a tiny desk, a comfortable chair, a sheepskin rug, a radio and a vase of flowers, Tardis-like it has expanded. When I'm inside it, it has all I need. I use it to get some peace to write, or just to sit and read quietly. In summer I sit in the doorway with a cup of tea and listen to the birdsong. In winter, I bring a blanket, light candles and cosy down to read a chapter of a book.

Here's an idea for you...
Write down what taste, scent, sensation, sound and sight immediately relaxes you and gather them in one place so they are always at hand. Velvet slippers, satin quilts, birdsong, pink light, roses. What sensual cues calm you down instantly?

Having a place you can call your own helps immeasurably with stress. I realised this on reading a book about sacred and meditation rooms around the world. The need for a quiet place is universal. I was intrigued by the ingenuity of those who clearly lived in the real world like me, where knocking out the centre of the house to build an atrium wasn't really an option. One woman had turned a fair-sized cupboard into her own sanctuary and filled it with objects significant to her. I was particularly taken by a sweet Sikh who kept his shrine on a breakfast tray and simply stuck it in a cupboard when it wasn't being used. (It was beautiful, too.)

Why bother? Because I think that in some very profound way having a corner where you can let your imagination run free and where you have control is deeply important to the human spirit. As a child did you have a secret place where you would hide away? Did you build 'shrines'? No? Think of the times you set up your favourite toys next to your bed, your dolls aligned looking just right on a shelf, 'special' power stones hidden in a secret place only you knew about? Children love talismans and can spend hours contemplating a feather, a flower, a broken bottle. This is how they destress away from their parents, in a world of their own where they choose objects that soothe them and where they decide their significance – not the grown ups.

Defining idea…

'You need a break from the frantic, noisy, overpopulated world. And permission to write, read, rest, draw, do yoga, listen to music, sit and stare – anything that evokes the deepest, most peaceful part of you.' – '**O**' Magazine

Creating a place where you can go that is uniquely yours, where you have chosen what you look at, what you feel, hear and smell will prove invaluable in your battle against stress. A room is ideal, a cupboard will do, a corner of a room – just one armchair will be enough. There you are in control and you can read, rest, dream, just be. It could be a seat in your garden, a daybed in the spare room, a dressing table, or simply a shelf or windowsill on which a simple cerulean vase holding a pink rose sits. But it should be so attractive to you that you long to sink into your sanctuary – that way you'll want to carve out a little time for yourself as often as possible so you can be there. And that's the essence of relaxation.

4. Leave the office on time

Reduce interruptions. Reclaim your evenings.

Take control. Don't let your working day be hijacked by others. The secret is to have your goals clear in your mind.

THINK WEEKLY, THEN DAILY

Don't be a slave to a daily 'to-do' list. See the big picture. On Monday morning lose the sinking 'I've got so much to do' sensation. Instead, think 'What are my goals for this week?' Decide what you want to have done by Friday and then break each goal into smaller tasks that have to be undertaken to achieve all you want by Friday. Slot these tasks in throughout your week. This helps you prioritise so that the tricky and difficult things, or tasks that depend on other people's input, don't sink to the back of your consciousness. It also means you are giving attention to all that you have to do and not spending too much time on one task at the beginning of the week.

Concentrate on three or four items on your 'to-do' list at once. You won't be overwhelmed.

WORK WITH YOUR ENERGY CYCLES

Some of us operate better in the morning, some in the late afternoon. If your job demands creativity, block out your most creative periods so that you can concentrate on your projects. Don't allow them to be impinged upon by meetings and phone calls that could be done anytime.

Make the phone call you're dreading Right now. That call that saps your energy all day. Just do it.

Have meetings in the morning People are frisky. They want to whizz through stuff and get on with their day. Morning meetings go much faster than those scheduled in the afternoon.

Check emails three times a day First thing in the morning, just after lunch and just before you leave are ideal times. Keeping to this discipline means that you don't use email as a distraction.

Limit phone calls Talk to other people when it suits you, not them. In my working life I receive around twenty phone calls a day. Answer machines don't help me personally – the call-back list is another chore. This is how I turned it around. The most time-effective way of using the phone is to limit your calls as you do your emails – to three times a day. Make a list of calls you have to make that day. Call first thing. If someone isn't there, leave a message and unless you have to talk to them urgently, ask them to call you back at your next 'phone period'. Just before lunch is good. That means neither of you will linger over the call. Your other 'phone time' should be around 4.30 p.m. for the same reason. Of course, you can't limit phone calls completely to these times but most of us have some control over incoming calls. I don't have a secretary any more to screen calls, but I very politely

Defining idea...

'Take a note of the balls you're juggling. As you keep your work, health, family, friends and spirit in the air, remember that work is a rubber ball and will bounce back if you drop it. All the rest are made of glass; drop one of them and it will be irrevocably scuffed, tarnished or even smashed.' – JON BRIGGS, voice-over supremo

say 'Sorry, I'm in the middle of something.' I tell the caller when I'll be free and most people offer to call me back then, saving me the hassle of calling them. No one minds that if their call isn't urgent. The point of all of this is to keep phone calls shorter by putting them in the context of a busy working day. Social chat is important and nice but most of us spend too much time on it. Time restrictions stop us rambling on. And this goes for personal calls too. Check your watch as soon a friend calls. Give yourself five minutes maximum. Or better still save personal calls as a treat for a hardworking morning.

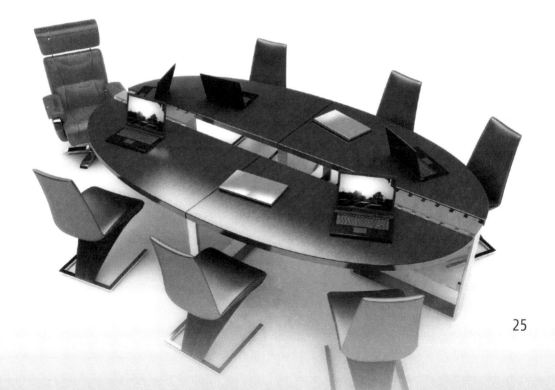

5. Are you too stressed to relax?

Stress saps energy and eventually our enjoyment of life. Stress makes us unhappy without us even realising it.

Do you accept the stressed-out state as just the way you are? Does it have to be this way?

Are you healthy? Hopefully, you'd answer 'yes' immediately. But if I told you that the World Health Organisation's definition of good health is not just an absence of disease but the 'presence of *emotional* and physical well-being' (my italics), you might hesitate. Few of us can remember when we last felt 100% emotionally and physically well. And the chances are that it's stress that's bringing you down.

One of the most pernicious things about stress is that we start to think the stressed state is 'just life'. We forget there was ever a time when we didn't get narked by the neighbours or feel guilty about how little we've achieved. These questions are geared to help you pinpoint how stress is affecting your well-being, perhaps without you realising it.

Imagine what it would be like to live without irritation and self-blame? Recognising these emotions as being the product of stress is the first step towards emotional well-being.

Here's an idea for you...

Lemon balm helps beat anxiety and irritability. You can buy lemon balm herb in supplement form at your chemist or find a supplier on the web.

STAGE 1

Do you have a sense of injustice or resentment against people you don't know such as big lottery winners or acquaintances who seem to have a much better life than you?

Do you say 'should', 'ought to', 'must' a lot?

Are minor niggles with neighbours or colleagues dominating your thinking?

STAGE 2

Do you feel guilty about being unhappy with your life?

Do you find it hard to motivate yourself?

Do you feel tired all the time?

Do you lack confidence and self-esteem?

STAGE 3

Have you had repeated problems for a prolonged period of time?

Do you have trouble remembering the last time you really laughed out loud?

Are the people around you a constant source of disappointment?

Do you think that life could be so much better if you could only resolve one negative issue?

Do you suffer from constant anxiety?

Do you think it is impossible to improve your situation?

If you ticked any statements in stage 1, you'll benefit from finding more pleasure in the life you've got – seeking out good feelings like a pleasure-seeking missile will make a huge difference to your state of mind.

Defining idea...
'Health is not simply the absence of sickness.' – HANNAH GREEN, writer

If you ticked any in stage 2, stress is having a serious effect on your mood and could be pushing you into depression. Read on, but consider talking to your doctor.

If you ticked any in stage 3 it's time to consult your doctor. You might benefit from counselling.

When repetitive thought patterns or overwhelming anxiety are making life miserable, you might want to consider a form of therapy known as CBT (cognitive behavioural therapy) which is designed to work in a matter of weeks. The therapist helps you explore and recognise thought patterns that are holding you back. CBT works on changing the way a person thinks about himself and how he fits in the world. These thoughts usually operate at the edge of a person's awareness and are often moulded in childhood. Once you have 'named' such thoughts, you can consciously change your thought patterns so that you begin to see the world through a different filter.

Whatever stage you're at, a very good place to start is by making your well-being a top priority. I've met many people who have suffered from emotional ill-health and one recurring theme when they talk about getting back to health is the importance of keeping it simple. They say that if they can just exercise a little, eat well and sleep at night, it helps immensely, even if they don't believe it will. Exercise and fresh air tires you out so you sleep. Brisk exercise three times a week for 30 minutes has been proven to be as effective as drug treatment in treating depression and only 8% of people who exercised became depressed again, whereas 38% 'relapsed' in the drug treatment group. Keeping to the same hours as the rest of the world means you don't get into the vicious cycle of living 'out of sync' which only heightens isolation even more.

10 instant calmers

1. Take off your watch. Work to you own agenda

2. Leave a hole in your diary on every day of the week. Use these gaps to relax.

3. Set your alarm 15 minutes early and just lie in bed.

4. Plant a tree, some bulbs, a flower.

5. Close your eyes: breathe in, breathe out. Do this nine times as often as you remember.

6. If you can't cook an entire meal from scratch, peel a carrot, toss a salad or steam some broccoli to eat with your ready-meal.

7. Bathe rather than shower in the morning.

8. Stand on the escalators rather than walk.

9. Take the bus rather than drive. Use the time to read or just look out the window.

10. Swap instant coffee for green tea. It's only the power of suggestion that makes you feel more zen – but it works.

6. Restoration day

When you're suffering from chronic, long-term stress. When your batteries are blown. When burnout is imminent, here is your emergency plan.

Book yourself a day out. By tomorrow, you will feel rested, stronger and more in control. (No, don't stop reading – you can make this happen.)

All you need is 24 hours. If you have children, ask someone else to look after them for as much of the day as possible. Remember that if you don't look after yourself, you will have nothing left to give to others.

The restoration day is based on three principles:

- Replenishing your body by giving it rest.
- Resting your brain by focusing on your body.
- Nourishing your soul with healthy simple food which will replenish the nutrients stripped away by stress.

BEFORE YOU GET UP
When you wake, acknowledge that this day will be different. Today you are going to shift the emphasis onto relaxation and releasing tension and replacing what stress has drained away from your body. Stretch. If you feel like it, turn over and go back to sleep. If not, read an inspirational tome – a self-help book, poetry, a favourite novel.

Here's an idea for you...

Go to bed at 9.30 p.m. today and every day this week if you can manage it. Don't watch TV if you're not tired – read or listen to music. People who do this have turned around their stress levels in a week.

Don't reach for your usual coffee or tea. Sip a mug of hot water with lemon: this, according to naturopaths, boosts the liver which has to work incredibly hard processing all the junk that goes into your body. Whatever, it's soothing. Every time panic hits because you're not doing anything – now and for the rest of the day – breathe in deeply for a count of eight and out for a count of eight.

WHEN YOU GET UP

Stretch for 10 minutes. A few yoga stretches are good, but it doesn't matter as long as you try to stretch every muscle in your body. You don't have to do this 'perfectly', it's not a work out, it's a reminder – you have a body: it carries tension and pain. Feel the cricks draining out. Finish with the yoga position known as the Child's Pose. Kneel with your legs tucked under you. Bend forward so your forehead rests as near to the floor as possible in front of you. A cushion on your knees might make this more comfortable. Take your arms behind you with hands pointing back and palms upward. Rest like this and breathe deeply. This is a favourite of mine because it releases tension in the neck and shoulders, which is where I store tension. I've been known to climb under my desk at work and do this for a few moments.

BREAKFAST

Try a fruit smoothie: blend a cup of natural yogurt with one banana and a couple of handfuls of other fruits; peach, mango, strawberries, pineapple. Thin, if preferred, with a little fruit juice. Sip slowly, preferably outside. Imagine the vitamin C zooming around your body replacing the levels depleted by stress. My advice today is to eat lightly and avoid (except for the odd treat) foods that strain digestion too much. Drink coffee and tea if you normally do; the last thing you want is a caffeine

Defining idea...

'Rest as soon as there is pain.' – HIPPOCRATES

withdrawal headache. But don't have more than, say, three caffeine drinks. Caffeine will make you jittery even if you're very used to it.

MORNING

Get outside – in the most natural surroundings you can manage. Ideally, lie on your back on the grass. Stare at the sky. Let your mind drift off. Or walk in the countryside, the park, sit in your garden. If you really can't bear to be still, do some gardening.

LUNCH

Have a huge salad combining every colour of vegetable you can think of – green, yellow, orange, purple, red. More vitamin C. Serve with a delicious dressing. This meal must include one absolute treat – a glass of wine, a dish of ice-cream, a piece of chocolate. Lie back. Indulge.

AFTERNOON

Go back to bed, or curl up on a cosy corner of your sofa. Watch a favourite movie, or a comedy show. A weepie can be great for this. A good cry is very therapeutic. Sleep if you can. Or if you'd prefer, listen to some favourite music.

DINNER

You should be hungry but feeling light. Eat another pile of vegetables – a salad or perhaps a stir-fry, following the 'eat a rainbow' advice given above. Have a fresh piece of fish grilled or fried in a little oil or butter. Think delicious but simple. Present your food beautifully; eat it by candlelight.

Go to bed early. Resist the temptation to watch TV. Read a book, listen to the radio or some music.

7. Turning Japanese

Learn from zen. The Japanese bath and tea ceremonies are as much about refreshing the mind and spirit as nourishing and cleansing the body.

Try this and you'll see why the Japanese consider having a bath to be a sacred experience.

This is my version of the Japanese bath and I try to make time for it once a week, mid-week, on a 'school night'. It works better than a simple candle-lit bath. I think that's because you have to put a (minimal) amount of effort in and that makes you feel you're taking back control. The Japanese bath has cumulative effects – the more often you do it, the more powerfully it works. There is a set pattern to it and the predictability is soothing in itself.

You will need: a balancing essential oil such as lavender or geranium or frankincense, an aromatherapy burner, a quiet place to sit, a clean bathroom (free of clutter), some soft towels (preferably warmed), a loofah or a body brush or sisal glove, a small bowl, comfortable clothes, a teapot, cup, strainer, loose-leafed tea, a candle, a blanket, and a minimum of one hour.

First, light the burner in the bathroom, lock the door and sit there quietly breathing in the fragrance, letting your mind quieten and be still. Lay your hands on your stomach, breathe in deeply and feel your stomach move out. Breathe out and feel your stomach contracting. Let go of all other thoughts. Now, and for the rest of this hour, keep your focus on what you can see, feel, hear and smell. Anxious thoughts

Here's an idea for you...

Invest in some special props that you keep purely for restoration. The sense of 'specialness' helps turn a bath into an event and with time you will be able to trigger relaxation with just part of the ritual. A cup of tea, a bath with the balancing oil or body brushing will in themselves be almost as good as the whole ritual.

will intrude, of course. When they do, imagine them drifting off in the fragrance rising from the burner.

When you're relaxed, undress and gently draw a brush or loofah over your body, working always towards the heart. Then step into the shower – it works best if it is at a slightly cooler temperature than usual. Lather up and get really clean. Concentrate on the noise of the shower. Let anxious thoughts disappear down the plughole with the soapy water.

Clean? Now step out the shower and run yourself a hot bath. Add a few drops of your balancing oil to the rushing water. Sink into the bath. When intrusive worrying thoughts interrupt, let them gently float away in the steam. When you're good and chilled out use the small bowl to ladle water all over your body. The idea is not to get clean but to focus your mind on pouring the water as gracefully as possible. Study the pattern of the falling water. Let yourself enter a sort of trance state, soothed by the repetitive actions. When thoughts of the outside world intrude, imagine them moving from your mind to being plastered on your body and then visualise them being swept away by the falling water.

Defining idea...
'There must be quite a few things a hot bath won't cure, but I don't know any of them.' – SYLVIA PLATH

When your mind is calm and you feel centred, emerge, wrap yourself in warm towels, dry off and dress in warm, comfortable clothing.

Hold this 'mindful' state. Go to a peaceful corner of your home and light a candle. (If you can do this whole ritual by candlelight, it will be even more restful.) Then make some tea, concentrating fully on every step. Watch the kettle boil, relax and breathe deeply and keep your mind as restful as possible. Concentrate on the candlelight if it helps. Make your movements as graceful and economical as possible.

Green tea gives the authentic 'Eastern' feeling. Herbal is good. But any tea will do. Finally, retire to your quiet place, cosy up with a blanket, sip your tea, inhale the fragrance, focus on the candle flame, keep your attention on it. Concentrate on the taste of the tea. Imagine anxious thoughts drifting away in the fragrant steam rising from your cup.

8. Runaway, runaway...

or to give it the grown-up name, retreat.

Some time alone with your own thoughts is deeply relaxing.

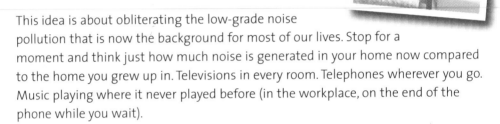

This idea is about obliterating the low-grade noise pollution that is now the background for most of our lives. Stop for a moment and think just how much noise is generated in your home now compared to the home you grew up in. Televisions in every room. Telephones wherever you go. Music playing where it never played before (in the workplace, on the end of the phone while you wait).

This constant barrage of noise is stressful. Here is a three-step plan to give yourself a break.

STEP 1: SWITCH OFF THE TV

TV will eat up your life. Some 9 year olds are watching up to four hours a day and these children perform less well on all measures of intelligence and achievement. TV does exactly the same thing to adults. It is such a very passive form of entertainment – it's been proven that just lying on the couch doing nothing burns off more calories than watching TV, presumably because without TV at least you're generating some thoughts in your head. Reclaim hours of your time by limiting TV to one or two favourite programmes a week. The rest of the time, switch it off. Listen to voice radio or music if you must have some noise.

Here's an idea for you...

Listen to some Bach, Chopin or Beethoven prior to falling asleep. It's been shown that people who listen to classical music in bed fall asleep more easily and sleep better than people who watch TV or listen to other sorts of music.

STEP 2: BE SILENT

This is difficult to manage if you live with other people. But take a day off work and experiment with no noise. No TV, no radio, no phone – switch them off. Silence is golden, honest. Not talking gives you the chance to listen to what your inner voice is trying to say to you.

STEP 3: RETREAT

The best way of doing this is to go on a dedicated retreat – all sort of institutions, religious or otherwise, run them. You can retreat and do yoga or dance or write or paint – or do absolutely nothing.

Of course, you don't have to leave home for that. It's much easier if you can escape but it's not impossible to put aside the hassles of everyday life and retreat in your own home. Clear away any clutter. Put away laptops, phones, diaries, PDAs – all work paraphernalia should be banished. Make your house as calm, restful and serene as possible.

Defining idea...

'Silence propagates itself and the longer talk has been suspended, the more difficult it is to find anything to say.' – SAMUEL JOHNSON

SEVEN STEPS TO RETREATING

1. Set aside at least 24 hours, preferably longer. Warn everyone you know that you don't want to be disturbed.

2. If you have family, do the best you can to escape. One way of doing it is to come back on your own a day early from a break, or leave a day after everyone else.

3. Get in all the food you'll need. Plan ahead. Make it especially tasty and nutritious. You don't want to have to venture out for supplies.

4. Switch off the phone. Don't open your mail.

5. Don't speak.

6. This is your opportunity to go inwards and not only relax fully but work out what you really want to do with your life. For that reason keep the TV and radio off. Listen to music if you like but make it classical and not too emotional. Limit reading to an hour a day.

7. Write in a journal, paint or draw, invent recipes. Do anything creative.

Better yet, be very still. Lie on the couch with a blanket and your thoughts. Breathe. Stay silent for as long as you can.

9. Perfect moments

The ability to create perfect moments is possibly the most valuable life skill you'll ever learn.

We humans are rubbish at predicting what will make us happy. We work our butts off to get the 'right' job. We scrimp and save for the big house and flash car. We think surely parenthood will make us really, really happy – and it does for a few years, until our adorable toddlers grow into worrisome teens. Human happiness is the holy grail, but no one yet has found a formula for it.

Or have they? In the last few years, neuroscientists have moved their attention from what's going wrong in the brains of depressed people, to exploring what's going right in the brains of happy people. And for the most part, it's quite simple.

Happy people don't get so busy stressing about building a 'perfect' tomorrow that they forget to enjoy this 'perfect' today.

It turns out that the surest, indeed, the *only* predictor of how happy you are going to be in the future is how good you are at being happy today. If you want to know if you are going to be stressed out tomorrow, ask yourself what are you doing to diminish your stress today? And if the answer's nothing, don't hold your breath. You won't be that calm and serene person you long to be any time soon.

Here's an idea for you...
Invest in an old-fashioned teasmaid. Waking up to a cup of tea in bed can get the day off to a good start for little effort on your part.

We can plan the perfect wedding, perfect party, perfect marriage, perfect career. But we have absolutely no idea if when we get 'there', a perfect 'anything' is going to be delivered. The only thing we can do is guarantee that today at least we will have a perfect moment – a moment of no stress where we pursue pure joy.

What is a perfect moment for you? I can't tell. For me it is whatever helps trigger me to remember that unknown, unquantifiable, profoundly peaceful part of myself. Let's call it 'the spirit'. We could call it 'Joe' but it lacks that certain mystical something that I'm aiming for. Anyway. When I'm having a perfect moment, I'm absolutely happy, absolutely content. That doesn't mean everything is alright in my life, but it does mean that for this one moment, I've got enough to feel joyful.

Some people slip in to a perfect moment as easily as putting on an old coat. But me, I'm a pragmatist. I think if you want to have a perfect moment, you have to plan for it early before your day is hijacked. So I try to start each day with a perfect moment. All debris, mess and clutter is banished from my bedroom the night before. When I wake just about the first thing I see is a bunch of fresh cut flowers – big squashy pink peonies are a favourite. Before my eyes are quite open, I reach out and grab a book of poetry from my side table and I read for five minutes. I choose poetry because it reminds me that life is a lot bigger than me and infinitely more interesting.

Defining idea...
'Happiness not in another place, but this place...not for another hour, but this hour.' –
WALT WHITMAN

But your perfect moment might be snatched late at night, listening to jazz by candlelight when the family are asleep. Or it could be a glass of chilled wine as the sun slips beyond the horizon. You might best be able to access a perfect moment by running round your park or through practising yoga. Listening to music while you exercise often heightens the sensations of being in tune with your body and tips you into joy. Preparing, cooking, eating food can give perfect moments. Gardening is a good one. Sex is reliable. We all know the sensation of feeling 'bigger' than ourselves. All you have to do is give yourself the space to feel it more often – ideally, at least once a day.

But ultimately, only you know your own triggers. Write down a week's worth and plan for them. Schedule them in your diary. It obviously doesn't have to be the same activity every day and sometimes despite your best intentions, it all goes belly up. (I only get to read poetry when I'm not woken by the kids clamouring for cartoons and cereal.)

But planning for perfect moments means they are more likely to happen. Even if you don't believe now that striving for perfect moments will destress you, try it. At least you will be able to say 'Today, there were five minutes where I stopped and enjoyed life.' Enjoying life today is the only certainty you have of happiness and your best chance of being less stressed tomorrow.

10. Burned out?

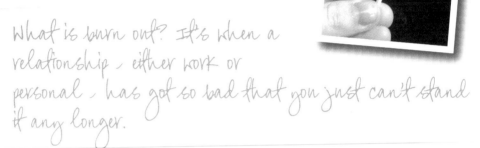

What is burn out? It's when a relationship, either work or personal, has got so bad that you just can't stand it any longer.

If the only route of action that appeals is hiding under your duvet until Christmas, it's time to reassess.

You're stressed. But just how stressed? Here are a few statements worth answering.

	Score
You fantasise a lot about your perfect life that doesn't include your dull/annoying partner/job	+1
You say 'I can't take it any more' at least once a week	+2
You feel unappreciated	+3
Tension is beginning to affect your health	+3
You wake up dreading the day ahead	+3
All you want to do in the evening is slump in front of the TV and sleep	+1

Score

4 or under = mild level of dissatisfaction. This indicates that the present situation is stressful but potentially saveable.

9 or under = life is not good and you know you need to act.

10 or over = burnout imminent.

Here's an idea for you...

Spend 10 minutes every evening planning your next day. It's proven that you get one-fifth more work done if you review what you want to accomplish the next day in advance. Plus what you do achieve will likely be of higher quality.

Dr Dina Glouberman, who has written on the subject of burnout, defined it as what happens when 'The love or meaning in what we are doing goes, but attachment drives us to carry on.'

It's this attachment that you need to question. It's clear that some situations are easier to leave than others but if you have tried all you can to fix your particular hell and nothing improves, it's time to admit the unhappiness to yourself and others, and move on. In our competitive world, it's hard to say 'I may have made a mistake.' The more time you've invested in the wrong life, the harder it is to give up on it. But the first step is simply admitting to yourself and perhaps a few trusted compadres that yes, you are human, you made a mistake.

There's nothing wrong with being unhappy with your life. See it as a positive. What it signals is that you have outgrown your present situation and that it's time to move on. Otherwise, the stress of living a life that isn't yours can be fearsome. You risk burn out – a state of collapse where you lose all joy in life. Your body gives out and your spirit gives up. It is extremely painful and can take months, even years to come back from.

Defining idea...

'*Stress is an ignorant state. It believes that everything is an emergency.*' – 'O' Magazine

But even if you do burn out, it's not an unmitigated catastrophe either. For many it's the beginning of a new more enlightened life. After spending their time in the metaphorical wilderness, they rethink their life and choose a new route.

11. What sort of time traveller are you?

Are you a P or a J? Finding out will turn your life around.

There are two main ways that human beings relate to time. Finding out yours could re-energise every aspect of your life, with no effort whatsoever.

Everyone's heard of Carl Jung, but few people realise the extent to which his ideas are still influencing us today. One of Jung's big ideas was to identify four pairs of 'preferences' – ways that human beings organise their world. A mother-daughter team of psychologists – Myers and Briggs – developed his ideas and Myers-Briggs theory was born. If you've applied for a job with a corporation, there's a good chance you've taken one of their tests of personality. Understanding where you fall in one of the preference pairs – what's known as the J-P dichotomy – could boost your energy by helping you understand how you use deadlines.

I won't bore you with what J and P stand for – it's irrelevant. What you need to know is that Js like things to be organised. It's essential for them to regulate and manage their lives. The want to reach decisions, get closure, move on. They need a plan, they need a timetable to achieve the plan and they need to be able to get on with the plan. If you are a J, your energy will be leached away if you're not allowed to follow your plan – usually by your P boss who won't sign off on it.

Here's an idea for you...
A quick test to find out whether you're P or J. Design a poster advertising an upcoming event. If you're a typical J, the date and time will feature strongly. If you're a typical P, you may have forgotten to mention them at all!

Ps value spontaneity and flexibility over organisation. They need the freedom to go with the flow. For example, they may plan to work all day and then when offered an invitation to lunch, accept it. Then they may well work doubly hard through the morning to make up time. Or they may not and miss their deadline. They'd rather experience life than control it and they feel confined by plans and definite commitments. They are energised by their resourcefulness in adapting to the demands of the moment.

You probably know if you're P or J by now, but if not, get a piece of paper and pen and write for a minute the answer to this question: What is really important about plans and planning?

If you're a typical J, you will have tackled the question with enthusiasm. If you're a typical P, your feelings will have ranged from slight feelings of dread and resistance to complete boredom.

How does understanding your attitude to time affect your energy levels?
Js need a lot of stamina. You'll worry about projects in advance, and although Ps seem to work harder right at the end to finish a project, you'll probably spend more hours on it because you'll set aside time and the job will expand to fill the hours. You need to exercise, eat well, sleep and do all you can to support yourself on the long haul, especially if your boss is a P because they will drive you mad by refusing to follow a plan.

relax and enjoy life

Defining idea…
'There is no pleasure in having nothing to do; the fun is in having lots to do and not doing it.' – MARY WILSON LITTLE, American writer
(She was a P if ever there was one. If this quote irritates you, you're definitely a J)

Ps, no matter how you buck against it, would benefit from a little bit of preparation each day, weeks in advance of a deadline. You will still leave significant amounts until the last minute because that's how you work best, but at least the groundwork will be done. In extreme cases Ps just don't 'see' deadlines anymore, but other people do and that's very stressful. Also, don't beat yourself up for being lazy because you work in fits and starts. The times Ps 'goof off' are just as vital as the times they work intensely.

Hell is other people

Another point worth making. Both groups often profoundly mistrust the other group's way of working. Js think Ps disorganised and simply making life more complicated than it needs to be; Ps think Js anal and missing out on the best bits of life. Take a minute to dwell on whether your colleagues and, most importantly, your boss are likely to be Js or Ps. How much energy are you expending in placating groups that are the opposite of yours? One P friend of mine transformed her working life by throwing a sop to her J boss. She started showing her complex schedules and plans of work. She continued to work in the same haphazard way, but her boss's attitude to her was transformed. It was a win-win because my friend was more autonomous and her boss felt there was some control.

Relax and take back control

QUIZ: **Are you in control of your life?**

Read the following statements and give yourself 2 points for every 'agree', 1 point for every 'not sure' and 0 for a 'disagree'.

If you want a job done well, do it yourself.
Agree   Not sure   Disagree

I seldom admit defeat.
Agree   Not sure   Disagree

I feel that I'm on top of my life.
Agree   Not sure   Disagree

I'm a 'cat' rather than a 'dog' person.
Agree   Not sure   Disagree

I could easily work from home.
Agree   Not sure   Disagree

There's not such a thing as 'destiny' – you make your own luck.
Agree   Not sure   Disagree

I feel I can achieve anything if I try hard enough.
Agree   Not sure   Disagree

'Insurmountable' problems can be solved one step at a time.
Agree   Not sure   Disagree

My life is on course.
Agree   Not sure   Disagree

I don't feel comfortable following the crowd.

Agree   Not sure   Disagree ☐

I operate on my own agenda at work.

Agree   Not sure   Disagree ☐

When I think of what I have to do, I feel energised.

Agree   Not sure   Disagree ☐

Big Brother may be watching but I don't let that change my behaviour.

Agree   Not sure   Disagree ☐

I am the captain of my ship.

Agree   Not sure   Disagree ☐

Scores

20 or over. You feel strongly in control of your life which should make it easier for you to make the changes necessary to slow down. Try *idea 8* for a shortcut to a sense of calm.

14–19. You feel moderately in control but still are likely to have your plans hijacked. Use the information in *idea 25* to help you see the long term consequences of not slowing down.

13 or under. You often feel powerless to take control. Try reading *idea 16* to get some insight into why you might be doing things you don't really want to.

12. Never procrastinate again

Procrastination is stress's best friend. It's not big, it's not clever but for most of us, it's a way of life.

Procrastination is slowing down, but not in a good way. Here is the best method I've ever found for overcoming it. It was taught to me by life coach Mark Forster. An interesting man, he achieves more in a day than most of us do in a week. But he used to be disorganised and chaotic (he says!). None of the advice on procrastination ever worked for him (we all know that feeling), so he invented his own techniques. (You can read more in his brilliant book *Get Everything Done*.)

Mark calls this the rotation method. You need pen, paper and a watch but a kitchen timer with a bell works best.

1. First make a list of your tasks. (Here is my list for this morning: write two ideas for this book, organise dinner party, do washing, make phone calls to pay some bills.)

2. Against each item write 10, 20, 30. These represent blocks of minutes that you are going to spend on each item in turn. So my list would look like
   Write book 10, 20, 30
   Organise party 10, 20, 30
   Laundry 10, 20, 30
   Phone calls 10, 20, 30

Here's an idea for you...

Scan your diary for big projects coming up. Tomorrow spend just 10 minutes working on each project. By giving a tiny amount of focused attention regularly to projects, well in advance, you accomplish them without even noticing.

3. Start with the task that puts you off least. Set the kitchen timer for 10 minutes. Do the task for 10 minutes. (I choose the laundry – a mindless chore that I quite enjoy. I have my load on comfortably within the 10 minutes.)

4. When the timer rings. Stop. Wherever you are in the task. Stop. Take a pencil and score through the 10 next to the task.

5. Set the timer for 10 minutes. Start the next task. (In my case, it's paying bills. It takes me the whole 10 minutes to get the paraphernalia together. Note: I'm no longer resentful about paying the bills, I'm irritated that I can't get on with it.)

6. Score through the 10 on the list and start the next task (Writing. The task that is most formidable, but buoyed on by the fact that I've made a start on the mundane tasks, I sit down, make some notes and start typing. The timer rings mid-sentence. Note: I'm disappointed that I have to leave my task and move on.)

7. Score off 10 and start the next task. (I look through recipe books for 10 minutes and make some notes on whom to invite.)

8. Score off 10 minutes. Now move on to the first task again but set the timer for 20 minutes. Repeat the entire process. (Laundry again. The first load isn't finished, so I sort the laundry so that it's ready to go in the machine. That takes 10 minutes but I score off the 20 next to laundry as there's nothing more I can do. I set the egg

Defining idea...
'Procrastination is the art of keeping up with yesterday.'
– DON MARQUIS, American humorist

timer to 20 minutes for the bills. For most of that time I listen Handel's Water Music played on a xylophone but I am halfway through paying the last bill when the timer goes. Score off 20. I move back to the writing with a sense of relief – that's the job that's most important but because of my 10-minute start I'm raring to go. When the timer goes after 20 minutes, I go back to the party, finalise the guest list and decide on the menu. Back to the laundry – 30 minutes. Unload and hang out the washing, set off the next load – well within the 30 minutes that they have now been allocated. Now I go back to my computer and complete another 30 minutes. After 30 minutes I pause and look at my list. All the chores have been completed. I don't need to do any more on the party – I've made a real start. And I'm where I want to be – sitting at my computer and enjoying writing, so I set my timer for 40 minutes and carry on, promising myself a cup of tea at the end. I'm so into it after 40 minutes that I bring the cup of tea back to my desk and carry on until lunch time.

WHY THIS WORKS FOR ME WHEN NOTHING ELSE DOES

- It helps you overcome resistance. You can assign a task 5 minutes to begin with – although I started on 10 here. Anybody can do just about anything for 5 minutes.

- It has built in end-effect. This is the phenomenon well observed in employees in the two days before going on holiday – they get more done in two days than they usually achieve in a month. The rotation method keeps you focused because you build in artificial 'deadlines'. In other words, you'll get more done in three 20 minute blocks than in an hour of unfocused grind.

- It has an innate momentum of its own. The easy tasks propel you into the difficult ones.

13. Never lose your keys again

Often you can't remember where you left the car keys. Sometimes you can't remember where you left the car.

Memory lapses aren't necessarily the first indication of Alzheimer's, so don't worry. But if they're increasing in frequency it could be that your memory is a casualty of a multi-tasking lifestyle.

Juggling a hectic schedule can have a disastrous effect on your memory. The 'fight or flight' response actually sharpens our cognitive abilities. But chronic stress over long periods of time is a different matter. If your mind is bustling ahead to deal with the day's problems it's concentrating on other things and you're not noticing what's going on around you. Not surprisingly you can't retrieve memories of what you did today because your mind was actually living in tomorrow. This in itself is deeply stressful.

WHAT THE HELL'S HIS NAME AGAIN?
The only answer is to be aware that when you're busy and stressed you're not taking in information in the same way and you're not going to be able to recall it. Make like a boy scout and be prepared. For example, on a busy day when you meet someone new, be aware that you are more likely to forget their name. Make more effort than usual during introductions. Repeat a new name inside your head. Use it again in conversation as soon as you can.

Here's an idea for you...
Try a supplement. There's some evidence that the herb gingko biloba improves blood flow to the brain and hence memory in the elderly, but it's likely that it will be proven to help younger people too. You can buy supplements containing gingko at chemists and health food shops. Sage is also good for memory.

This repetition is important. When learning anything new during a stressed period, repeat it to yourself and if possible say it out loud three or four times, increasing the amount of time between each repetition. This 'repetition, pause, repetition' pattern strengthens memory.

This technique also works for items or tasks that you have to remember – and always forget. If you're fed up going to the supermarket to buy tomatoes and coming back with everything else but tomatoes, try the above. If it doesn't work, then make allowances and leave notes in your purse or on your toothbrush, places where you will certainly check. Don't rely on your memory.

WHERE ARE MY KEYS?
What few people realise is that most routine actions will cause memory problems if you do them differently every day. The very fact that we do some things over and over again can make them easy to forget. That's because when you put items you use frequently in different places from one day to the next, you have to block the memory of what you did with them yesterday and the day before in order to find them today. Which is why it seems you've spent a half of your lifetime looking for your keys and wallet.

Defining idea...
'Happiness is nothing more than good health and a bad memory.'
– ALBERT SCHWEITZER

THE ANSWER

The easiest thing is to create a memory pot – a bowl or basket near your front door where everything goes as soon as you get home, and which you check before you leave the house. This is not as simple as it sounds – it takes about two or three weeks before it becomes second nature. And even then, it makes sense to keep a spare set of keys somewhere separately.

DID I SWITCH OFF THE IRON?

The phenomenon of worrying endlessly if you've done something that you've done a hundred times before is down to something called 'social misattribution', the fancy name for recalling the action but not realising that you performed it on another occasion. Again, it's because you're not focusing on the action while you're doing it.

THE ANSWER

No matter how tied up your brain is with problems, take the time to check what you're wearing. As your arm reaches out to switch off the iron, note 'Oh yes, blue shirt.' When you get the doubt that you've done an action, recall what your arm was wearing when you did it. Look down. Blue shirt. Check. On you go with your day. Again, just like the above habit, it takes about two or three weeks for this to become second nature when we're undertaking all those activities that we do on automatic pilot – locking the front door, switching off the oven, picking up the children...OK, scratch the last one.

14. What's your Plan B?

Take the insecurity out of your life. All you need is a Plan B.

The life you're living is Plan A. Plan B is what happens if it all goes pear-shaped. Know how you'd get from A to B and you remove a huge chunk of the stress that is caused by worry about the future.

It was a former boss who taught me the value of having a Plan B. Magazine editors have one of the most glamorous jobs going – great pay, company car, free holidays, free clothes...

And they have one of the most insecure jobs you can imagine. The higher they climb, the faster they can fall. Their job is highly stressful and they routinely work their butts off for an employer only to be shunted to the side in a matter of hours if they don't deliver. 'How do you stand it?', I asked my former boss. 'Always, always have a Plan B,' she told me breezily.

DECIDING ON PLAN B
Every life has its fair shares of upsets and reversals of fortune. An essential of the Plan B is to be able to look at your life dispassionately and see potential stress lines – where your life is likely to come apart.
For instance:

Here's an idea for you...
Tomorrow open a completely new bank account for your Plan B. Start a direct debit and pay in until you've built up your emergency fund total of three months' expenses. Knowing you've got enough money to finance your dream makes your present life a whole lot more fulfilling.

- If you work in a volatile industry, it's work. Your Plan B is what you'll do if your dismissal slip lands on your desk.

- If your relationship is struggling, your Plan B is what you'll do if you split up.

- If your health isn't good, your Plan B is to research methods of financing your life if bad stuff happens.

Now please, don't get cross. I'm not trying to rain on your parade or say that your happy world is about to fall around your head. I'm merely concerned with stress proofing your life, and Plan Bs are brilliant for this. No one says you'll ever need Plan B but having one is invaluable comfort when you wake in the middle of the night and can't get back to sleep because of catastrophic thoughts swirling around in your brain. You know those nights? Well, with a Plan B, you worry for about 30 seconds, go 'Oh, I remember, I've got a plan B', roll over and doze off again.

For Plan B to work it has to be a fantasy built on reality. By that I mean it's not just a vague 'Oh, I'll sell the house and move to France.' It's more concrete than that.

BUILDING THE DREAM
First, decide on your Plan B and start a file. Add cuttings, pictures, information to it. Suppose you were going to sell your house and move to France. Your file for this would include information on people who had done the same thing, and research on how much you'd need to live on per year in France if you were mortgage-free. You'd also put in notes on the school system if you have young children.

relax and enjoy life

Defining idea...

'Reality is the leading cause of stress amongst those in touch with it.'
– JANE WAGNER and LILY TOMLIN, comic writers

Your Plan B should be realistic, but it should be awesome. It shouldn't be a case of 'Oh well, I could always move back in with Mum.' It should be training to become a chef, starting your own business, backpacking around Mexico. It should make your heart sing. Plan realistically but dream big.

BUILDING AN EMERGENCY FUND

Think about the financial position you'd need to be in to make it work, and take steps to achieve it. The ideal sum for a 'just-in-case fund', whatever your Plan B, is eight months' worth of living expenses. Go through your bank statements, adding up your outgoings for a year – this is truly frightening – take the total, divide by 12 to get your average per month and then multiply by eight.

Still reeling? Yes, it does that have effect. OK, eight months is ideal but it's that – an ideal. However, I'd say that a priority for anyone who wants to stress proof their life is to build up at least three months' living expenses. That's the bare minimum that you should have easily accessible in a bank account according to the experts.

What happens when you spend more of your time thinking about Plan B than worrying about Plan A? Then it's time to move your life on.

15. Achieve the life–work balance in ten minutes

I refuse to call it work–life. It should be life–work. And that's what achieving it entails - a life–work.

Unless of course, you've read this idea.

Just a small point, but have you ever met anyone who felt they've achieved the perfect work–life balance? I've been thinking about it since lunchtime and I'm still struggling to come up with a name.

One of the most pernicious things about stress is the way we don't notice how it switches our attention away from what we value and love in life until it's too late. So here are some clues to work out if stress is stomping all over your life–work balance...

1. Do you feel like your day is spent dealing with difficult people and difficult tasks?

2. Do you feel that those you love don't have a clue what's going on with you and you don't have a clue what's going on with them?

3. Do you regularly make time for activities that nourish your soul?

4. Do you feel you could walk out the door of your house and no one would notice you were gone until the mortgage had to be paid?

Here's an idea for you...
Designate Saturday 'family' day and Sunday afternoon 'selfish' time. We can usually find an hour or so on Sunday afternoon to spend on ourselves – just don't let it get filled with chores or your partner's agenda.

Yes, you guessed it? Number 3 was the trick question. Answer yes to that one and you're probably alright. Answer yes to the rest and you could be in trouble.

In a nutshell: make sure you're putting time and effort into the people and activities that make your heart sing and it really is very difficult to buckle under the effect of stress.

But I think too much emphasis is put on the stress caused by the 'work' part of the equation and not enough placed on the stress caused by the 'life' bit. Everyone assumes that all we need is less work, more life and all would be harmonious balance. Hmmm.

Where it has gone all wrong for so many, women especially, is that they've cleared enough time for the 'life' part of the equation but not taken into account that it isn't necessarily restful or enjoyable. This is no idle observation. Research shows that men's stress hormones tend to fall when they get home whereas women's stay high after the working day, presumably because they get home to confront a dozen chores and hungry kids. Your children may be the reason you get out of bed in the morning but you need to accept that spending time with them is not necessarily any less stressful than work – in fact, it often makes work seem like a walk in the park. More time with your kids is not necessarily the answer.

Defining idea...
'The best and safest thing is to keep a balance in your life, acknowledge the great powers around us and in us. If you can do that, and live that way, you are really a wise man.' – EURIPIDES

More time with yourself, very probably, is.

That old saw is true – if you don't look after yourself, you can't look after anyone else. And all it takes is just ten minutes a day.

And ten minutes of selfishness every day is enough to make a profound difference in your ability to achieve a life balance that works. Try it.

16. A shortcut to coping with obstacles

For every behaviour or action, there's a payback. When you work out the payback you often drain away a lot of stress from a situation.

OK, this is a brutal one. Don't read on if you're feeling fragile. This is where we take the gloves off.

These are some of the random (cruel) thoughts that have crossed my mind during conversations with friends and acquaintances in the last couple of months:

- **If you're over 35 and still trying to please your mother**, it's time you stopped, not least because acting like a child isn't going to advance your chances of ever having a half-decent relationship with her.

- **If you're a man (or, indeed, woman) who uses work as an escape route** to get out of going home, it's pretty obvious to everyone what's going on, including the folks back home. Maybe that's why your family are so darned unpleasant when you bother to show up?

- **If you're single, over 40, and unhappy about it**, then you made choices even if these didn't feel like choices at the time. Your choice was to run from the people who wanted to commit to you in favour of those people who didn't want to commit to you – all of whom, incidentally, you invited into your life.

Here's an idea for you...
Write down three situations in the last week that have stressed you out. (Say, missing the train to work, arguing with your sister, staying late at work.) Then work out what the payback was. Make a game out of working out the payback for your actions on a daily basis. It's interesting to observe when you're 'running a racket' (which is life coach speak for kidding yourself).

If you're a mother in the developed world still breastfeeding a year-old child several times a day, you're doing it for reasons of your own that may have little to do with your child's needs and everything to do with your own. The fact that you're exhausted and your relationship with your baby's father is shaky isn't all that surprising.

If you're feeling awful because you've had an affair, you deserve to. Not for the mindless sex but for neglecting your primary relationship in the first place. You were too cowardly to address the problems and are too cowardly now, having precipitated a crisis instead in order to force your spouse to make decisions.

If your child is using explicit swear words to your mother-in-law you probably should feel guilty. Not for giving birth to a delinquent but for being disrespectful to the old bird behind her back even if she is a pain in the neck, even if it is good fun to laugh at her.

Remember I didn't actually say these things. These people were distressed and the last thing a distressed person needs is a know-it-all. My friends wanted sympathy and that's what they got. However, if we were really serious about sorting out our stress levels, we could start by taking our share of the responsibility for creating them.

Defining idea...
'I think of a hero as someone who understands the degree of responsibility that comes with his freedom.' – **BOB DYLAN**

TAKE RESPONSIBILITY

When you realise the great truth that you create a lot of your stress by your choices, then you're in a position to work out the payback – your 'reward', what you're getting from the situation. And I guarantee that there will always be a payback. Sometimes the payback is worth the stress. You choose to look after your ill child. Nothing could be more stressful. The payback is, of course, self-evident.

But others are more tricky and take great honesty. Sacked from your job? But remember, you decided to stay when the company started looking dodgy because the pay was good and it was near your home. Being chased by the taxman? Hmmm, you did wonder why your tax bill seemed low, but weren't concerned enough to double-check your accountant's figures.

So whatever your stress source, look carefully at what choices of yours led to it: excitement, money, security, perpetual childhood, a sense of competence. You might decide that the payback is worth the stress.

But just by recognising that in every single thing you do, every single relationship you have, every single habit you've got, you are getting some sort of payback *or you wouldn't do it* is incredibly liberating. Recognising the payback gives us immense self-awareness. Obstacles melt away because we stop blaming everyone else. Once we're self-aware we tend to change of our own free will. The truth will set you free. Honest.

17. Stress proof your Christmas

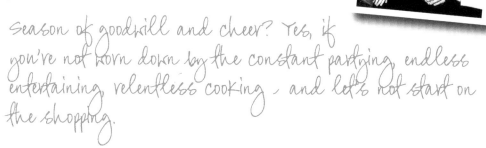

Season of goodwill and cheer? Yes, if you've not worn down by the constant partying, endless entertaining, relentless cooking - and let's not start on the shopping.

This year, let's make it different. Let's find the time to enjoy Christmas.

> 'Dear Santa
> All I want for Christmas is that you transform my family into a perfect one full of sweetness and light, and, most of all, appreciation. Also, despite the fact that I feel pressurised into buying enough presents for a small European state, cook a four-course feast and put up with a drunken father-in-law, let it be stress-free. Oh, and if you could see your way to sprinkling the whole season with magic dust so I get excited because it was a bit of an anticlimax last year, that'd be terrific.'

Would your letter to Santa read like this? You wouldn't be alone. One survey discovered that we rate Christmas as one of the most stressful life events, just after moving house, changing jobs and divorce. Two-thirds of us are mentally and physically drained after Christmas.

Here's an idea for you...
Get the worry out of your head and on the page. Buy a beautiful notebook and keep it with you at all times from November on. Scribble down ideas for presents, stray thoughts about the menu, addresses of friends for cards, baby-sitter numbers...anything you'll need.

So to avoid 'crash and burn', try this countdown. I must have written about fifteen articles over the years on 'stress proofing' Christmas, and this is the *crème de la crème* of the tips that worked for me.

START EARLY
For me, Christmas cards were always a complete chore, not to say bore. But then I started following the advice of my friend, Kate. 'I have an old box covered in Christmas paper and each year I fill it with Christmas cards and stamps. It stays on the kitchen table all through November and I'll sit down most evenings, put on some nice music, pour a huge glass of wine and get stuck in.' I, too, now have a box and from the middle of November, I 'do' five cards a night. It takes 20 minutes max – including the inevitable calls to check addresses which mysteriously haven't made it into my address book.

THE ONE-DAY SHOPPING BLITZ
I spend one day shopping for my family and one day shopping for everyone else. I have a good idea what I'm buying for my family so it's not too stressful. For everyone else I do it in one day, in one store. To make this fun, go with a friend. Take a day off work and meet in the best department store in town for breakfast. Then at 10 a.m. sharp spend three hours shopping and meet again for lunch in the store's restaurant. Then split up for another two hours and meet up for afternoon tea. Finally, split up again and meet for cocktails in the bar across the road at 6 p.m.

You can adapt this idea to suit yourself and your environment. If you do everything via the internet, allow yourself just one day to do it all. This method focuses the mind. You have to make decisions quickly.

THE CUT-OFF POINT

Christmas Eve is magical. I often enjoy it more than Christmas Day. For me Christmas Eve is about missing the last-minute rush. I like to take the day off, build a big log fire, listen to carols on the radio and heat up some mince pies so the smell wafts through the house. Pretend I'm a domestic goddess for just one day, basically.

But if you have to rush around, or even like to rush around, at least give yourself a cut-off point after which you down tools, pour yourself a glass of something bubbly and take an hour or so to admire your tree piled high with presents. The end-point focuses you and, funnily enough, you'll get it done by then.

18. Blitz your home in a weekend

Decluttering. Space clearing. Life gets slower when you give it room.

Get rid of your clutter and you're free to redefine yourself. Life becomes a lot simpler. Everything I own fits pretty neatly into the average living room – and that includes my car. I started decluttering about ten years ago, and I haven't stopped since. It's addictive, it's life affirming. Nothing makes you feel so serene and in control of your life as chucking out stuff you don't need.

Smug? You bet. Life wasn't always this way. For all of my twenties and most of my thirties I had all the furniture, plants, ornaments, designer clothes and bad taste costume jewellery you'd expect of someone who reached her majority in the 80s. Then in the early 90s I thought I'd write about this new gimmick I'd heard rumours about – feng shui (remember that!). And that's how I ended up inviting space clearer Karen Kingston into my less than fragrant home. She told me to clear out the wardrobe, clean out the junk under my bed and get rid of my books – 'let new knowledge in'. Then the magic started to happen.

Life picked up a pace. In the three years following my meeting with Karen, I moved out of the home I'd lived in for years, travelled extensively and reorganised my working life so I earned enough from working half the hours.

My job is to research and write about what is called self-help or 'mind, body, spirit'. I've done it all from meditation to colonic irrigation. But nothing transformed my life like decluttering or to give it its esoteric name, space clearing.

Here's an idea for you...
Try the 'one in, one out' rule. For instance, if you buy a new pair of shoes, then you must get rid of an existing pair. An added bonus is that this system protects you against impulse purchases of stuff you're not really fussed about as you have to focus your mind on what you'll chuck out when you get home.

CHUCK IT OUT, LOSE THE GUILT

How does it work? Most of us live among piles of ancient magazines, defunct utensils, clothes that neither fit nor suit us. The Chinese believe that all these unlovely, unwanted things lying about haphazardly block the flow of energy – the chi – in our homes. My theory is that by losing them, we lose a ton of guilt – guilt that we'll never fit into those hellishly expensive designer jeans again, guilt that we spent all that money on skis when we only go skiing once a decade, guilt that we never cook those fabulous dinners in those two dozen cookbooks. You get my point. Just about everything in your home probably engenders some sort of guilt. Cut your belongings by 90% and you do the same to your guilt.

THE BIG CLEAR UP

'Useful or beautiful, useful or beautiful' – that's the mantra. If any single object doesn't fulfil one of these criteria, bin it. Cultivate ruthlessness. If you haven't worn it, used it or thought about it in a year, do you really need it?

Have three bin bags to hand as you work. One for stuff to chuck out, one for stuff to give to charity, one for things you want to clean or mend. Visit the charity shop as soon as you can – make it a priority. Give yourself two weeks to tackle the 'mend or clean' bag.

Something neither useful nor beautiful, but that you don't like to get rid of for sentimental reasons? Put it away for a year. Time out of sight makes it easier to get rid of.

Defining idea...

'If more of us valued food and cheer and song above hoarded gold, it would be a merrier world.' – J. R. R. TOLKIEN

Do this little but often. Try a couple of one-hour sessions per week. I operate the 40–20 rule: 40 minutes graft followed by 20 minutes sitting around feeling virtuous. You get better at decluttering. Soon it's second nature. Do two to three sessions a month.

Find a home for everything you own. You're allowed one drawer that acts as a glory hole for all the odd items.

19. Hug your home

It's hard to change when your home is filthy. And even if it's clean, keeping it that way often means we're working late.

There is no secret to having a fragrant, immaculate home. It takes time – either yours, or your cleaner's. But even if you have a cleaner, at the end of the day we all have to do a bit of cleaning – unless we've got the luxury of a housekeeper 24/7.

So here are some ideas for making housework stress a thing of the past. It will benefit two groups of people.

- The owner of a messy home – your house will be cleaner.

- The owner of an already immaculate home, but the price for it is you find yourself polishing kitchen units at midnight. This will help you slow down, but you can skip through the first bit snorting with derision.

I am not a slob, but neither am I a perfectionist. So given that I'm busy, domesticity is way down on my priority list and my house gets dirty – certainly far below the standards acceptable to my grandmother. It used to upset me until I found www.flylady.com. I urge anyone domestically challenged to seek it out. A bit hokey, but sweet, it's a support group for those who have felt overwhelmed by the ceaseless round of domestic duty and fed up struggling with it alone. They have rules. One of them is that the minute you get up, you make your bed, get dressed (including shoes), wash your face and get your make-up on and/or shave.

Here's an idea for you...
When cooking, fill the sink with hot soapy water and dump stuff in as you go along. Yes, even if you have a dishwasher. It helps you keep surfaces clear and then you enjoy yourself more too.

Try this and you'll be amazed at how much more productive you are. I have adapted some of their other rules to suit me. (Hint: the first tip here changed my life.)

ALWAYS HAVE A CLEAN KITCHEN SINK

With a shiny sink, you feel you're in control. Wash dishes by hand if necessary (yes, shocking, but it's a skill you won't have forgotten). A shiny sink reflects back a vision of yourself as a domestic goddess (or god) in stunning control of your world. Don't leave home or go to bed for the evening without clearing the sink area. It really is best to clear your kitchen straight after the evening meal – or get your kids to do it. Before bed you can't always be bothered and it sets the morning off to a bad start.

ADOPT THE LASER BEAM APPROACH

Divide your home into clearly defined areas. You will clean one of these areas thoroughly every week. No area should take more than an hour. This could look like: hallway and bathroom; kitchen; reception rooms; bedroom and spare bedroom; children's bedroom(s). Now make a list of what you need to do to each area to get it cleaned to your satisfaction. Keep a master list for each room in a file. The reason for this? With a list you get to tick off items and that's immensely satisfying. First thing Saturday morning is a good time to clean, not least because if you have children they can get involved.

Defining idea...

'At the worst, a house unkept cannot be so distressing as a life unlived.'
– ROSE MACAULEY, writer

BLESS YOUR HOME

The flylady website calls it the Weekly Home Blessing hour – and this is the superficial cleaning you do to keep your home bearable. It takes an hour a week – or you can split it up. I do 10 minutes morning and evening, three times a week That on top of the hour a week I spend on one area is usually enough to keep my (small) home bearable. You may have a larger home and need to put more time in. During my 10-minute sessions I do one of these activities: sweep and mop floors; vacuum; dust; clean bathroom; polish all reflective surfaces; get rid of all rubbish – purge magazines, empty contents of recycling bins.

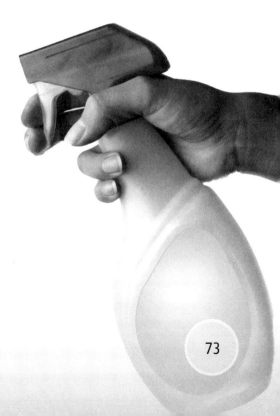

20. Zap those piles

No, not those kind of piles. We're talking about the avalanche of paper, magazines, unpaid bills, flyers for pizza houses, the general detritus of 21st-century life that threatens to overwhelm you.

This idea is very personal to me. Following it has reduced stress in my life by a factor of 10. When my daughter, then three, was asked what her mother did for a living she said 'My mummy tears bits of paper out of newspapers.' Which is actually quite an accurate description of what I do for a living – it's called 'research'. I spend hours tearing out, but it's never enough. All my working life, piles of paper have dragged down my spirit and proven to be a stressor in my domestic life. My partner objects to hefting piles of magazines off chairs before he can sit down.

This is the system that works for me, culled from reading and interviewing just about every organisational guru on the planet. The only drawback is that it takes time to set up. But if you have a day to spend or ten free hours, give it a go. Ten hours can work magic. You will probably have to make a few adjustments to suit your life.

Here's an idea for you...
Chuck out files regularly: it's a good way to keep on top of paperwork. Every time you open a file, put a pencil mark on the corner of it. At the end of six months or a year, you'll be able to see in a moment which files you've barely opened. Most of their contents can be chucked out.

STEP 1
Gather together everything that you will need to create order in your world. For me that's cardboard magazine holders, folders, pens, labels, stapler, a couple of hard-backed address books (personal and business) and a huge industrial-strength binbag. I also keep the family calendar and my diary at hand so I can put dates directly into them as I reveal the invites and school dates in my pile.

STEP 2
Work systematically. You are going to go from one side of your desk to the other, or one side of the room to the other. Gather together one pile of paper and assorted junk and place it bang in the middle of the room or your desk. Start sorting. Every single piece of paper that you touch must be actioned.

- If it contains a phone number that you might need in the future, then put the number straight into one of your *address books*.

- If it is a bill that has to be paid, or anything which must be acted on immediately, then create a file for *urgent and unpaid bills*. (I carry this file with me, in my handbag and work through it every day when I have a down moment.)

Defining idea...
'We can lick gravity but sometimes the paperwork is overwhelming.'
– WERNER VON BRAUN, rocket engineer

- If it is an article or piece of information that you might need in the future but which is not urgent, start creating files for these (*named files*) such as 'pensions', 'holidays', 'general interest'.

- If it is a piece of information that you need to act on or read or make a decision on but not now, put it in a file marked *'To Do'* and make an appointment in your diary sometime in the next week when you'll deal with it. This file should be somewhere accessible and you should clear it not less than once every two weeks or it gets out of control.

Keep a *tickle book*. Tickle as in 'tickle my memory.' Mine is an A4 hardbacked notebook. In it I note down the names of anything I might need in the future: the idea of an article I might write or a savings account offering a good rate of interest. The point is that I don't have to hold on to endless bits of paper just in case I ever want this information – there's enough in the tickle book to help me trace it. I also keep the tickle book by my side at work and if anyone calls me with a piece of information I may need but don't know for sure, then I scribble down their number and a couple of explanatory lines so that I can follow up later. Same with my emails. The tickle book means I have been able to throw out dozens of pieces of paper almost as soon as they reach my desk.

21. End ' stop and collapse' syndrome

You take holidays. You know how important this is if you want to slow down.

And then you spend the first week in bed recovering from some dreaded lurgy. You've got leisure sickness – aka 'stop and collapse' syndrome.

The guy who first identified leisure sickness was a sufferer. Professor Ad Vingerhoets of Tilburg University noticed he always got ill on the first days of his holiday. So he did a study of nearly 2,000 men and women aged between 16 and 87. And guess what? He wasn't alone. A small but significant number of his subjects regularly got ill at the weekend or on holidays. (I think his numbers must be an underestimate because most of the people I know are affected.) He discovered that those who got leisure sickness complained mainly of headaches, migraine, fatigue, muscular pains, nausea, colds and flu (especially common when going on holiday).

Those who got it shared certain characteristics: a high workload, perfectionism, eagerness to achieve, an over-developed sense of responsibility to their work – all of which make it difficult to switch off.

One theory is that those who work hard simply get so bored on holiday that they start to notice the symptoms they've been suppressing while at work. It could also be a case of 'mind over matter': we don't allow ourselves to get sick until the work is done. Yet another theory is that when you're working (stressed) your immune

Here's an idea for you...
If you're prone to weekend sickness, try exercising on a Friday evening. Exercise is a stressor but one your body loves. This acts as a transition between work and time off, and helps you unwind quicker.

system is actually working better than it does when you're relaxing. When you relax, the immune system slows down, your defences relax, and kaboom!, you're calling the concierge for a doctor.

So what can you do about it? I'm going to suggest a two-pronged attack.

1. SUPPORT YOUR LOCAL IMMUNE SYSTEM
As a very bare minimum, eat a minimum of five fruit and veg a day and take a good-quality multivitamin and mineral supplement (I like Bioforce, Solgar, Viridian, Vitabiotics). If you drink too much alcohol or are a smoker, you also need more vitamin C – so supplement that too. I'm also a fan of echinacea, so give this a try as well (but read the instructions carefully: if you take it for too long, it loses its effectiveness).

2. PLAN FOR HOLIDAYS WITH MILITARY PRECISION
You really need gradually to begin to wind down in the two weeks before you go.

Cue hollow laughter. You think I don't understand, but I do. In August 1998, the day before my holiday, I worked in the office from 6 a.m. until 11 p.m., went home, packed, slept for three hours, went back to the office at 4 a.m., worked until 8.30 and took a cab straight to the airport to get on a plane. That's not smart. That's borderline lunacy. So let's have no more of the workaholic nuttiness.

Defining idea...
'Those who don't take the time to be well eventually have to find the time to be ill.' –
Anon.

Here are some ideas (I am assuming everyone in your household has a valid
passport. Young children's passports don't run as long as adults. Not sure about
this? Go and check right now. This one small action could save you bucket loads of
stress down the line.)

Three weeks before you go. Make a packing list. Write down everything you need
to take with you and then allocate each lunchtime this week to completing any
errands.

Two weeks before you go. Sort out work. Take a look at all your projects and decide
at what stage you want to pass them over. Set goals with each project and allocate
deadlines for reaching them, preferably all to be tied up the day before your last day.

One week before you go. Start packing. Put out your bags or suitcases in a spare
room if you've got one and start the washing and ironing nightmare in the
weekend before you go. Do a little packing each night. Also
start winding up projects and writing up
your handover notes to whichever
colleague is taking over your
responsibilities. You can always
amend them on the last day if
you get further with a project
than you planned to. Amending
is a lot better than starting them
at 8.30 p.m. on your last day.

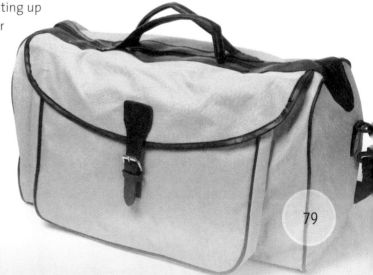

22. Have a holiday at your desk

Take time to imbue the old nine-to-five with a certain glamour and you'll be amazed to see the tension seep away.

You'll be raising your standards and that means lowering your stress levels. Forty years has taught me that there are two ways to have a perfect day. One is in the grand tradition of the Lou Reed song. You hang out for a whole day with someone you really, really love who is loving you right back – or at least tolerating you. You don't have to do anything because just being with the beloved is so blissful it blocks out the boring little problems that usually stress you out. If you manage twenty days like this in your whole life time, you're doing pretty well.

And then there's the second way. You build a perfect day for yourself and by adding grace and glamour to your life, you remove stress. It takes a little thought. But it is more reliable than true love. You can have a holiday of the 'mind' on even the most mundane day.

REBOOT YOUR COMMUTE
Give your journey to work an overhaul. Set yourself targets. Instead of a drag, see it as a purposeful part of your day. If it involves walking, buy a pedometer. Learn a language. Use the time to repeat your mantras for the day. Be creative: write a page of free-hand prose on the journey in (not if you drive of course!). Start working up the characters for your novel. It's a terrific time to practice mindfulness, which can deliver the benefits of meditation. The list is endless.

Here's an idea for you...
Clothes can play a huge part in improving the quality of our life. Every morning choose one thing that makes your heart sing – a colour you love, a fabric that embraces you, a piece of jewellery with sentimental attachment. Next time you're shopping buy clothes that help you radiate confidence.

BOOST YOUR ENVIRONMENT
Your starter question: what five changes would make your work environment more pleasant. Here's mine. Getting rid of piles of papers and magazines that need to be filed. Investing in a china cup and no more sharing the office's grubby, chipped ones. Cheering up my desk with a bunch of pink tulips. Cleaning my keyboard – so filthy it's a health hazard. Turning down the ringtone volume on my phone. Everyday find some way to make your surroundings more pleasant.

BEAT THE MID-AFTERNOON SLUMP
When you feel the slump kicking in, stop working and get away from your workstation if you can. Go for a short walk in the sunshine, or take a nap. If you can't, try this: palm your eyes in your hand for a few minutes and visualise a calm and beautiful place. See this in as much detail as possible.

THE JOURNEY HOME
This needs a different mood from the journey to work. If you listen to music, make it different from the tunes you play in the morning – slower, deeper. Small stuff like that really helps to emphasise that this is your transition period. Have a project that you work on at this time (planning your holiday is good). And if you read, keep the tone light. If in the morning you read French verbs or the novels of Dostoyevsky, read P.G. Wodehouse on the way home.

Defining idea...
'You can make more friends in two months by becoming interested in other people than you can in two years by trying to get other people interested in you.'
— DALE CARNEGIE, founding father of the self-help movement

SPREAD LOVE
When you pass someone in distress send them 'serenity' or 'calm' as a thought. Spread good and happy thoughts wherever you go. Smile. Be gracious. Be kind, compassionate, a force for good.

Not every day can be a high day or holiday, but changing your mindset, looking for grace and sheer fun in previous black holes of misery turns you into a force for light and transforms your day-to-day grind – it's the art of living lightly and it gets easier the more you look for opportunities to practise your skill.

23. Stop acting on impulse

Focus, concentration, sticking to what you've started. Earn time for yourself.

'Yes, yes, yes, but how?' I hear you say.

Some days I run around like a frantic hen. Charging to work, rushing home early to spend time with the kids, doing chores, doing research, phoning my mother. I react to events and whatever crisis looms next. I don't do anything properly. I don't do some things at all.

When I get to bed I remember the stuff that I didn't get round to and feel disappointed and frustrated with myself. When that happens it's time to go back to basics and use this idea. It helps you finish what you start and makes you feel on top of your life. Besides helping you become more focused, it also helps you curb your impulse to wander off and do other stuff rather than the one task that you have set yourself. It will show up the numerous times you have just got started on a project when it suddenly seems terribly important to water the plants, call your mum or make a nice cup of tea. But now you will be prepared and will observe your impulses as just that – impulses. And you will stay put with a wise 'Oh there I go, looking for ways to waste time again.'

Here's an idea for you...
Making a promise to yourself every night and keeping it the next day is the route to mental toughness. Every time you keep a promise to yourself, stick some loose change in a jar. It's a good visual record of your growing focus and strength – and, of course, you get to spend the cash at the end of it.

Besides training you to focus and resist the impulse to waste time, this idea will achieve two further objectives: (1) It will build your self-esteem by fostering your sense of yourself as a person who follows through on their word. (2) It will clear your life of a ton of annoying little irritations that have been stopping you mentally from moving on.

Step 1 Before you go to bed tonight, think of something you want to achieve tomorrow. Keep it really small and simple. It doesn't matter what it is, but you have to do it. Make it something restful – you're going to read a chapter of a favourite novel. Make it useful – you're going to clean the cutlery drawer. Make it worthy – you're going to take a multivitamin. Take this promise extremely seriously. Promise yourself you'll do it – and follow through. If you don't, no excuses. You've failed. But you're aiming too high. Make your next promise easier to achieve.

Step 2 Make a promise to yourself every evening for a week. And follow through.

Step 3 OK, now you're going to make a list of some tasks that you need to undertake but have been putting off. You will need seven, one for every day of the week. Some ideas: starting on your tax return; making a dental appointment; cancelling the gym membership you never use; sorting out your wardrobe; cleaning out the inside of the car; tackling just one pile from the many piles on your desk; grooming the dog; making a start on the garage.

Defining idea...
'He who every morning plans the transactions of the day and follows out that plan, carries a thread that will guide him through the maze of the most busy life. But where no plan is laid, where the disposal of time is surrendered merely to the chance of incidence, chaos will soon reign.' – VICTOR HUGO

Step 4 Write these down and keep them by your bed. Each night for the next week, pick one and promise yourself you'll do it tomorrow.

Step 5 Write another list. This time put on it things that are worrying you and driving you mad. Suggestions: discover if your pension plan will pay out enough for you to live on; write a letter to that friend you're upset with; paint the kitchen. Put on the list everything that is driving you nuts. Then pick one and break it down into manageable steps. Promise yourself to do the first of these steps tomorrow, and every day from now on, make a promise to take another step forward. Don't let impulse drive you off course.

This is an exercise in mental toughness. Making promises to yourself that you never keep brings you down and, over time, breaks your heart. But by breaking difficult tasks down into manageable chunks and building the strength of character to follow through and get them out the way, you take a huge step forward in reducing stress in your life.

Warning: don't make more than two or three promises a day. Keep it simple.

24. Dealing with interruptions

other people and their agendas - they suck the energy right out of you. But there are ways of dealing with interruptions.

It's been one of those days. This morning I had a clear day to get on with writing this. And then it all went wrong. I've taken two phone calls and been side-tracked at the school gates by a friend wanting a coffee and a chat. I've agreed to pick up another parent's kid, which shouldn't be a problem but, somehow, now it is. It's now 12.45 pm and I've written 100 words. (That's not good, by the way.)

I'm reminded of the definition of an optimist: someone who believes that today will be better than yesterday. What's the definition of a fantasist? Someone who believes today will be better even if she doesn't make any changes. Sure, I can be an optimist, imagining I'll zip through everything I want to achieve today, but if yesterday was constantly hijacked by other people, and I don't do anything to change that today, I'm living on Fantasy Island if I think I'll get everything done.

And that feeling of having wasted time is a total energy bummer. So it's time to start making some plans to ensure that I don't let other people interrupt me. My trigger points will be different from yours – as you've probably guessed, mine is being seduced by my friends into going off-track. Below we explore some possible energy drains, and what hopeless cases – and that means me – can do about it.

Here's an idea for you...
Over the next week, note down when you were interrupted, by whom and for how long. At the end of the week, go through marking those interruptions that you couldn't put off because they were too important. How long did you have to spend dealing with them? Next week be aware when you're planning your week's workload that that amount of time may 'disappear' from any day because of critical interruptions. Keep a note to see if it's the same next week. Planning for interruptions that can't be avoided means your week will flow more easily.

YOU WORK IN AN OFFICE

The average office worker is interrupted every three minutes, according to research undertaken in California. It's a wonder that we get anything done at all. If you're lucky enough to have your own office space, how about operating a one-hour-door-open, one-hour-door-shut policy, when you can't be interrupted. It's also worth learning some great exit lines for bouncing the interrupter back to the drawing board until it suits you and/or they find someone else to help them. You could try 'Sorry, got to finish this project; can we talk about it tomorrow?' or 'Sorry, this week is impossible; what about next week.'

YOUR HOBBY IS CHATTING

Yep, this is me. The answer is simple. Just say no. Personally, knowing how weak I am, I don't engage in conversation. Tomorrow, unlike today, I won't answer the phone but let the machine pick up. I'll check messages for urgency at noon and five o'clock.

YOU'RE A 'SOCIAL E-MAILER'

This tag is the invention of my friend Jane Alexander, a wonderful writer who admits that one of her occupations is 'social e-mailer'. She lives in the depths of Devon, so for her there's some excuse: e-mail is her window on the world. For the rest of us, it's probably nothing but a huge distraction. One radical idea that works

Defining idea...

'I choose to ... live so that which came ... to me as a blossom, goes on as a fruit.'
– DAWNA MARKOVA, poet

for me is not to look at e-mails first thing in the morning. Instead, spend that first hour doing the most important task of the day. Often that first hour is the calmest you'll get, and what do you spend it doing? 'Chatting' to your friends – it's just that the written word fools you into thinking you're working. Or else you're answering other people's banal requests. Try ignoring your e-mails until you've done some serious work, and check them no more than three times a day.

YOU CAN'T SAY 'NO'

Perhaps you need to look at whether you are just being helpful or are hooked on being needed. Next time, when you're tempted to let yourself be distracted, ask yourself 'if I respond to this distraction, who am I disappointing?' It might be your boss, it might be you, it might be the child that you won't be able to take to the park at the weekend because you'll be making up time on a work project instead. Seeing the human cost of allowing yourself to be interrupted can help you decide if it's worth it or not.

25. Stop dithering, start living

Here's how to make swift, smart decisions.

Learn this vital decision-making formula. You'll free up your mind from niggling worries in seconds, saving your mental energy.

I've had a bit of a dilemma today. I'm staring at an e-mail advertising a two-day self-development course that I'd love to attend. There's just one problem. The weekend in question is the one (of admittedly many!) on which we will be celebrating my partner's fortieth birthday. I've promised to take him out for dinner that night and since the course is near my home, I could do both – attend the course during the day and take him for dinner that night. But ... but ... I've got that sneaking suspicion that by trying to pack too much in, I'm taking too much on. I'll be rushed and late for dinner.

In the past, this is the sort of dilemma I would have spent time on. I would have weighed up the pros and cons, written lists, talked to my partner about it, talked to friends perhaps, spent valuable time dithering when I could have been getting on with my life.

But that was before I learned the magical qualities of what I call 'the power of 10' question.

relax and enjoy life

Here's an idea for you...
The very quickest form of this idea is brilliant for procrastinators. Think of a task that you're putting off. Imagine what the consequences will be in one month (or whatever time span is relevant) if you *don't* act. If the consequences don't frighten you, go to the pub; if they do, get on with it now. Worrying about it even subconsciously is sapping your energy.

When faced with any dilemma simply stop and ask yourself: what will the consequences be in:

10 minutes?
10 months?
10 years?

When you're faced with a problem where there's no win-win situation and someone will end up unhappy, at least in the short term, 'the power of 10' helps you cut through the emotions of the moment and focus on what is really important.

Let's take my present dilemma.

If I decide to go to the self-development course, what will be the repercussions in 10 minutes? None. I'll explain to my partner, he won't really register it – it's down the line and as long as I'm not actually cancelling dinner, he won't care. I'll be happy.

In 10 months? That depends. If there are no mess-ups and I get there on time, probably it will be fine. But if I am late for dinner, in 10 months' time, he'll still be making sarcastic comments.

Defining idea...
'But all will be well, and every kind of thing will be well.'
– JULIAN OF NORWICH, medieval mystic

In 10 years? You know, that's the tricky one. Even if I manage everything, I think he's still going to remember that on the weekend of his fortieth, I wasn't really around. That's the general impression he'll have long after he's forgotten the presents, the party and all the other gestures I'll make to 'big' up his birthday and distract his attention from the fact that I'm not actually there very much. Would I be better off attending the course? I might learn a lot. I might make some lifelong soulmates. But there's no way of knowing if it will be worth it, or not. And there's potentially a lot to lose. So this time, I think I'll have to pass.

It took me as long to make that decision as it took to type it, and now my mind is free to get on with writing this, and everything else I have to do. I won't waste any more time thinking about it.

This is a variation of an old idea – imagining yourself one year, five years, ten years down the road is commonplace. 'What will it matter in twenty years' time?' we say to each other. But I find 'the power of 10' particularly elegant and easy to use. Try it when you're not sure what route to take and know that either will end up making someone unhappy. The three different timescales help you see through the emotional turmoil of yours or somebody else's short-term unhappiness to what the potential benefits could be when disappointment has passed. It helps you cut through the emotional 'fuss' that occurs when your plans are unpopular with some people, and to see clearly if they're worth the grief.

Life skills for the terminally busy

Develop the attitudes that allow a calm and focused life.
Here is the remedial work for those who don't know where
to start when it comes to relaxing.

QUIZ: **Too stressed to relax?**

If there's too much adrenaline coursing around your body, it's going to be very hard to relax. It's also going to be very hard to be effective because adrenaline has you bouncing off walls like a demented blue-bottle. So are you energised by stress, or overwhelmed? Our quiz can help you decide. Just tick the statement that you most closely identify with.

1. **You are woken in the night. What are the chances you would roll over and go back to sleep?**
    a. Very high – you always sleep well.
    b. Usually good, but right now you're stressed
    c. Very low. When you waken in the night you nearly always start turning over worries in your head and get anxious.

2. **Your boss calls to say there's a sudden emergency. You have six hours to solve a big problem, but solving it will be a terrific boost to your profile. Your reaction?**
    a. Fired up – on all cylinders
    b. Tired at the thought, but you'll pull it off
    c. Ready to cry.

3. **Your family think of you as...**

   a. Good fun.

   b. Stressed and tired.

   c. Irritable and/or absent.

4. **Your fantasise about...**

   a. Living your own life only more so.

   b. Living your own life only calmer.

   c. Running away to a different life.

If you answered mostly 'a' you are energised and coping well with stress. Read the ideas beginning with *idea 35* to take your health to a new level.

If you answered mostly 'b' you are dangerously stressed but it seems to be a temporary problem. Go back to *idea 1* and start carving out some time to relax.

If you answered mostly 'c' you need to turn to *idea 10* on burn-out. You may be a candidate. Time to slow down fast.

26. The perfection trap

Your need to 'get it perfect' isn't about perfection. It's about staying in control.

Staying in control is not a virtue if it's making you miserable. I have a friend who ran her first marathon. And she did run the whole way, never once slowing down to a walk. She felt fabulous for about six hours afterwards – she deserved to. Then before she'd even had her evening meal, the self-doubt began – she should have run faster, pushed herself more, achieved a better time. All she'd wanted beforehand was to complete the race but now that she had, she couldn't stop beating herself up for not doing it 'better'.

When she told me this story, I sat dumbstruck by her perfectionism. She looks better than me, earns more than me, achieves more than me, but the price for her success is a small voice inside telling her endlessly that she's just not good enough. Does it have to be that way? I think perfectionists can achieve just as much if they let that voice go for good. They tend to think not. They know their perfectionism is neurotic but they cling to it because they think they are lazy and that without the voice they would just give up and slope around the house in old tracksuits not brushing their teeth.

This is unlikely. However, only you can learn to ignore the little voice. What I do know is that if you don't ignore it, you'll never be free of stress. Often that little

Here's an idea for you…
Restrict your 'to-do' list to seven items only. Less a 'to-do' list than an 'I absolutely have to do' list. Chinese medics say that any more and you get stressed out by the sheer volume and fed up when you don't complete them.

voice belongs to someone we know, often someone who brought us up, who has no idea of the complexity of our world. In their world, with one role to fulfil it was easy to do it perfectly. In the world we live in, chocka with choice, where we can fulfil so many roles, there's no way we can do all of it perfectly. And even if you did, you still wouldn't be happy. Give it up!

Ration your perfectionist behaviour. You probably won't ever lose it completely. However, you can limit it. One woman I know whose energy levels had plummeted finally made the connection between her habit of staying up late reading and answering emails and her inability to get to sleep (duh!). So now she allows herself two nights a week to check emails late. Go through your own life working out where you can cut down or cut out perfectionist habits.

Lose your fear of the person who made you this way. Even if you were always the sort of kid who liked to colour code your books, no one becomes a perfectionist unaided. Someone somewhere had high expectations of you. Accept something pretty basic: if you haven't earned their unconditional approval by now, you probably never will. Let it go. And if you can't, get therapy.

Walk barefoot in the park. Remember Jane Fonda begging Robert Redford to stop being such a stuffed shirt and to walk barefoot in Central Park. You could try the same – just to see if you like it. You probably won't – but it might teach

Defining idea...

'The question should be, is it worth trying to do, not can it be done.'
– ALLARD LOWENSTEIN, political activist

you something valuable: that nobody cares but you. Whatever your version of mad devil-may-care spontaneity – asking friends to dinner and ordering a takeaway curry, or letting your roots show, or putting on a few kilos, or refusing to take the kids swimming on Sunday morning because you simply can't be fagged – go on: *do it*. The kids will not implode with disappointment. The world will not fall apart. Slip up and nothing happens.

No one cares if you're perfect but you (and the person who made you this way, see above, but we've dealt with them already).

27. Finding work to make your heart sing

What do you do if your job is dragging you down?

It's really, really hard to feel energised when five days out of seven are dedicated to an activity that bores you stupid – or worse, saps your self-esteem. Yup, we're talking about work.

At any one time, 40 % of us are looking for a new job. If you're one of them, the chances are that your present job is sapping your strength.

Do you basically love your job but need to move on for promotion, more money or simply for a change? Then terrific. It's just a matter of time, sending out enough good quality CVs and brushing up on your interview technique.

But this idea is for those people who know at heart that they are on the wrong track; that changing job may give a temporary fillip to their mood, offer new challenges and a change of environment, but really, deep down, it is going to be more of the same. You're the people who haven't yet found your dream job. You're the ones who fantasise about winning the lottery because it's the only way off the treadmill.

Here's an idea for you...

Phone a friend – or three. You almost certainly know people who have transferred skills and started working in another career. Pick their brains on how they financed it, got their family onside, garnered the qualifications, coped with problems. Those who have pursued their happiness are going to have more practical advice, on coping with the good and bad, as well as more enthusiasm, than those who haven't taken a similar leap.

To find work that will energise, excite and stimulate you, you will have to do some soul-searching and perhaps face some hard decisions. Use the five words, often called 'the journalist's best friends', that are the start of any investigation – namely, when, what, why, how and where.

1   ***When do you lose yourself?*** Think back to the last time you were so completely engrossed in what you were doing that you didn't notice time passing. Were you painting a room, listening to your friend talk, dancing at a wedding, decorating a cake? Were you driving, shopping, helping your child with their homework, volunteering for your local charity? Write it down. Try to remember a few more occasions. It might help to remember what you used to love as a child. Did you love to wander about the garden examining flowers and rocks? Were you always at the swimming pool? Did you prefer to be alone, or hang out with friends? Search for your passion. Seek out your joy. Look at your list, and mull on it.

2   ***What do you dream about?*** Another version of step 1 is to think about what you'd do if you won the lottery and didn't have to work anymore. How would you choose to spend your time? Any clues there?

Defining idea...
'The brain is a wonderful organ. It starts working in the morning and doesn't stop until you get into the office.' – ROBERT FROST, poet

3   ***Why are you scared?*** Ask why you're not fulfilling your dream. At the root of it will almost certainly be fear. That could be fear of telling your spouse you want to give up your lucrative job to become a windsurf instructor or it could be the fear that giving up a profession into which you've invested a lot of time makes you look a fool. The longer you've studied or worked at a profession, the harder it is to give it up. Think of it this way: you're not giving up, you're transferring skills; you're not wiping years off your CV, you are using past skills to find a parallel career that gives you satisfaction.

4   ***How much value can you add?*** It may take a while. In the meantime, try putting your most into the job you've got. Bringing a good attitude to work will almost certainly result in you doing well because most people simply don't – their work is mediocre – and that makes it easy to shine if you put in some effort. Being enthusiastic will energise you.

5   ***Where are the soulmates?*** Go back to your step 1 list. While you're looking, or retraining for your dream job, include more of what makes you happy in your life. Pursuing what makes you happy means you'll meet other people who share your interests, and who knows where that will take you? Listen to your instincts. While I was listening to a casual business acquaintance describe the re-training she wanted to pursue, the thought popped into my head: 'I should do that'. Two years later, I did.

28. Who you are is what you get

To transform your life you have to understand how to take full responsibility for what you can make happen. And this means learning the difference between what you can control and what you can't.

I've wasted a lot of my life trying to control the things over which I had no control and getting more and more stressed when I failed.

It was always important to me how people treated me and if they didn't treat me in that way I spent lots of time trying to get them to do so – I thought it was my right.

UNDERSTANDING THE DIFFERENCE

As a group exercise on my Personal Leadership Programme I ask people how they'd like to be treated by everyone they meet. Together we come up with a list that almost always includes things such as with respect, honestly, openly, kindly, as an equal, with integrity, as an individual, and so on. I then ask them, 'Can you make people treat you this way?' Of course, the answer is absolutely not. We might be

Here's an idea for you...
Look for someone in your family or team at work who's not performing as you
think they could. Think about what you could give them that would enable them
to improve their performance. It may include things like truly listening to them to
understand their needs, giving them some more information, supporting and
encouraging their ideas more, giving them appreciation or developing their skills
and knowledge.

able to influence them, but we certainly have no control over making them.
How often in life do we spend time trying to get others to treat us in the way we
think we deserve to be treated and getting upset when they don't? I certainly
behaved this way, especially with my children. The reality is this. We have no control
over 'get', we only have control over 'give'. So the conclusion that we come to is that
if we want people to treat us in the ways that are important to us, then we in turn
need to be respectful, honest, open, kind, treat others as equals, behave with
integrity and show that we think each person is unique. This doesn't necessarily
mean that they'll then treat us in the same way, but it's certainly going to make it
more likely. The key here is recognising where you do have power and where you
don't. You can't control the way people treat you and if you can't control it, then
why spend lots of time worrying about it? The only place where you have power is
in areas where you do have complete control.

Defining idea...
'From what we get, we can make a living; what we give, however, makes a life.'
– ARTHUR ASHE

MOTIVATION – WHOSE JOB IS IT?

How often at work do you hear managers questioning how they could motivate their teams more effectively? However, where does motivation come from? It comes from inside of you. So, how can anyone push a button that's inside of you. The knack of motivation is getting them to motivate themselves. If you believe your role is to motivate them and you do a really good job, what happens when you're not there? So turn your thinking the other way round. Instead of thinking about how you can get them to perform better, how can you get them to be more creative and how you can raise levels of awareness, think instead about what you can give them to enable them to perform better, what you can give them to enable them to become more creative, what you can give them to help raise their levels of performance.

There's a huge amount of research supporting the effectiveness of this approach, often known as 'servant leadership', and you'll find books and articles about this everywhere. The guru of servant leadership is Robert Greenleaf, and he believes that you should turn an organisation on its head so, for example, the CEO is at the bottom and his focus is on what he can give his directors to enable them to become more effective in every way. And the directors are thinking, 'What can we give to our direct reports?', and so on. At the 'top' the people at the coalface are totally focused on what they can give to their customers to enable an even more fulfilling and profitable relationship.

This works in exactly the same way in your home life. What is it that you can give your partner or your children to enable them to become happier, more loving and more fulfilled?

29. Are you two people?

Do you live life as though you are two people? Is there one person for work and another one for home? Or one for strangers and another for friends?

When you are with your boss, do you behave as you would at home? Do you talk about your feelings and instincts or do you resort to facts and figures?

THE AWAKENING

I know a business consultant who, ten years ago, stepped out of her job for a while. This was for two emotional reasons and one business one. The business reason was the most complex. For many years she had been a trainer, which involved considerable management training. "As a company we were very successful", she says, "but something that always concerned me was that no matter how great people said the training was, once they returned to work they seemed to forget most of what they had learned before they had begun to put it into practice. This was unacceptable to me and I decided that I wanted to get out of the business. It was at this point that I left my husband."

Here's an idea for you...
Ask yourself whether you behave at work as you do at home. If you behave differently then ask yourself why. Which is the person that you are comfortable with and which is the person you want to be? It may be that you would like to include elements of both. Now ask yourself what is stopping you from becoming one person. Identify each side's strengths and plan how you can take those strengths into both situations.

"The following year was a difficult one. I gave myself time to heal and did many things to keep me occupied. I qualified in massage, sports massage, aromatherapy and reflexology. I became a Reiki healer, an AuraSoma therapist and qualified in hypnotherapy. It was a busy year! I also went on some personal-development workshops, ranging from the very intense to the seriously wild and wacky, including Date with Destiny, Landmark Education and Mind Control. The thing that began to fascinate me was this. There were countless business people at these

Defining idea...
'You cannot expect the world to change until you change yourself.'
– ROBERT MULLER, co-founder of the University of Peace, Costa Rica

workshops, and I asked several how they applied what they were learning to their work lives. The response was usually, 'We don't. This is for me not for work.' This response challenged me because it meant people were deliberately choosing to be two people – the home person and the work person. I then began to question whether it was possible to link the two halves and take personal development into the business world in a truly pragmatic way that would be acceptable."

HEAD OR HEART?

She has a good point. At most management training programmes, trainers are appealing to people's heads. Trainers are getting people to think about the best ways to lead, inspire and motivate, and they give them all sorts of models that make this easier to understand. Consequently, when people finish the programme, all that they have learned makes sense and what they need to be doing seems obvious. However, as soon as they get back to work, life takes over. Urgent work has built up while they have been away and needs to be dealt with. When they do eventually get the opportunity to look back at all the good things they have learned, a considerable amount has been forgotten. Why? Because their hearts haven't been engaged. The training was aimed at head level. We should be asking the question 'What sort of leader do I want to *be?*' and not just 'What do I need to *do* to be a good leader?'

This consultant now only runs programmes that affect the whole person, and everything learned can be used at both home and work.

30. Creating your own reality

A positive mental attitude can transform a glass from being half empty to being half full and then actually help to fill the glass.

Your attitude towards the things you have to do makes the difference between getting the most out of them and seeing them as chores that are impossible to enjoy.

A SILLY STORY

Imagine there are two women who are both married to successful men. They live in the suburbs from where their husbands commute to the city every day. Their husbands come bursting in from work one day with the news that they've won the Salesperson of the Year Award. The reward is a week in San Francisco in a five-star hotel with a pool and all the luxury you can imagine. Not only that, but wives are invited.

Both men suggest that their wives head to town on a shopping spree to buy some new clothes, especially something stunning for the dinner and dance and gala presentation.

The first wife is excited and thinks, 'Brilliant, a day in town. I'll park in the car park, probably not too near the station because the commuters will have got there first, but it'll be safe and I won't need a taxi. I'll go up by train, which I love especially as I

Here's an idea for you...
Choose a task that you're not looking forward to. Firstly, remember that whether or not you do the task is your choice. Now imagine having completed the task and how much you enjoyed doing it. Feel the pleasure of having completed it. Next set aside a time to do the task. Remember that you choose your thoughts, so it's down to you whether you feel depressed or energised about the task. If you feel depressed, the task will become more of a chore and the quality of the thinking you put into it will be reduced.

love people-watching. It's fun trying to work out what they all do by how they look and the newspapers they read. I'll also be able to have a nosey at people's gardens and see the different things they all do with the similar space. And when I get to the centre, there'll be millions of people of all different cultures and just the energy of the place will be exciting. Then I'll get a taxi and even though there'll probably be a queue, you never know who you'll get talking to and the cabbies are real characters. I might get some tips from them about where to go. Then I'll explore the shops, which I really enjoy. The challenge will be not to buy too much because I know there'll be so many things that I'll like. What fun, I can't wait.'

The second wife thinks, 'Oh no, I hate the city. I'll never find anywhere to park at the station because the commuters will have got there first. It'll probably be raining so I'll be wet and cold before I even get there. I probably won't get a seat and I bet no one will offer me their seat. Commuters are so boring, they just stare at their newspapers and ignore you. And when I get there, it'll be a nightmare with hundreds of people pushing and shoving. There's bound to be a long queue for a taxi and cabbies always take you the long way round and charge a fortune. Then I'll have to traipse round the shops. Shop after shop because I'll never find something I

Defining idea...

'Life is the movie you see through your own eyes. It makes little difference what's happening out there. It's how you take it that counts.'
– DENIS WAITLEY, trainer and motivator

want, and the service is never as good in the big city stores. It's going to be awful but I suppose I'll have to go because I've got to find something to wear.'

So, both women do go to the city. And what sort of day do they have? It's obvious isn't it – the first has a brilliant day and the second has an awful one. But just think about it – everything outside of themselves is identical, and yet they have a very different experience.

What you can say here is that these women created a day in their life by the way they were thinking. So, let's pause a minute and think about this because if we can create one day then perhaps we can create two days, a week, a month, a year or even a lifetime. This is actually amazingly exciting because it means that we have everything that we need to transform our lives. Change your thinking and you'll change your life.

31. What do I think about me?

Beliefs can have both negative and positive effects on our lives. Recognising that a belief can be changed can be liberating and is the way forward to a more fulfilled life.

Our upbringing and what we witness in our early years can dramatically effect how we live our lives. We can end up repeating useless patterns and believing that 'life has it in for us'.

WHAT WE DON'T WANT

Imagine you were born into this life as a pure spirit – a blank sheet of experience soaking up knowledge from the world around you. Say you're born into a family where the father is violent and, from a very young age, you hear raised voices and the noise of slaps and punches. You may actually see your father knocking your mother about. At a very young age you may begin to acquire the subconscious belief that all men are violent. And every time you hear or see your father hitting your mother or your older siblings it reinforces that belief. As this is your only experience of men, the unconscious belief may continue to develop.

Now you've grown up a bit and go to school where you meet lots of lovely little boys – great kids who care about their friends and treat them kindly. But one day, in break time, you see two older boys bullying a younger child. Here's another reinforcement of your subconscious belief that men are violent. All the lovely boys you've seen count for almost nothing.

Here's an idea for you...

Is there something holding you back from achieving something you've always wanted to achieve? Perhaps there's a subconscious belief that's stopping you. See if you can find it by asking yourself what you're assuming about this situation. Write down whatever responses come into your mind, however crazy they might seem. You may then choose to ask yourself a question along the lines of, 'If I could change my life to be exactly as I want it to be, what would I do differently, right now?'

Later as a teenager you could be receiving abuse yourself – maybe physically, maybe sexually. Sadly, there's a real possibility that you'll assume that this is the way of the world. But as you grow older still, and spend time with friends and their families, you begin to realise that what you're experiencing isn't normality at all. Many of your friends have never been hit and neither have their mothers. You begin to realise that the pain you're going through is the exception not the norm.

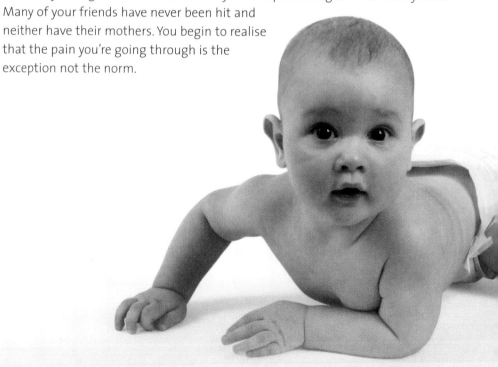

Defining idea...
'The self is not something ready-made, but something in continuous formation through choice of action.' – JOHN DEWEY, US philosopher and educator

SO LET'S CHANGE

At this point you may swear that the one thing you'll never do is treat your own children in this way. You'll be a very different person because you'll never allow children of yours to suffer in this way.

The statistics on this are scary. According to current police evidence it appears that around 82% of abusers have been abused themselves. Crazy isn't it? At a conscious level, who'd ever want to put others through the pain that they themselves experienced? At a subconscious level, one can get some understanding of what's happening. In a much less dramatic way, and because of my early childhood experiences, I had the belief for years that I wasn't good enough. I kept trying to change the circumstances outside of me so that I could improve my life – I changed husbands, homes, ways of living, etc. It was a long time before I realised that nothing would change until I changed the belief itself. Another thing that appals me is something I learned recently. Research shows that about 80% of young offenders reoffend within two years. We keep trying to change them and give them new skills, a new environment, a new family. But perhaps we are working in the wrong area. Perhaps we need to help them to change their inner world and get them to explore the beliefs that may be holding them back from the change so desperately needed.

7 steps to achieving work-life balance in a week

There is nothing more depressing than a 'to do' list that never gets any shorter. The usual reason is that we are unrealistic about how much time we have. This method not only helps you prioritise *what* you have to do, but ensures you assign time to actually *do* it.

1. Make a master list of everything you have to do.

2. Divide the list into three categories – work, 'buffer', free time.

3. Buffer is everything that isn't urgent but makes life flow more smoothly – all the admin jobs that need to be done but you never find time for – filing receipts, dental check-ups, searching for cheaper car insurance.

4. Now take your diary and set aside at least half-day for 'buffering' per week, as many work days as you need and at least one day a week free time (this is reserved for total enjoyment – no guilt or duty outings (those are buffer activities). Free-time is about total enjoyment.

5. Into every work day and buffer period, assign tasks for each day of the week. Be realistic and obviously start with the most important stuff. If you can't get round to the important stuff because you have so many appointments, perhaps you need to think about curtailing meetings. Your 'to do' list is simply fantasy if you don't have any time to complete tasks.

6. As you achieve each task, colour it in highlighter pen. This isn't strictly necessary but it's cheerful and as the page becomes more colourful, you heighten the sense of achievement.

7. Now you have prioritised what you have to do, but most importantly found slots of time in which you can achieve them. This method also means you remember to take time off, essential for you to recharge, and also find time for 'buffering' by attending to the non-essential but important tasks that we ignore until they become critical. Leaving buffer activities until the last minute makes us harried – dealing with them little and often helps us feel in the flow.

See idea 36 for another way to tame to do lists.

32. Don't live your life by accident

We do have a choice about how we live our lives. For example, we can choose to focus on work. Alternatively we can place a higher priority on family and leisure. Whatever our choice, how do we get the balance just right?

Here's a way of establishing whether you have the balance you want or whether you need to make some changes.

CHECK THE CURRENT SITUATION

There are 168 hours in a week, and you probably spend around 56 of them in bed. So, this leaves 112 hours for living in. Draw a table comprising three columns and three rows, resulting in nine square boxes. In each box write down an activity or area of your life where you currently spend your time, such as Friends, Relationships, Family, Alone Time, Work, Spirituality, Vision, Personal Growth, Health, Hobbies, Leisure, Creativity. If you need more squares just add them. Also include areas that you wish to get involved in, such as Fitness or Travel.

Now add the number of hours in a typical week that you spend in each of these areas. Then convert these numbers into a percentage of 112 and write the percentages into the appropriate boxes.

Here's an idea for you...
Create an action plan. All too often we talk about wanting to get fitter, visit friends or take up a new hobby, but another year passes and we never seem to get around to it. Head up columns with the areas you wish to work on, then create two rows for listing exactly how you intend to go about the change and when you intend to achieve this by. Also include a 'completed' box. The key is to break the path to success down into small, realistic and achievable steps.

That's your starting point. You may wish to ask your partner or a work colleague to take a look at what you've written to make sure that you're not indulging in any wishful thinking. If the percentages are just as you'd like them to be, then well done – there's no need for you to continue with the rest of this idea.

One person I did this exercise with decided that he was spending too many hours watching television and too many hours working. The area that suffered as a result was his box marked Wife and Family. Following this realisation he resolved to refrain from watching TV between Monday and Thursday. He also committed to telling his boss that he was only going to work late three evenings a week and that he was leaving each Wednesday and Friday at five o'clock. He decided to ask for support from his team at work and to sit down with them to look at their work–life balance and to ask them what he could do to help them get their ideal balance. He planned to take his wife out for dinner once a month and decided he would tell his two sons that every other weekend they could have half a day of his time to do anything they wanted to do, provided it didn't cost more than a couple of DVDs. His commitment to action made this exercise really work for him and his family.

Defining idea...

'We're so engaged in doing things to achieve purposes of outer value that we forget that the inner value, the rapture that is associated with being alive, is what it's all about.' – JOSEPH CAMPBELL, US expert on mythology and comparative religion

PLAN THE FUTURE SITUATION

Now look at your own table and decide on the areas where you want to make adjustments. Remember that you'll need to counterbalance each area where you wish to raise the percentage. And resolve to get started on any activities that you've added that you currently don't do. Now translate the percentages into hours and see whether you think you have a feasible plan.

33. Who is in charge of your life?

It's too easy to live your life the way others want you to live it. Even scarier, you may not even recognise that you've doing it.

It took a long time for me to realise that I didn't know who I was and that I didn't actually own my life.

WHO AM I?

It starts when you are a small child, when you do what your parents tell you to do. Because your parents are older and therefore wiser you automatically assume that they knew best. Even when you rebel, you don't truly feel that you are your own person. You are just rebelling because you resent the rules that are being imposed, not because you are choosing who you really want to be. You can spend most of your life trying to be what you think others want you to be, and always trying to fulfil their expectations.

Here's an idea for you...
Pick one day next week to be your day to do whatever you want. Decide not just what you're going to do, but also how you're going to feel and look. Set aside thinking time to ask yourself, 'If I knew that I own my life 100%, what might I be or do differently right now?' You could do this while taking a walk, lazing in a bubble bath or playing golf. Don't write your answers down yet – just open your mind to new possibilities.

It doesn't work. Take the case of an 'extreme wife', trying to be all that she thinks a wife should be. On top of the standard things like washing, ironing and cooking, she runs her husband's bath, puts out his clothes each day, drives him to and from the station to save him from having to park, and so on. The more she does, the more he expects of her. But as soon as she has several young children, she no longer has the time to continue doing all these things. He complains and she feels a failure.

Defining idea...
'Most powerful is he who has himself in his own power.' – SENECA

THE STARTING POINT
I've found myself in situations like this where I've completely lost sight of who I am. In fact, I'm not sure I ever knew who I wanted to be. This was when I sat down and did some exercises – including writing my own obituary! – so that I could recognise who I wanted to become. And I tried to visualise my future life, in order

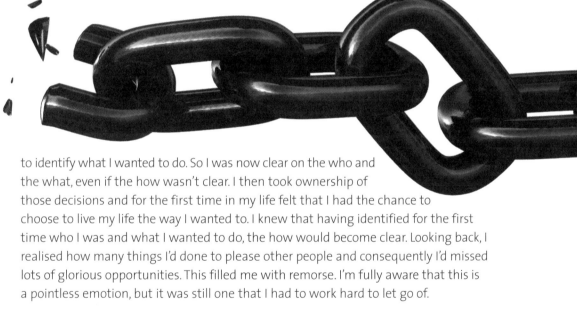

to identify what I wanted to do. So I was now clear on the who and the what, even if the how wasn't clear. I then took ownership of those decisions and for the first time in my life felt that I had the chance to choose to live my life the way I wanted to. I knew that having identified for the first time who I was and what I wanted to do, the how would become clear. Looking back, I realised how many things I'd done to please other people and consequently I'd missed lots of glorious opportunities. This filled me with remorse. I'm fully aware that this is a pointless emotion, but it was still one that I had to work hard to let go of.

I now own my life totally and whatever the circumstances I recognise that this is actually where I'm choosing to be, how I'm choosing to feel and how I'm choosing to react. If it's off track then I'm choosing it to be that way. If I'm in an abusive relationship, that's my choice. If I'm behaving in a way that denies my values, then that, too, is my choice.

34. No more indecision

We don't often ask ourselves who we really want to be. Yet this is fundamental to how we live our lives.

If you were no longer here, what would you want people to say about you? How would you like people to think about you? If you could be listening at the keyhole, what would you like to hear?

HOW DO YOU WANT TO BE REMEMBERED?

A good friend asked me these questions about ten years ago and gave me an exercise to do that was probably one of the most uncomfortable and most life-changing exercises that I've ever done. She asked me to write my obituary! In two steps. The first step was to think of the person that knew me the best, and write my obituary as though I'd just died and that person was writing it. I did this, imagining what Hazel might say. It contained many good things – how loving I was, what a caring and supportive friend and mother I was – and I felt proud to read these. However, there were some serious negatives that I didn't like writing or reading, including never fulfilling her potential, never being strong enough to stand up for what was right for her, putting others first and then blaming them when it all fell apart, never being really clear about what she wanted in life, and an awful lot more. I then asked Hazel to read it and she said that it was pretty accurate. Oh dear! This was not how I wanted to be remembered at all, so I knew I needed to do something about it.

Here's an idea for you...
Write your own obituary and then pick one of the values that this has highlighted. For example, take 'Living your life with integrity'. Now list all the behaviours that you'll be demonstrating that will allow anybody you meet to say that you're a person with integrity. It may be things such as always telling the truth even when difficult, doing things that you say you're going to do, only agreeing to do something for someone else if you know you're not going to let them down, only talking about people to their faces and not gossiping behind their back, always dealing with issues that need to be dealt with, not blaming others for your mistakes, and so on. Do this with each of your values because unless you're clear about what behaviours support your stated values then nothing is likely to change.

Step two was to write some more obituaries as though I died at a wonderful age – at least ninety-five! I wrote four, from the point of view of one of my children, a loving partner, a business colleague and a special friend. These included very different things from those I'd written previously, such as 'As a mother she was a living example of how I want to be – she always encouraged me to be who I am, even if sometimes it wasn't what she would have wished...', 'As a business colleague she was always there for me and I could trust her with my deepest secrets knowing they would go no further...' and 'As a partner she always listened to me and loved me unconditionally...'.

Defining idea...

'Knowing others is intelligence; knowing yourself is wisdom.' – LAO TZU

SO WHAT NOW?

When I looked at the difference between my first and second steps it became apparent that I wasn't being the person that I wanted to be. A whole lot of my values had become muddied. Did I really love unconditionally? Was I really allowing my children to fulfil their dreams or was I trying to make them how I wanted them to be? Was I really living my life with integrity? The answers made me fundamentally shift my values from my unconscious mind to the conscious. I became fully aware of how I wanted to be and totally committed to getting there. I still have that exercise and I look back at it occasionally to see how very far I have come.

35. Why plan your life?

I spent most of my life believing that I was doing what I wanted with my life. Then I realised that I wasn't my own person at all as I'd never actually sat down and thought hard about how I really wanted my life to be.

Do you really have a vision for how you want your life to be or do things just happen? Do you ever feel as though life is passing you by? And are there times when you say 'If only...'?

HOW MUCH DO YOU VALUE YOU?

I spent a large part of my life focusing on what I didn't want – getting myself into situations and knowing that I didn't want to be there. If anyone asked me what I did want, by the second sentence I was telling them what I *didn't* want! If anyone suggested creating a vision for my life I thought, 'What a waste of time and how would that help?'

Here's an idea for you...

Set aside an hour and find a pen, some paper and a quiet place. Now imagine the best six months of your life. Not six months that you've already lived or the next six months, but six months of your dreams. Picture yourself at the age of ninety-five telling your great-grandchildren about this incredible six months that you're living, what you're achieving, how happy you are, what a fantastic job you're in, what wonderful relationships you're enjoying, what a beautiful house you're living in, and so on. Describe all this in as much detail as possible. Now put this somewhere that you can see it every day, read it each morning and see what happens. Even better, each day ask yourself, 'If I knew that there is one thing that I can do today that will move me closer to my vision what might that be?' Then do it!

I have faced a time when I found myself with debts and no confidence. I have been an emotional wreck and I suspected that this wasn't entirely what I'd envisaged when I was younger! When a good friend and colleague suggested I do a vision, I never thought that it could change my life. If I'm completely honest, I did it to humour her! After I'd completed the task, I laughed at what I'd written because it seemed a complete impossibility and was so far from where I was at that point in my life. In the ten years since, I've rewritten my vision three times because I have exceeded it each time. How I wish I'd met that friend years earlier.

Think of it this way. Have you ever bought a new car thinking it's not a car that everyone else has, yet the day you collect it and start driving it's as though everyone else has had the same feeling. Suddenly there's twice as many of the

Defining idea...
'The great thing in this world is not so much where we are, but in what direction we are moving.' – OLIVER WENDELL HOLMES

same car on the road. The reality is that they were always there; you just didn't notice them before. The same thing happens when you create your vision for your life. Suddenly opportunities begin to appear as if by magic. But they were always there, you just didn't see them before.

STEALING YOUR DREAMS

It's so easy to have your dreams stolen, and sadly the people who steal them the most, after you of course, are the people closest to you. I know an eighteen-year-old girl whose dream was to become a jockey, but when she went to live with her father he persuaded her that this wasn't a viable future. He loved her so much that he wanted the best for her and he thought that being a jockey would be a tough life where she would earn no money and have to be in the top of her profession to get anywhere. He also thought that it wouldn't be good for her back, which was weak owing to an accident she'd had when she was younger. After becoming an extremely successful sales manager, she came to work with me and began to rethink her dream. She worked shorter hours to qualify as an amateur jockey, came second in the first race she ever ran and then went on to win the second race! Unfortunately she'd left it too late to ever qualify as a full jockey. Effectively, loving her, her father stole her dream. Are you allowing the people closest to you to steal your dreams or could you be stealing theirs? Think it. Dream it. Do it.

36. Revamp your 'to do' list

'To do' lists are essential for most of us but they can be a huge drain on energy.

The list that never seems to get any shorter is not so much an *aide-memoire* as a horrible reminder that we're running fast but getting nowhere.

And what could be more dispiriting than that?

The other side, of course, is that 'to do' lists are incredibly useful tools for motivating us and making us more productive. Having a clear plan for the day ahead focuses the mind and puts you in control like nothing else. Whether you're a CEO, freelance, stay-at-home parent or student, the well run 'to do' list will give you a sense of full-capacity living.

But for it to work, you have to have a definite system. Try this one. It is based on the advice given to 1930s magnate Charles Schwabb by a young man he challenged to double his productivity. The young man told him to write down the six most crucial tasks for each day in order of importance and work down the list. Then teach his staff to do the same. After a few weeks, the story goes that Schwabb sent a cheque for £25,000 to the young man, which was a huge sum then.

This idea works on the principle that we put off important stuff (or we work to others' agenda so we don't get round to what's important for us) and keep ourselves busy with lesser tasks to distract ourselves. But if we don't do the one

Here's an idea for you...
Switch off your mobile for as long as you can comfortably get away with, but aim for at least an hour in the morning and an hour in the afternoon. These should be your high productivity times when you aim to really motor through your tasks. The act of switching of your mobile sends an unconscious message to your brain that this is time when your interests are the priority, and it helps to focus your mind on the task at hand.

important thing, no matter what we achieve, we'll feel dissatisfied at the end of the day. Instead of an abstract list of things to do that you attack randomly, switch the angle from what you *must* do to when you are *going* to do it.

HOW TO REVAMP YOUR 'TO DO' LIST
In your diary or a separate notebook, draw a line down the left hand side of the page to form a column and mark in the working hours of the day. This can be precise (9.30 to 10.30, 10.30 to 11.30) or loose (morning, afternoon). Now you're set to go.

- At the end of your working day, brew a cuppa, sit for a second, take a deep breath and gather your thoughts. Pat yourself on the back for what you have achieved today. Now. Swing your mind forward into tomorrow.

- Ask yourself what regular scheduled tasks or meetings you have for tomorrow. Block them off on your diary page.

- Remember to add in travelling time, lunch and relaxation.

- What is your major task? What *must* you do tomorrow? That gets priority and should be done first thing if possible. Set aside a realistic block of time (err on the side of caution). Be precise.

Defining idea...

'Energy and persistence alter all things.' – BENJAMIN FRANKLIN

- Put in specific times for phone calls/e-mails. It is more time effective to do these in two or three blocks rather than breaking concentration and doing it ad hoc during the day.

- What's your next most important task? Is there room in your day? If you have time left, you can schedule in other tasks, but be realistic.

- For each week have a short list of brief one-off tasks (phone calls, paying bills, birthday cards) and if you have a few down minutes, slot them in.

2

Part two

Going deeper...
prioritise yourself

Imagine how it would feel to know that you were making time for the important stuff. We all know we should be taking care of our health and our future security but we're too busy fighting fires today to worry about tomorrow. Our authors know that feeling and here are their ideas on how you can be as healthy as possible, and as secure as you need to be – with very little effort. The result will be a calmer (dare we say smugger) you. Here's how to make yourself the priority.

Turn back the clock...

QUIZ: **Are you younger than you think?**

How fast you age is a process that's under your control far more than was thought before. How long your body and mind stay fit, active and healthy is determined by the choices you make. It's thought that you can have a biological age of 50 in your 70s.

Start with your chronological age and add or subtract

1. Do you get at least 30 minutes of moderate exercise (such as walking) on most days?

    Yes – subtract 1 year

2. Do you exercise intensively on a regular basis?

    Yes – add 3 years

3. Do you rarely, if ever, do any physical exercise?

    Yes – add 2 years

4. Are you more than 10% over the recommended weight for your height?

    Yes – add 3 years

5. Are you the correct weight for your height?

    Yes – subtract 1 year

6. Are you under stress or pressure on a regular basis?

   Yes – add 4 years

7. Do you actively practise stress-reducing techniques such as meditation or yoga?

   Yes – subtract 3 years

8. Have you experienced three or more stressful life events in the past year (for example, divorce, bereavement, job loss, moving house)?

   Yes – add 3 years

9. Do you smoke?

   Yes – add 6 years

10. Do you have a cholesterol level of 6.7 or higher (or has your doctor told you that you should think of reducing your cholesterol levels)?

   Yes – add 2 years

11. Do you have blood pressure that's 135/95 (or has your doctor told you to that you should think of reducing your blood pressure)?

   Yes – add 3 years

12. Do you eat five or more portions of a range of fresh fruit and vegetables every day?

Yes – subtract 5 years

13. Do you regularly eat processed, packaged or fast food?

Yes – add 4 years

14. Are you a vegetarian?

Yes – subtract 2 years

15. Do you eat oily fish three times a week?

Yes – subtract 2 years

16. Do you drink two or three small glasses of red wine, up to five days a week?

Yes – subtract 3 years

17. Do you drink more than 21 units of alcohol a week (if you're a man) or 14 units (if you're a woman)

Yes – add 5 years

18. Do you have an active social life and a supportive network of friends and family?

    Yes – subtract 2 years

19. Do you have an active sex life?

    Yes – subtract 2 years

20. Are you happily married?

    Yes – subtract 1.5 years.

If you're younger than your biological age, keep up the good work. Exercise is the best way of knocking off more years so if you don't already exercise, turn to *ideas 52 and 55*.

If you're older than your biological age, and want to do something about it, then it's time to start relaxing. Start with the *idea 38*.

37. Ageing explained

We've undergoing a quiet revolution in our understanding of ageing. It may not be inevitable — and one day may even be reversible.

Slowing ageing down, right now, is something we can all do. It can be as easy as simply eating more vegetables.

What, exactly, is ageing all about? It's the subject of hot debate among scientists. Some see it as an unavoidable process that we can only slow down by postponing ageing-related diseases as long as possible. Others see it as a specific biological process that one day we may learn how to switch off.

For decades, it was thought that ageing was a way of getting rid of a generation of people who had already reproduced and so were no longer useful to the survival of the species. But in 1956 US scientist Dr Denham Harmon came up with the theory that ageing wasn't simply a sign that our time was nearly up – it was the result of the build-up of faults in the body. And these faults are caused by damage from unstable molecules called free radicals.

Free radicals are by-products of normal bodily processes – like breathing, eating and drinking – which are 'unstable' as they lack an electron, so they career around the body looking for spare electrons to bind with. In optimal health, the body simply

Here's an idea for you...
What's the simplest way to add more healthy years to your life? Drink more water. Drink more than five glasses a day and you'll halve your risk of certain cancers. But according to one recent survey, most of us drink fewer than four glasses of water every day. Why not buy a filter jug that fits in the fridge? Then you'll have cool, clean tasting water 'on tap'. Aim for two litres (around ten glasses) a day.

mops up free radicals and makes them harmless. But if the body's self-repair capabilities weaken, free radicals, and the damage they cause, can accumulate, leading to serious diseases, muscle and bone wastage, reduced skin elasticity, weakened sight and hearing and slower mental reactions. Everything we associate with getting old. But this can be slowed down by eating more vegetables – they contain antioxidants which bind with free radicals and make them harmless.

One of the newest theories is called the cross-linking theory of age or the glycosylation theory of ageing. It's all about how glucose (sugar) binds to protein, causing damage. It's thought that a lot of skin-ageing and heart problems may be due to cross-linking. One theory is that sugars binding to DNA may cause damage that leads to malformed cells and thus to cancer. Excessive cross-linking is thought to be the reason why people with diabetes (who often have excess amounts of glucose in the body) tend to age quicker. So simply cutting back on the sugar in your diet may help keep you younger for longer.

Recently, we've learned more about the role our DNA plays in the ageing process. Our DNA is our individual blueprint, passed to us from our parents. It means that we are born with a unique code and a predetermined tendency to certain types of physical and mental functioning that regulate the rate at which we age.

Defining idea…
'Just as we can alter the lifespan of a car by how well or badly we drive and maintain it, we alter the ageing of our body by how well, or badly, we take care of it.' **– Top UK longevity expert DR TOM KIRKWOOD**

These days, not a week goes by without a 'gene' headline hitting the papers: 'Researchers find the breast cancer gene', 'Colon cancer gene isolated'. This has given all the fatalists among us a new excuse for avoiding healthy lifestyle choices by saying, 'What's the point? It's all in the genes anyway.' It's the current equivalent of 'you could get run over by a bus tomorrow'. Yes, scientists have discovered that genetic mutations occurring in what are known as our 'germ line' cells, those that become the egg and sperm, can be passed from parent to child, creating a higher risk of developing certain diseases. And it's undoubtedly true that our deepening understanding of DNA will have far-reaching effects on our health in the future. But it's also important to keep it in perspective. The vast majority of diseases are caused by environmental (i.e. lifestyle) factors rather than genes. In breast cancer, for example, genetic predisposition is thought to account for less than 4% of cases. Inheriting a gene that increases your risk of developing a certain disease does *not* mean you're destined to get it.

Scientists all over the world are studying these and many other theories in the hope that one day, we'll find a foolproof way to stop the ageing process. But until that day there is much you can do to influence the rate at which you age – simply by adapting the way you live your life.

38. What a difference a day makes...

Motivated by instant results? These simple lifestyle changes could add years to your life in one day.

There are many different ways to stay younger for longer – eating different foods, cutting others out of your diet, exercising, getting out and about, watching your stress levels, taking the right vitamins.

It can seem overwhelming, but in practice it comes down to common sense. Most of it is even fun! To give you a better idea, here's what an ideal anti-ageing day could look like.

7.30 a.m. ALWAYS START YOUR DAY WITH BREAKFAST. People who eat breakfast live longer than people who don't – as long as they choose wholegrain-based cereals. Add a cup of green tea and a piece of fruit to boost your levels of disease-fighting antioxidants.

7.45 a.m. DRINK A GLASS OF WATER AND TAKE A MULTIVITAMIN. Most people don't get the recommended daily allowance of many essential vitamins and minerals. You're more likely to remember to take a supplement every day if you take it with breakfast.

8 a.m. BRUSH AND FLOSS YOUR TEETH – it can take six years off your biological age. The bacteria that cause gum disease also cause furring of the arteries which can lead to heart disease. And bad teeth never helped anyone look younger!

Here's an idea for you...
Defining your anti-ageing goals will make them more achievable. Try conjuring up an image of yourself as you'd like to be in a year's time. Someone who enjoys exercising three times a week, cooks imaginative, healthy dishes and has a fulfilling social life? Someone who's 12 kg lighter, who's given up smoking and who sticks to 14 units (or 21 if you're a man) of alcohol a week? Write down weekly steps that will get you to your goal. This week, it could be buying a new recipe book and learning to cook with pulses. Next week, it could be joining a local running group.

8.30 a.m. WALK TO WORK. Exercising for at least thirty minutes every day is the best way to keep your heart and lungs in good shape (not to mention the rest of you).

9 a.m. DRINK A GLASS OF WATER and try to have six more throughout the day.

10 a.m. HAVE ANOTHER CUP OF TEA. Always squeeze your teabag – you'll release twice as many antioxidants that way.

10.30 a.m. CONNECT WITH YOUR FRIENDS and colleagues by email or phone. People with a strong social network of friends and family live longer and healthier lives than more solitary types.

12.30 p.m. DO SOME LUNCHTIME YOGA. It balances out all the body's systems and gets your organs working efficiently. Ever wondered why yoga teachers look so young?

1.30 p.m. HAVE A RAINBOW SALAD FOR LUNCH. Use as many differently coloured vegetables – red peppers, watercress, grated carrot and courgette, young spinach leaves, cherry tomatoes – as you can. Dress with olive oil and balsamic vinegar, and sprinkle with a handful of toasted sunflower and sesame seeds for the perfect antioxidant-packed, disease-fighting lunch.

Defining idea...
'The best thing about the future is that it comes only one day at a time.'
– ABRAHAM LINCOLN

3.30 p.m. TAKE THE STAIRS. Climb up and down a flight six times a day and you'll prevent weight gain of 2 kg a year. You take 36 days off your life for every 5 kg overweight you are.

6 p.m. MEDITATE ON THE TRAIN HOME. You'll lower your blood pressure and slow your heartbeat, both of which are good for your heart's health. Close your eyes and breathe deeply, in through your nose and out through your mouth. Try to empty your mind and simply concentrate on what the breath feels like as it enters your nostrils and leaves through your lips. Feel it filling your lungs and pushing out your abdomen. Keep this focus for around ten to fifteen minutes.

7 p.m. HAVE A SMALL GLASS OF RED WINE. Go for a deep red like a Pinot Noir for a maximum boost of disease-fighting flavonoids. Just be sure to stop at one or two.

8 p.m. HAVE SALMON FOR DINNER. Oily fish like salmon – or mackerel, sardines, trout or tuna – keeps your brain healthy and can stave off Alzheimer's if eaten at least twice a week.

9 p.m. WATCH A FUNNY VIDEO. Laughter boosts your immune system and reduces the ageing effect of stress hormones on the body. So switch off the news and watch a comedy instead.

10 p.m. HAVE SEX. People who have sex more than twice a week live longer than those who don't.

11 p.m. SLEEP! It's your body's chance to release growth hormone and repair itself from the inside out. So never skimp on your shut-eye – aim for at least six to eight hours a night.

39. Boost your immune system

You can't live younger for longer without a strong immune system, it's your private army fighting off invasion by foreign organisms that can lead to disease.

Every day, hordes of bugs (bacteria, viruses, parasites and fungi) are doing their best to get inside your body. To a bug, you're a very attractive proposition: a bijou residence offering warmth, safety and food.

Luckily the body has developed a highly effective defence system for keeping these bugs out. Inside you is an army of scavenging white blood cells, constantly roaming the body looking for invaders. If a scavenging cell spots one, then it's immediately transported to the nearest lymph glands (situated in the neck, armpits and groin) and destroyed before it's even had a chance to wave a white flag. (You can feel this brutal elimination process taking place when your lymph glands become swollen.)

A healthy body with a fully functioning immune system sees off potentially dangerous organisms and carcinogens every day. It's even thought that cancer cells grow and are destroyed by the immune system on a regular basis. It's no surprise that a recent study of healthy centenarians found they had one thing in common: a healthy immune system.

The danger comes when the immune system is weakened, and invaders remain undetected and start to multiply. Some pathogens, such as HIV, are so powerful they simply trample over your body's defence system. But in most cases there are

Here's an idea for you...
Regular massage not only reduces stress and anxiety, it can also boost the immune system by increasing levels of infection-fighting cells. Can't coerce someone into doing it? Don't have the time or spare cash to see a professional? No problem – simply get a tennis ball, lean against a wall and roll the ball around between your back and shoulders and the wall. Try it – you'll be hooked.

three main factors which lead to weak links in your inner defences: a less than ideal diet (an army marches on its stomach, after all), the environment in which you live (constantly challenging your defences over and above what's normal by smoking, sunbathing or breathing in toxic fumes), and mental well-being – feeling under stress on a regular basis.

YOU ARE WHAT YOU EAT

Your immune system works best when you keep it supplied with a full range of micronutrients such as vitamins and minerals. But even people who eat a balanced diet often show deficiencies and there are two theories about why. When we evolved, we were designed to lead active lives, hunting, gathering and escaping predators, and consuming 3000–4000 calories a day. Now we're mainly sedentary, and need around 2000 calories, we may not be able to eat enough to get the full range of micronutrients we need. The second theory is that today's intensive farming methods have depleted our soil of key minerals (such as selenium) and our food processing methods further deplete food of micronutrients. We now know that a large number of people are regularly missing out on vitamins A, D and B12; folic acid, riboflavin, iron, magnesium, zinc, copper and omega-3 oils. Plus, nutritionists think we're more likely to have deficiencies as we get older, because the digestive system becomes less efficient at absorbing micronutrients from the food we eat.

So strengthening your immune system starts with taking a good multivitamin and mineral supplement every day. By the way, simply buying the bottle and leaving it in the kitchen drawer doesn't work! You need to top up your micronutrients every

Defining idea...
'Hope, purpose and determination are not merely mental states. They have electrochemical connections that affect the immune system.'
– NORMAN COUSINS, writer

day (so a bottle just lasts as long as it says on the label – 30, 60 or 90 days. Not all year). This really helps: there was a US study of older people with weakened immune systems. After taking a daily nutritional supplement they had fully functioning immune systems within a year.

BE AWARE OF YOUR ENVIRONMENT

Your body has a regular army designed to fight off everyday invaders, and it also has a troop of 'special forces', called T-cells, held in reserve for extraordinary circumstances. But if you bombard your body with extra invaders on a regular basis, the effectiveness of these special forces is inevitably weakened, allowing disease-causing bugs to multiply. And while you can't control the many bacteria and viruses that assault your immune system every day, you do have control over additional toxic invaders such as cigarette smoke (whether first-hand or passive) and, to a lesser extent, environmental pollution.

THE MIND/BODY FACTOR

Undergoing stress on a regular basis is like offering a personal invitation to foreign invaders to walk through the chinks it causes in your defences. Many of the hormones involved in your body's fight or flight response – how it responds to stress – are actually immune suppressants, slowing down its natural disease-fighting mechanisms. Ever noticed how you're more prone to colds when you feel under pressure? It's not just your imagination. People in one study were most likely to develop a cold if they had experienced a negative life event in the past year. It's also been found that the effectiveness of a pneumonia vaccine was reduced if recipients were suffering from stress.

40. Fighting free radicals

You don't need to get radical to stave off ageing – you just need to help your body do its housework.

When you put petrol in your car, you create energy – and noxious exhaust fumes. It's a similar story in the body. When you breathe, oxygen enters the bloodstream and combines with fats and carbohydrates to create the energy that every cell in your body needs in order to function. But a by-product is created during the process – an unstable molecule called a free radical or oxidant. This roams the body, bombarding your body's cells, trying to steal electrons to make itself 'stable'.

According to one estimate, free radicals attack each cell up to 10,000 times a day. If they successfully attack the DNA, stored in the cell's nucleus, they can cause cancer. If they successfully attack the mitochondria, or the energy factories of the cell, they can stop them working efficiently. And, as the mitochondria supply energy for all the bodily organs and systems, the knock-on effect is felt as ageing in the body.

It's only been in the last two decades that we've really begun to understand the role that free radicals play in the ageing process. Free radical damage is thought to be the main cause of Alzheimer's, cancer, heart disease and inflamed joints, as well as wrinkles and liver spots. In fact, the rate at which you age is directly related to how well your body deactivates these oxygen radicals. It might explain why pigeons live 35 years, twelve times as long as rats, animals that are about the same size: for the amount of oxygen they take in, pigeons produce only half as many free radicals as rats. Some experts believe that if you can boost your defences against free radicals, you can extend your life.

Here's an idea for you...
Here's a simple way to see the free radical effect working. Take an apple, cut it in half. Rub one half in lemon juice and leave both halves out for a couple of hours. When you come back, you'll have one brown half and one that's stayed white. The browning is the oxidation process at work. But rubbing cut fruits with lemon juice (which contains high levels of vitamin C, an antioxidant) delays the browning process. Now imagine what that vitamin C could do inside your body.

Luckily, most free radicals are neutralised by an army of good guys in the body known as antioxidants. It's like a house always getting dirty, and the antioxidants always tidying it up. The best way to stave off ageing is to help your body keep on top of its housework. Here's how.

KEEP YOUR DEFENCES UP BY BOOSTING YOUR ANTIOXIDANTS
The easiest way to do this? Eat more fruit and veg! They're packed with antioxidants – which is why nutritionists are always banging on about getting your 'five a day'. Try to choose differently coloured fruit and vegetables every day and eat local and seasonal produce. The sooner fruits and vegetables are eaten after picking, the more nutrients they contain (imported produce can take anything from a month to a year to arrive in the UK after picking). Home-grown is best but visiting your nearest farmers' market or having an organic box delivered are great choices too. Check labels for origin in your supermarket and buy food produced locally.

DON'T ADD TO THE FREE RADICAL LOAD
That means giving up smoking, which loads the body with millions of free radicals every time you inhale. The free radicals in cigarettes cause the fat in your blood to oxidise and form plaques on the artery walls, which is why smokers have a raised risk of heart disease.

Defining idea...
'Life is better than death, I believe, if only because it is less boring and because it has fresh peaches in it.' – ALICE WALKER, writer

DON'T SUNBATHE
Exposure to ultraviolet light floods the skin with free radicals and causes 80–90% of skin ageing.

EXERCISE REGULARLY
Keep it moderate, though – great news for anyone who hates painful, red-in-the-face, exercise sessions. Intense exercise uses up large amounts of oxygen and produces large amounts of free radicals as a by-product. The body can't mop up the free radicals quick enough and damage can occur, which is why athletes can suffer from depressed immune systems. But this isn't carte blanche to become part of the sofa – *moderate* exercise stimulates the production of the body's antioxidant enzymes and slows the ageing process. Aim for a minimum of around thirty minutes of brisk walking a day.

41. Upping the anti

Antioxidants could add years to your life by fighting free radical damage — if you're getting enough.

It's always important to know your enemy and in the war against ageing, it's free radicals, the unstable molecules that are a by-product of breathing and which damage the body's cells. There's nothing you can do to stop free radicals forming (except stop breathing, which would be a bit, well, radical), but antioxidants can eliminate them.

One half of the antioxidant army consists of compounds and enzymes that the body makes itself, using micronutrients found in the diet such as selenium, zinc, manganese, copper, iron, lipoic acid and glutathione. The other half are antioxidants delivered in the food we eat including vitamins A, C, E and B, and the vitamin-like compounds flavonoids, carotenoids and coenzyme Q10.

When you eat a diet high in antioxidants, a protective shield is created around each cell which fights off and destroys the attacking free radicals. But if you're depleted in any of these micronutrients, there will be cracks in the shield. Many scientists believe the rise in heart disease, Alzheimer's and some cancers can be directly linked to micronutrient depletion. Our intake of selenium, for example, has fallen by 50% in the past 50 years due to intensive farming methods that leach it from the soil.

When it comes to their antioxidant content, not all foods were created equal. Meat, fish and dairy products do contain antioxidants but they're destroyed by cooking. Fruit and vegetables, however, contain high levels of antioxidants that survive the cooking process (as long as you don't boil them to mush). For very basic good

Here's an idea for you...
Black really is beautiful when it comes to staving off ageing. The darker the pigment – think plums, prunes, bilberries, blackberries, dates and raisins – the higher the ORAC rating. It's thought the pigment is a rich source of antioxidants. To maximise the benefits, wash rather than peel the skin of fruits and veg – the pigment is often concentrated in the skin or outer leaves. Try to eat a dark red, purple or black fruit or vegetable every day. And if you love wine, go for deep reds – they contain the most flavonoids.

health, you need 'five a day' – five portions (a portion is around a handful) of fresh fruit and vegetables a day. But to fend off ageing you need to step up a level and pack in as many antioxidants as possible.

It's easier to do than you might think, thanks to the brilliant scientists at Tufts University in the States who have very helpfully rated the antioxidant value of every food. It's a system known as ORAC: oxygen radical absorption capacity. The higher the ORAC, the more powerful a food is at mopping up free radicals. In fact, eating plenty of high-ORAC foods could raise the antioxidant power of blood by 10–25%.

One Tufts study of 1300 older people showed that those who had two or more portions a day of dark-pigmented vegetables such as kale and spinach were only half as likely to suffer a heart attack – and had a third of the risk of dying of cancer – compared with people averaging less than one portion a day. Other research has shown that a diet of high-ORAC foods fed to animals prevents long-term memory loss and improves learning capabilities. It may be no coincidence that this high-ORAC diet is very similar to the one eaten by the Hunza people of the Indian Himalayas, who commonly live beyond 100.

Defining idea...

'The amount of antioxidants that you maintain in your body is directly proportional to how long you will live.' – **DR RICHARD CUTLER, anti-ageing researcher**

Visit your health-food store and you'll see you can buy antioxidants as a supplement. But the researchers at Tufts think it's the whole foodstuff and the way the hundreds of micronutrients within it (some of which they're yet to identify) react *together* that provides its powerful antioxidant punch. If you're the cautious type, take a belt-and-braces approach – aim for a high-ORAC diet and add a good antioxidant supplement just in case.

THE TOP ORAC-SCORING FOODS

The following figures are the number of ORACs that 100 grams of each food provides. A high-ORAC diet will provide 3000–5000 units a day.

Prunes, *5770*

Raisins, *2830*

Blueberries, *2400*

Blackberries, *2036*

Garlic, *1939*

Kale, *1770*

Cranberries, *1750*

Strawberries, *1540*

Spinach, *1260*

Raspberries, *1220*

Brussels sprouts, *980*

Plums, *949*

Alfalfa sprouts, *930*

Broccoli, *890*

Beetroot, *840*

Avocado, *782*

Oranges, *750*

Red grapes, *739*

Red peppers, *710*

Cherries, *670*

Kiwi fruit, *602*

Baked beans, *503*

Pink grapefruit, *483*

Kidney beans, *460*

Onion, *450*

White grapes, *446*

42. Your anti-ageing diet

Every meal you eat is an opportunity to fend off ageing, so eat the right foods.

If feeling and looking younger than your years is important to you, you'll have already made the connection between your health and your fridge. There's a good chance there'll be broccoli, spinach and carrots in there. You won't have to rely on the lettuce in your burger for one of your five-a-day portions of fruit and veg. You probably know from experience that some foods give you energy and make you feel full of vitality, and others drag you down. You're well on the road to the perfect anti-ageing diet. Now it's time for an upgrade.

Food is our most important weapon in the war against ageing and disease. You only need to look at the differences in life expectancy around the world for proof. It's why those Japanese living in Japan, eating a diet rich in fish, vegetables and soy, and low in fat and sugar, have the longest lifespan and the lowest levels of heart disease. It's also why women in Scotland are nine times more likely to die from a heart attack than women in France.

A disease-fighting, anti-ageing diet means cooking from scratch, buying fresh ingredients and including as many foods as possible that have been identified as 'superfoods'. Here are just a few of the easiest to find and cook with. Try introducing one or two a month and experimenting with ways to eat them.

SPINACH
It's all in the colour – spinach and other dark green vegetables such as kale, watercress, rocket and spring greens are packed with hundreds of disease-fighting micronutrients. Spinach is good at protecting eyesight as well as keeping the arteries clear of cholesterol, reducing blood pressure and lowering the risk of

155

Here's an idea for you...
Grow your own superfood at home – you don't even need a garden! Sprouts are young green plants germinated from the seeds of vegetables, nuts, grains or beans and they've got antioxidants in super-concentrated amounts. You can buy sprouting kits or just use a large jar and some clean muslin. Simply soak the seeds overnight, place in your sprouter, then rinse with water twice a day. Keep in a dark warm place and they should be ready to eat within three days – give them a boost of sunlight before eating, then just grab a handful to add fresh crunch to salads or sandwiches.

almost every type of cancer. Try using baby spinach leaves as a base for salads (it contains 90% more antioxidants than iceberg lettuce), adding them to stir-fries (right at the end – it barely needs cooking), or steaming them and serving as a side dish sprinkled with fresh lemon juice.

BROCCOLI
Broccoli is cancer's worst enemy. It comes from a family of cruciferous vegetables (including cabbage, kale and Brussels sprouts) that contain high levels of sulphur compounds which increase the enzymes that stop cancer cells growing. They also contain high levels of the antioxidant vitamin C and cholesterol-lowering fibre. If there are any leaves left on the stalk, don't discard them before cooking – they contain more carotenoids than the florets! Simply steam and serve, making a perfect accompaniment to meals.

ONIONS
Onions are high in the flavonoid quercitin, which can cut heart disease risk by 755%. Flavonoids also boost the immune system. One study showed a strong link between regular consumption of onions and a reduced risk of stomach cancer.

Defining idea...
'Are you getting enough sweet potato?' – **A popular greeting among Okinawans, one of the world's longest-lived people**

SWEET POTATOES

While white potatoes provide low amounts of antioxidants, the orange-skinned sweet potato is packed with anti-cancer antioxidants. They can be baked in their skins, or boiled and mashed – or try cutting them into chunks and roasting them in the oven in a little olive oil to make chips.

NUTS

Nuts got a bad reputation during the 1980s fat-free diet craze – we still think of them as a naughty treat. They are high in calories, but in moderation (a handful, a few times a week) they can reduce your risk of having a heart attack by up to 50%. They're packed full of monounsaturates, which lower 'bad' LDL cholesterol and raise 'good' HDL cholesterol. Go for them raw rather than salted or roasted. They're delicious simply chopped, or toasted in a dry frying pan, and added to salads or sprinkled on soups.

WHOLEGRAINS

White, refined carbohydrates such as white bread, rice and pasta – plus refined flour products such as cakes, pastries and biscuits – have little to offer an anti-ageing diet. Refined flour is stripped of its disease-fighting fibre and nutrients. But foods that come from the wholegrain, those that still contain the antioxidant-packed wheatgerm, will help to lower your risk of heart disease, hypertension and certain cancers. So if 'whole' isn't the first word in the list of ingredients, ditch it.

YOGURT

Live bio-yogurt is a good anti-ageing food as it's full of probiotics or 'good bacteria' essential for healthy digestion and boosting the immune system. Getting your digestive system working effectively means you'll also get the most out of the other anti-ageing foods you're eating.

43. The anti-ageing store cupboard

It's time to go shopping. Supermarket shelves are full of anti-ageing superfoods, if you know what to look for.

Stock up your store cupboard with these everyday items that are all actually superfoods in disguise. Here are your shopping essentials.

TINNED SARDINES/HERRING/MACKEREL

A cheap, convenient and delicious way to get the all-important oily fish into the diet. No one should be without a stack of cans of sardines and similar oily fish, preferably in tomato sauce (a good source of cancer-fighting lycopene). If you're ever stuck for a simple supper idea, simply mash up a can with a squirt of lemon juice and serve on wholegrain toast. Delicious.

TINNED TOMATOES

In the 1980s studies revealed that people who ate a lot of tomato-based foods were less likely to get prostate cancer. It's the lycopene, which gives the tomato the red colour, that makes it a superfood. What's more, this powerful antioxidant is most easily absorbed by the body when it's cooked – so tinned tomatoes (or tomato-based pasta sauces) are actually a better anti-ageing choice than fresh. Try them warmed and served on toast for breakfast.

TINNED BEANS

Beans or pulses are all full of polyphenols, an important antioxidant. Just eating beans four times a week could cut your risk of heart disease by 22%. They're also a great source of fibre which helps to reduce 'bad' cholesterol and raise 'good'

Here's an idea for you...
Don't forget to chew! Unchewed food is hard to digest and its micronutrients pass through our systems. The less you chew your superfoods, the less their micronutrients are absorbed. Aim to chew each mouthful fifteen times before swallowing.

cholesterol, and are good sources of potassium, calcium and magnesium which help to reduce hypertension. Soaking and cooking dried beans is more economical than using tins, but keeping tinned beans means you can easily add them to a salad, stew or soup. Which to choose? According to one study, the darker the bean, the higher the antioxidant levels, but they're all a good bet. Cooked, mashed kidney or black beans make a good tortilla filling – add a slice of avocado and a fresh tomato salsa for a nutritious taste boost. Or make home-made houmous – a tasty snack.

FROZEN VEGETABLES
Pack your freezer with frozen vegetables and there's no excuse for not eating them with every meal; they may even contain more nutrients than fresh vegetables that have been transported long distances. Most commercially produced frozen produce is frozen immediately after harvest when nutrient concentrations are at their highest. But bear in mind that the way you cook vegetables has a big effect on their nutrient content – lightly steamed is best. All vegetables boiled in large amounts of water for long periods of time lose far more of their nutritional content compared to vegetables that are lightly steamed.

FROZEN BERRIES
Berries, including bilberries, blackberries and cranberries, all contain high levels of anthocyanins – powerful antioxidants that work synergistically with vitamin C. Studies have shown that berries may slow or even reverse the ageing of the brain, preventing dementia. Keep a bag of frozen ones in the freezer and you can simply throw a handful into yogurt and blend for a ready-chilled smoothie. Frozen berries are also great added to hot porridge.

relax and enjoy life

Defining idea...
'It's clear that up to 70% of strokes and 80% of heart disease can be prevented by changes in diet and lifestyle.' – DR BALZ FREI, director of the Linus Pauling Institute which researches the role of diet in disease

DRIED FRUIT
Prunes, currants, cranberries and raisins all have a high ORAC rating – which means they're good at counteracting the damaging effects of free radicals in the body. Opt for organic varieties when you can (pesticides can be concentrated in dried fruits). Grab a handful as a snack, sprinkle them over a salad or add to your breakfast cereal in the morning.

PEANUT BUTTER
It's packed with healthy monounsaturates and may lower your heart disease risk by 21%. Go for a brand that has no added sugar or salt and no hydrogenated vegetable oils (trans fats). Try spreading it on wholegrain toast instead of margarine or butter or spread two tablespoons on half an apple for a satisfying snack.

CANNED PINEAPPLE
This is loaded with vitamin C, which can help maintain a strong immune system, and potassium, which protects your heart by regulating blood pressure. Add it to a stir-fry for sweet and sour flavour.

SOBA NOODLES
A Japanese staple, these noodles are made from buckwheat, a good source of two cancer-fighting antioxidants, quercetin and rutin. Use them in place of less nutritious egg noodles in stir-fries and soups.

44. The veggie question

Studies show that vegetarians live longer and suffer less heart disease and cancer. Is it time to ditch the meat?

If you're a vegetarian, it's time to feel smug. You're already a winner when it comes to anti-ageing. You can look forward to ten extra years of disease-free living than meat-eaters and you're 39% less likely to die from cancer. You're also 30% less likely to die of heart disease.

Anti-ageing scientists think meat doesn't do you many favours – and they point to the world's longest-lived communities to prove it. A famous study called the China Project highlighted the difference between mainly vegetarian Chinese from rural areas, who stay disease-free late into life, and their meat-eating urban counterparts who succumb to heart disease, stroke, osteoporosis, diabetes and cancer.

But hang on, you're thinking, if we're designed to munch plant food only, how come our cavemen ancestors ate meat? It's a good point. Trouble is, although the human race did evolve as omnivores, we now eat more meat in a week than our ancestors did in months. Obviously, this is partly because we no longer have to chase our meat with a spear before eating it. But it's also due to changes in farming patterns that mean meat and dairy products are cheaper and more readily available than ever before.

Here's an idea for you...
It's a myth that meat is the best source of protein – it's also found in some surprising foods, like brown rice for instance. Add a small tin of mixed beans (rinse them in a sieve under the tap first) to cooked, cooled brown rice and sprinkle with a few drops of sesame oil to taste. Garnish with fresh coriander and you've got a delicious, anti-ageing salad that contains all eight of the vital amino acids that protein supplies.

If you're tucking into a burger right now, you may want to read the following paragraphs some other time. There's a theory that humans have a long colon, like a horse or cow, and a relatively slow food transit designed to break down grains and grasses. Too much meat introduced into the system literally rots before it reaches the end, releasing toxins into the bloodstream.

Defining idea...
'It always seems to me that man was not born to be a carnivore.' – ALBERT EINSTEIN

Dr Colin Campbell, chairman of the World Cancer Research Fund, believes 'animal protein is one of the most toxic nutrients there is' and that 'the vast majority, perhaps 80 to 90%, of all cancers, cardiovascular diseases and other forms of degenerative illness can be prevented, at least until very old age, simply by adopting a plant-based diet'. Still eating that burger? The theory is that animal fats are high in saturated fats which raise levels of bad (LDL) cholesterol, increasing the risk of heart disease. Vegetarians, by contrast, tend to eat a lot of plant-based foods which are high in disease-fighting antioxidants.

Most meat-eaters also eat too much protein (even those who aren't on the Atkins diet). According to the World Health Organization, we need around 35 g of protein a day, but the average meat-eating woman eats around 65 g and the average man, 90 g. We do need to eat some protein with every meal but you don't always have to add meat to ensure you get it. If your meal contains fish, lentils and beans, grains like rice, quinoa, and bulgar wheat, eggs, yogurt, cheese, nuts or seeds, you're probably already eating enough.

But what if you're a diehard meat fan who can't bear the thought of life without a Sunday roast? Don't despair – omnivores who eat above average amounts of fruit and vegetables can cut their risk of most cancers by 50–75%. And by increasing the amount of plant foods you eat, you'll probably find you naturally cut back on meat consumption.

45. Time for an oil change?

Don't be afraid of fats, the right kind have a vital role to play in the anti-ageing process.

Confused about fat? Join the club. It's hardly surprising most of us don't quite know which way to turn, but it's not as complicated as you might think. It's all about getting the balance right.

In the last few years, we've cast off our fat phobia and joyfully indulged in an Atkins-fuelled fat frenzy, convinced we can feast on saturated fat with total impunity. But now the bubble has burst, rumours that diet guru Dr Atkins himself died obese are rife, and the company behind Atkins has been forced to temper its advice on fat, telling people to reign back on the amount of saturated fats and red meat they're consuming. So here's an easy four-step guide.

1. USE MORE OLIVE OIL
Olive oil lowers bad cholesterol and raises good, is essential for healthy cell formation and improves digestion. It's also packed with antioxidant vitamins A and E, as well as vitamins D and K, vital for strong bones. So it's no surprise that in those Mediterranean communities where people live the longest, where rates of heart disease are astonishingly low, olive oil is used with abandon – it's poured over salads, used instead of butter on bread and drizzled over cooked vegetables. Some anti-ageing experts say olive oil is the only oil they have in the house – they use it for all cooking and dressings.

Here's an idea for you...
When shopping for olive oil, look for 'extra virgin'. It means the oil is pressed from olives that are not damaged, bruised or subjected to adverse temperatures or too much air, or that have had additional treatment such as heat or blending with other oils. What is simply termed olive oil is often a blend of lesser-quality refined oils with some virgin oil added to give the right balance of flavour. Extra virgin olive oil, however, has the highest concentration of cancer-fighting antioxidants.

2. CUT BACK ON SOLID FATS

A diet high in saturates can raise levels of LDL ('bad') blood cholesterol and increase the risk of heart disease. Saturated fats tend to be solid at room temperature (think butter, margarine, lard, suet and dripping) or come from animal sources (meat, eggs, milk, cheese, yogurt), although two vegetable oils, coconut and palm oil, are also high in saturates. Limit this to small amounts such as a knob of butter on vegetables or some cheese crumbled on a salad. But don't try to cut it out altogether – it's the best source of fat-soluble vitamins A and D, vital for healthy skin, teeth, hair, bones and vision.

3. KEEP POLYUNSATURATED OILS TO A MINIMUM

Polyunsaturated vegetable oils have been sold as a healthy choice but anti-ageing experts keep them at arm's length. While polyunsaturates from natural sources such as nuts and fish are essential for a healthy heart and brain, once they are processed to become oils, their natural antioxidants are removed. The end result can be toxic – they form lipid oxidation products (LOPs) in the body which can attack the arteries. Keep soy, peanut and corn oils to a minimum (often these are just labelled 'vegetable oils'). Sunflower oil is a better choice as it contains higher levels of the antioxidant vitamin E, but the best choice of all, for cooking and dressings, is olive oil.

Defining idea...
'Spaghetti, a love of life and the odd bath in virgin olive oil.'
– Sophia Loren's explanation for her youthful good looks at 70

4. AVOID TRANS FATS

Trans fats are a form of polyunsaturates that are made when oils are processed by hydrogenation. This is used by the food industry to provide moistness in foods such as cakes, biscuits, pastries, pies and sausages. It's also used to stop margarines melting at room temperature and is found in many polyunsaturated margarines marketed as 'healthy'. But studies have shown that trans fats raise levels of LDL cholesterol in the body to a greater extent than saturated fats, while simultaneously reducing levels of 'good' HDL cholesterol. Around 30,000 heart-attack deaths a year in the US can be attributed to high levels of trans fats in the diet. Trans fats have also been linked with free radical damage to body cells that can lead to cancer and heart disease. Play safe by avoiding all products that contain trans fats – look for hydrogenated vegetable oil in the ingredients list. (It's also sometimes labelled as 'partially hydrogenated' or 'shortening'.)

46. Get hooked on fish

Simply opening a tin of sardines can stave off wrinkles (if you eat the sardines)

Your grandmother was talking sense after all – fish really is good for your brain and a daily dose of cod liver oil will keep you strong and healthy.

But what she may not have realised is that fish can also fend off ageing and help you look and feel younger. It all comes down to some special fatty acids found in fish called omega-3s. These oils are vital for the functioning of every cell in our bodies, and yet our bodies cannot make them – we have to get them from food. Ready for some long words? Two particularly valuable omega-3s are docosahexaenoic acid (DHA) and eicosapentaenoic acid (EPA) and you'll find high levels in salmon, herrings, sardines, pilchards, mackerel, tuna and trout.

A recent best-selling book recommended eating salmon three times a day instead of having a facelift. Converts swore that it reduced wrinkles. Omega-3 fatty acids do contain a chemical that stimulates nerve function and encourages the muscles under the skin to contract and tighten. But you don't have to eat fish as often as that to help you *feel* younger for longer.

Here's an idea for you...
Stuck for easy fish ideas? What about fresh salmon, grilled or poached in a little milk and garnished with fresh dill or parsley? Whole mackerel is a great fish to cook on a barbecue or try them stuffed with lemon chunks and herbs and baked in foil for a stylish dinner. Or try adding ready-to-eat smoked trout fillets to a salad, giving a lunch that's high in cancer-fighting selenium as well as omega-3s. Tins are also good – add a tin of anchovies to tomato-based pasta sauces or use as a pizza topping. Or mash a tin of sardines, herring or pilchards onto multigrain toast for a speedy snack or simple supper.

Take the Inuit. Did you know they don't have a word in their language for heart attack because it's so rare among them? This is thought to be thanks to their diet – and some doctors are now recommending that we copy it. But if you don't fancy whale or seal blubber all winter, don't worry – you get the same benefits from eating the fish that whales and seals eat: salmon, herring, anchovies, mackerel and tuna. The omega-3 fatty acids 'calm down' the artery walls, as well as reducing production of bad LDL cholesterol, raising levels of good HDL cholesterol, lowering blood pressure and reducing irregular heart beats.

Thanks to reams of other studies, we now know that these valuable oils play a role in staving off stroke and breast cancer, fighting asthma and protecting joints. There's scientific research to back up what our ancestors knew by instinct – that fish is good for the brain. One study found that older people who eat fish or seafood once a week have a significantly lower risk of developing dementia.

Omega-3s work best as part of a double act with another group of essential oils called omega-6s, found in vegetable oils such as sunflower, soy, hemp and linseed, which are important for lowering blood cholesterol and supporting the skin. Thanks to the widespread use of sunflower oil in food processing, few of us are deficient in omega-6s, but at the same time, intake of omega-3s has dropped by

Defining idea...
'Fish, to taste good, must swim three times: in water, in butter and in wine.'
– Polish proverb

more than half (we don't eat so much fish and tend to go for low fat varieties such as cod and haddock rather than herring and mackerel). Scientists now believe that too many omega-6s in the diet can undo the good work of omega-3s. To redress the balance, try to cut down on fried and processed foods and margarines and eat more oily fish – aim for a minimum of twice a week.

47. Have a cuppa

Now here's something we can all do to improve our chances of living a longer, healthier life — drink a cup of tea. Put the kettle on!

It's almost too good to be true. Just by curling up in a chair with a cup of tea, you're lowering your blood pressure, fighting cancer, osteoporosis, heart disease and wrinkles.

Tea is one of our most ancient drinks but only recently has research revealed its remarkable anti-ageing powers. It's packed with flavonoids, disease-fighting compounds that reduce the damaging effects of free radicals on your body's cells. Tea contains a particularly potent variety called catechins which have been shown to be more powerful antioxidants than vitamins C and E in laboratory tests. But they're just one of tea's nearly 4000 phytochemicals which are thought to work synergistically to fight disease.

It seems there's no end to the ways that tea can help you live longer. It can lower your risk of having a heart attack and stave off cancer. In one extraordinary study, green and black tea rubbed onto precancerous lesions reduced the growth of the cells. In mice, tea has also been shown to slow the development of lung tumours and colon cancer. It also keeps your prostate healthy. Men in East Asia who drink lots of green tea have much lower rates of prostate cancer than men in the rest of the world, thought to be due to green tea's antioxidants.

Here's an idea for you...
Here's how to get the most from your cuppa. Tea should be made with freshly
boiled, but not boiling water, which can reduce its antioxidant capacity. So let the
water sit in the kettle for a minute before pouring it on the tea. Allow the tea bag to
steep for three to five minutes to bring out its catechins. Then give it a good squeeze
– this can double the amount of flavonoids released. Green and white teas taste
best drunk without milk. If you prefer to add milk to black tea, go ahead – a recent
review of tea studies suggests it doesn't affect the health benefits.

Tea also protects your joints. Researchers have found that two compounds in green
tea block the enzyme that destroys cartilage. Other studies have shown that tea
can even play a role in strengthening your bones and reducing the risk of hip
fractures. And it's good for your teeth – it fights the bacteria that cause gum
disease and contains fluoride which helps fend off decay.

It also reduces skin damage. The compounds in green tea fight DNA damage
induced by ultraviolet light – the source of skin ageing (and skin cancer). It's why
green tea extract is a favourite ingredient in anti-ageing cosmetics.

And just in case you're still not sold on the idea, if not already in the process of
making a cup – tea may even help you lose weight! A preliminary study has found
that an extract from green tea may help with weight loss by speeding up fat
metabolism.

Defining idea...

'If you are cold, tea will warm you. If you are heated, it will cool you. If you are depressed, it will cheer you. If you are excited, it will calm you.'
– **WILLIAM GLADSTONE, nineteenth-century British Prime Minister**

But what's the best type of tea to opt for? It all comes from a single plant (*Camellia sinensis*), but differences in processing after harvesting produce different 'colours' of tea. And it seems that while all true teas (herbal or fruit teas aren't true teas) have health benefits, some have more than others. The classic cup of black tea, usually drunk with milk, is made up of leaves that have been left to ferment after harvesting, which darkens them and allows them to develop a stronger flavour. Green tea is much more lightly processed than black and contains slightly more flavonoids than black (316 mg per cup compared with 268 mg). It also contains a higher percentage of catechins. Recently, there's been big excitement over white tea – it's been hailed as the most antioxidant-rich tea of all. It's made from very small buds picked in the early spring, before they have opened. It's the rarest tea in the world, produced on a very limited scale in China and Sri Lanka – which is reflected in the price.

But green, black or white will all give you a powerful antioxidant boost if you drink around four cups a day. Which colour you opt for is a matter of taste, although many people prefer the 'kick' of black tea at breakfast and the lighter, more refreshing taste of green or white throughout the day. Adding four or more cups a day is probably one of the cheapest, easiest and most enjoyable ways to fight ageing.

48. The good news about booze

Here's some news to drink to , people who have two to three small glasses of red wine a day live longer than people who don't.

Scientists are finally coming up with an explanation for what people in France, Spain, Italy and Greece have known for centuries – that a couple of small glasses of wine a day keep you young and healthy.

While it's well-established that moderate drinking can fend off heart disease, an exciting new study suggests it may actually fight the ageing process itself. This was carried out by scientists at Harvard Medical School, who found that the potent antioxidant called resveratrol found in red wine could extend the life of yeast in a laboratory experiment by 60–80%. Although we've known for some time that resveratrol is a great ally in the battle against damaging free radicals, what got the scientists so excited was that this study showed it might have another, quite different effect. They think that it stimulates special enzymes in the body called sirtuins that prevent cell death.

The only other way this has been made to happen has been in studies of very restricted calorie diets. And, given the choice, most people would rather drink more red wine than starve themselves!

Here's an idea for you...
A simple way to cut down on your wine consumption without feeling deprived is to buy some traditionally sized, 125 ml wine glasses to use at home. They may not be as trendy as the bucket-sized glasses now in vogue, but they'll help you keep track of your units. One of these glasses is around one unit and most people say they sip their wine more slowly if it's in a smaller glass. Always ask for a 125 ml glass in bars or restaurants too.

Although more research is needed to find out if red wine has the same effect on human cells, it fits in with other studies that give moderate wine drinking the thumbs up. According to a recent report the more wine you drink, the lower your risk of death – not just from coronary heart disease but from all causes of death, including cancer.

The French habit of drinking a glass of wine with meals is thought to explain the so-called French paradox: their high intake of saturated fat but low rate of heart disease. In fact, regular wine drinking is credited by cardiologists for the low rate of heart disease generally in Mediterranean countries. It's thought that red wine interferes with the production of a body chemical which clogs up arteries and increases the risk of a heart attack. And when given to cancer-prone mice in another study, red wine increased lifespan by 50%, thought to be due to the anti-cancer properties of two powerful flavonoids.

Defining idea...
'Wine is constant proof that God loves us and loves to see us happy.'
– BENJAMIN FRANKLIN

But it goes without saying that moderation is the key. The proof that too much booze speeds up the ageing process can usually be found propping up a bar! Too much alcohol *increases* your risk of heart disease and cancer (not to mention liver disease). Plus, as anyone who's ever had a hangover can testify by simply looking in the mirror, too much alcohol has a severely dehydrating – and ageing – effect on the skin. It's essential to stick to two or three small drinks a night, stay within the recommended weekly limits (21 units for men and 14 for women) and have at least two alcohol-free days a week. Try to drink while you're eating food and sip water as well. Opt for the deepest red wines made from these grapes to get maximum flavonoids in every glass: Merlot, Cabernet Sauvignon, or Pinot Noir. Stick to these simple rules and drinking can be one of the most enjoyable ways to stave off ageing. Cheers!

49. Less cake, more birthdays?

Reducing your calorie intake can stave off ageing and reduce your chances of getting serious diseases. But how can you do it without feeling deprived?

If you want to live longer, practise hara hachi. It means stopping eating when you're 80% full. By doing so, you naturally cut 10–40% of calories from your diet.

It's a tip from the longest-living people on earth, the inhabitants of the island of Okinawa in Japan. Starving has never been good for longevity. But eating just enough, rather than too many, calories can help you live younger for longer. In fact, reducing calorie intake is the one thing that anti-ageing scientists can definitely say has an impact on lifespan at present. In lab experiments, mice live twice as long as normal if their daily calorie intake is halved. They also stay younger for longer (apparently it's perfectly possible to tell if a mouse is young for its age).

The theory is that calorie restriction inhibits the creation of free radicals, those destructive particles that harm genes and proteins. Others speculate that a reduced calorie diet catapults the body into a survival mode that retards the ageing process.

Here's an idea for you...
No good at mental arithmetic? Then ditch calorie counting and use this 'handy' guide to portion control instead.

- a portion of meat or fish: the size and thickness of your palm.
- a portion of hard cheese: the length and width of your thumb.
- a portion of cereal: the size of your fist.
- a portion of vegetables: two cupped handfuls.
- a portion of cooked rice, pasta or potatoes: one cupped handful.
- a portion of jacket potato: the size of your fist.
- a portion of butter or margarine: the tip of your thumb (from the knuckle).

In the States converts to calorie restriction for longer life call themselves 'cronies', and they say the benefits are low blood pressure and cholesterol levels, abundant energy and an imperviousness to colds and flu. Cronies eat around 1400 calories a day if they're female and 1800 if they're male (compare this to what the average woman eats – around 2000 calories a day – and the average man, around 2600). The Okinawans eat around 1500 calories a day.

Reducing your calorie intake by a third is probably worth considering if you're overweight. But do get advice from a qualified dietician if you're restricting calories and you have any health problems, to make sure you don't miss out on any vital nutrients. The key to success is making sure every single one of those calories delivers a maximum nutrient punch. That means saying goodbye to nutritionally empty fast food, processed food, alcohol, sweets and cakes and basing the bulk of your diet on wholegrains, pulses, fruit and vegetables. A high-nutrient, low-calorie diet both limits the amounts of free radicals generated *and* provides large amounts of antioxidants that neutralise the effects of free radicals on the body.

Defining idea...
'Hara hachi bu.' – **Okinawan saying meaning 'eat until you're only eight parts full.'**

The latest research has found that you can also fend off ageing with intermittent fasts. It's thought that fasting produces mild stress which triggers the production of substances known as stress-resistance proteins, which are resistant to disease. In addition, it increases the production of a brain chemical which promotes learning, memory, and the growth and survival of nerve cells.

You can get these effects by cutting back to 500–600 calories one day a week or fortnight – by just having one meal on that day. But it doesn't mean the rest of the week can be a junk food binge; that would undermine all your efforts. Try to base the bulk of your diet on fruit, vegetables, wholegrains, nuts, soy, olive oil, lean meats, fish and low-fat dairy products.

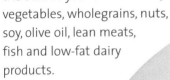

50. Supplementary benefits

Most nutritionists believe everyone will benefit from taking a good multivitamin and mineral supplement every day.

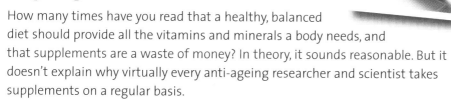

How many times have you read that a healthy, balanced diet should provide all the vitamins and minerals a body needs, and that supplements are a waste of money? In theory, it sounds reasonable. But it doesn't explain why virtually every anti-ageing researcher and scientist takes supplements on a regular basis.

Let's face it, we never quite live up to our healthy intentions. We know we need five portions of fruit and vegetables a day, but average consumption is just about half that. On top of this certain lifestyle factors, such as smoking and heavy drinking, can deplete your body of nutrients, and stress can also take its toll on the B vitamins which are required to keep the nervous system healthy. Plus, as we age, we require fewer calories on a daily basis, and so our chances of getting the right amount of nutrients from food are reduced. Add to that the fact that modern farming and food processing techniques have reduced the vitamin and mineral content of many foods, and you can see the problem.

But walk into any health-food store and you can be overwhelmed by the choice of supplements on sale. It's not simply a case of 'more is better' – your body (and your bank balance) will thank you for making an informed choice of a select few. Here's a simple four-step guide to successfully negotiating the supplement maze.

Here's an idea for you...

When's the ideal time to take vitamin supplements? Nutritionists say it doesn't matter, as long as they're taken at roughly the same time every day. This is to ensure that levels of nutrients are consistently topped up. You're also most likely to remember to take them if it's become part of a daily routine. Many people find the easiest way to remember is to take their supplements with breakfast, as it's the meal most regularly eaten at home. Keep your bottles next to the kettle as a reminder!

1. START WITH A DAILY MULTIVITAMIN/MINERAL SUPPLEMENT

This will make up for any deficiencies caused by trace elements missing from your diet. You don't have to spend a fortune or buy it from an obscure mail order company – you can get an affordable, good quality multi from most supermarkets and high street pharmacies. Look for one that includes selenium – a mineral needed in trace amounts that's thought to boost the immune system. One study found that 100 mcg of selenium taken daily reduced the death rate among cancer patients. Ideally, it should also include around 50 mg of magnesium, which helps to lower blood pressure.

2. BOOST YOUR VITAMIN C

Vitamin C's main job is to enter your cells and lie in wait to eliminate opportunist free radicals looking to damage your DNA. When it has a spare moment, it also helps heal artery walls that have become damaged, reduce cholesterol and lower blood pressure. It's also vital for boosting the immune system and plays a big role in fighting cancer. Making sure you eat some citrus food or berries every day is essential, then add a vitamin C supplement of up to 1000 mg a day – the current recommended safe upper limit. Some anti-ageing experts recommend taking up to 3000 mg a day, although it has been known to cause diarrhoea in high doses. Try starting with two daily 500 mg doses, six hours apart.

Defining idea...
'Every human being is the author of his own health or disease.' – THE BUDDHA

3. BOOST YOUR VITAMIN E

Vitamin E can lower the risk of heart attack in women by as much as 40% and in men by 35%. If vitamin E is given to people who already show signs of heart disease, it can reduce the risk of heart attack by as much as 75%. In an ideal world, vitamin E likes to work with vitamin C – they complement each other as E is fat soluble, and C is water soluble, so between them, they've got the body covered. Make sure you're eating wholegrains such as wholegrain cereals, bread, rice or pasta several times a day, and green leafy vegetables at least once a day. Then add a supplement of up to 540 mg a day.

4. BOOST YOUR BS

Homocysteine is an amino acid which builds up in the blood as you age. Now scientists are linking high homocysteine levels with a higher risk of heart disease. But simply taking a supplement of 400 mcg of folic acid every day is usually all you need to substantially reduce your homocysteine to safe levels. Folic acid is a B vitamin that likes to work synergistically with the other Bs, so look for a B complex supplement.

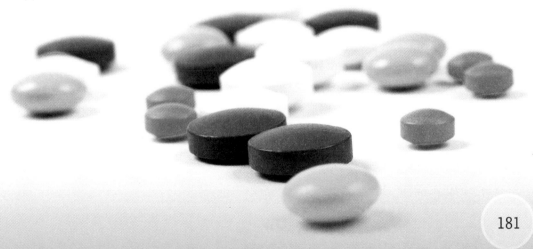

51. Queue up for Q10

could boosting the levels of Q10 in your diet help you stave off ageing?

It's not often that scientists get really excited, but recently there's been a lot of jumping up and down over a micronutrient called co-enzyme Q10. In fact, so much exciting research is emerging on its anti-ageing benefits, that it's beginning to look like a miracle pill. In Japan Q10 is as popular as multivitamins are; in Scandinavian countries, it's treated like gold dust – in Norway in 1994 a group of armed robbers broke into a health supplement factory and made off with 17,000 packets of the stuff, leaving the office safe behind!

Although it was discovered in 1960 (in Britain, where it was promptly ignored), it's only recently that the true extent of its anti-ageing powers has been understood. In one experiment, Q10 supplements extended the lifespan of mice by up to 45%. If humans responded like mice, this could mean an additional thirty to forty years of life.

So just what is this wonder substance and how exactly does it stave off ageing? Q10 is a naturally occurring substance known as a quinone, produced in small

Here's an idea for you...
Heavy drinking slows the body's production of Q10. Not sure if you're exceeding the recommended weekly limits of 14 units for women and 21 for men? Then try keeping a drink diary for a week. You may be surprised at how quickly your units add up.

amounts by the liver and found in trace amounts in certain foods such as sardines and offal. It has two main roles in the body – it's a potent antioxidant and it's central to energy production. The problem is that it can't be made efficiently in a body that has a deficiency in any one of six vitamins and minerals, including the B vitamins (and most of us are lacking in at least one of them). Heavy drinking also affects production, and it begins to slow down altogether after the age of 40.

Some experts now believe that many of the symptoms of ageing can be linked to this slowdown in Q10 production and recommend that anyone interested in longevity take Q10 supplements. The theory is all tied up with how our cells burn food to create energy. The relevant bits of the cells are called mitochondria – the cell's energy factories. Nutrients are burned in these energy factories to produce a substance called ATP which is rather like petrol for your muscles. But, as with an engine, there are nasty by-products produced – free radicals. Co-enzyme Q10 not only helps the mitochondria produce ATP efficiently, but also helps to neutralise the destructive free radicals as they are produced. If there's a deficiency in Q10, less energy is available and more free radical damage – which ages the body from the inside – occurs. One visible side-effect of damaged mitochondria is wounds that are slow to heal.

Defining idea...
'Studies show that as many as 97% of the adult population is low in Q10. And if you look at the figure for heart disease, you can see the end result.'
– PROFESSOR KARL FOLKERS, pioneering Q10 researcher

Scientists are also getting very excited about the link between Q10 deficiency and heart disease. Q10 has been used as an experimental therapy for patients suffering from heart failure, angina and hypertension around the world. In one study involving people with congestive heart failure – a condition in which the heart becomes progressively weaker – 75% of those on Q10 survived for three years, compared to only 25% on conventional medicine. Q10 could also help your body fight gum disease, which we now know has been linked with heart disease.

Although it will be some time before there is definitive evidence of Q10's anti-ageing benefits, it also offers short-term effects that help you feel younger. It's a great energy booster and a popular (legal) pill used by athletes to increase stamina. One study even found it improved fitness levels in people who did not exercise – middle-aged Japanese women complaining of constant tiredness found that 60 mg of Q10 a day improved their fitness by over 30% – and reported being much less tired.

52. Get moving

The right kind of regular exercise can extend your life – but the wrong kind can shorten it.

Lead an inactive life, and you increase your risk of several serious diseases. But exercise carefully, regularly, and you can slow down the ageing of the entire body.

Fact: the human body is designed to move. Regular exercise lowers blood pressure and cholesterol, produces antioxidant enzymes and cuts heart attack risk by up to two-thirds. In fact, some researchers believe that not exercising is as great a risk factor for heart disease as a twenty-a-day cigarette habit.

In fact, being fit and exercising can make up for a multitude of other sins – even smoking or eating a high-fat diet (although it's a much better idea to ditch these habits altogether). If you're fit, you're over one and a half times less at risk from premature death than someone who lives a healthy life, but who doesn't exercise.

And consider this: exercising will give you prompt – and noticeable – returns. Within a week of beginning a regular exercise programme, you improve your sense of well-being. Your energy levels rise and your muscles feel stronger, so every movement feels easier. The result is that you feel, and look, younger.

Here's an idea for you...
Here's a simple way of checking your fitness level. Find your resting heart rate by taking your pulse in the morning before you get up. Press your fingers (not your thumb) on the main artery in the side of your neck, just below the jawbone. Using a watch with a second hand or a stopwatch, count the number of heartbeats in six seconds. Multiply this by ten to get your resting heart rate. Now, step up and down on a step or low bench, alternately leading legs for three minutes. Rest for thirty seconds then take your pulse for six seconds and multiply the result by ten. This is your recovery heart rate. The nearer it is to your resting heart rate, the fitter you are. If it takes more than ten minutes to return to your normal rate, your fitness level is ageing you.

It's also never too late to start – studies have shown even nursing home residents in their nineties can improve their mobility by exercising. And the American Council on Exercise cites a study of five men who took part in an aerobic capacity test in 1966 when they were 20. Researchers revisited these five men in 1996. At 50, the men were an average of 25% heavier than they had been at 20, and their aerobic capacity had declined by 11%. Back on a monitored exercise programme for six months, the men increased their aerobic capacity by an average of 15% – in other words, they were more cardiovascularly fit than they had been thirty years previously.

Defining idea...
'Those who think they have no time for bodily exercise will sooner or later have to find time for illness.' – EDWARD STANLEY, US Congressman from 1837–1843

Aerobic exercise improves your ability to process oxygen. From the lungs, oxygen travels down to the haemoglobin of the red blood cells and through the circulatory system to every cell in the body. The fitter you are, the more oxygen you can take on board and the better your body functions at a cellular level. Plus, the increase in free radicals triggered by using extra oxygen to exercise causes the body to boost production of its own antioxidant enzymes. These remain active even when the exercise stops, which means you get better protection against the oxidative stress that causes heart disease and cancer.

But moderation is the key. Forget 'no pain, no gain'. Very intense exercise can actually *increase* your risk of disease, leading to premature death, as it produces excessive amounts of free radicals that the body doesn't have a chance of mopping up. The result is a suppressed immune system that's more prone to infection and, some scientists believe, developing cancer. (If you're an athlete, don't think you're doomed to an early grave – you can minimise the effects of the free radicals you're producing with a diet high in antioxidants.)

The truth is that just half an hour of moderately intense activity can bring about the anti-ageing effect. It also has an accumulative effect so you could simply do three ten-minute sessions a day to gain the benefits. Now, what's stopping you?

53. Walk the walk

Walking is the simplest way to improve your fitness level and fend off the ageing process.

It's easy to incorporate walking into everyday routines, so it's the exercise you're most likely to do consistently and stick at.

Want to add years to your life in an instant? Walk! The great thing about physical activity is that its anti-ageing effects are immediate. So no matter how unfit you've been in the past, if you start exercising now you will live a longer and healthier life. But you've got to do it consistently, and you've got to keep it up. (Don't think you can rest on past athletic laurels – no matter how fit you were once, after five years of being sedentary, you have the same fitness – and body age – as someone who's never exercised at all.) This is why walking is such a great anti-ageing exercise choice.

At this point, you're probably thinking one of two things: walking isn't real exercise, and that you do a lot of walking anyway and you're still not fit. Well, brisk walking – the pace you'd go if you were late for an important appointment – raises your heart rate to between 60–80% of its maximum, the level of activity necessary for strengthening the heart and lungs. But it does so without putting undue strain on your joints – in fact, it can help strengthen bones and stave off osteoporosis. Regular walking will also reduce your risk of heart disease, stroke, diabetes, high

Here's an idea for you...
Want an easy way to keep track of your walking to make sure you're doing enough to stave off ageing? Buy a pedometer or step counter, a cheap little gadget that you wear on your waistband to count every step you take. Aim for 10,000 steps a day (roughly equivalent to five miles). Experts say that's the minimum you need to do to encourage weight loss and bring with it the many anti-ageing benefits associated with lower body fat. But that doesn't mean setting out on a daily hike – every step you take throughout the day counts, be it indoors or out, fast or slow.

blood pressure, bowel cancer and arthritis – as well as psychological conditions such as anxiety, stress and depression. Now studies have shown that regular walking is also good for the brain and can help stave off Alzheimer's. It can also help you lose weight – one study tracked a group of walkers who did a two-mile, hilly route, three times a week. They lost an average of 6.5 kg (14 lb) in three months – without dieting.

Think you already do a lot of walking and aren't fit? You won't get results by walking the kids to school if you go at snail's pace. You should feel warm, sweaty and slightly breathless. Ideally, you should schedule some walking sessions three to five times a week, and work up to doing an hour at a time. On other days, try to fit in three ten-minute walks throughout the day.

For best results, invest in a good pair of trainers and wear comfortable clothing – it doesn't need to be sports kit. Dress in layers – for example a T-shirt, then a sweatshirt which you can take off and tie round your waist when you warm up. A lightweight running jacket is a good investment as it keeps out rain and wind without weighing you down.

Defining idea...
'How do you live a long life? Take a two-mile walk every morning before breakfast.'
– HARRY S TRUMAN

Always warm up with five minutes of easy walking before picking up the pace. Then cool down with five minutes of easy walking at the end, and do some stretches. During your walk, keep your tummy muscles pulled in tight to support your back. Think 'tall' – don't slump into your hips. Relax your shoulders and let your arms swing naturally by your sides. Use your natural stride – don't try to lengthen it – and strike the ground with the heel first, rolling through the foot then pushing off with the toe.

Complete beginners should start with short bursts of walking interspersed with rest periods. Try walking briskly for five minutes, walking slowly (or completely resting) for three, then walking briskly for five. Do this three times a week for two weeks, then start to add a minute a week to the brisk walking bursts. When you feel your fitness improve, begin cutting back on the rest periods. Your aim is to walk briskly for thirty minutes.

Still not convinced it'll get results? When one of the world's most respected anti-ageing scientists, Professor Jay Olshansky of the University of Illinois at Chicago, was asked which single product people should buy to stave off ageing, he replied 'a good pair of walking shoes'.

54. Good morning, sunshine

Here's the simplest yoga routine, that's been energising people for thousands of years.

Time spent mastering this move could be one of the best investments you make in terms of energy.

One reason its fans love yoga so much is that it gives them energy. This specific effect on energy levels has been backed up by research. The *Journal of the Royal Society of Medicine* reported on the effects on participants' mood and vitality in three groups of volunteers: some did relaxation exercises, some visualisation and some yoga. Those doing a 30-minute programme of yoga reported an increase in both mental and physical energy. They also reported a lift in their mood. They were more alert; the other groups reported feeling more sluggish and less happy.

You don't have to do much yoga to benefit. The 'Salute to the Sun' is just that – it's meant to be carried out while facing the rising sun. But wherever you do it, it's specifically designed to increase your energy. That said, this is a brilliant way of starting your day: it releases tension, limbers up the body after sleep and stimulates circulation before your day.

Here's an idea for you...
Yogic breathing has been shown in some studies to 'wake up' your brain, specifically those parts responsible for creativity and logical thinking. Close off your right nostril with the thumb of your right hand and breathe in through your left for the count of four. Now close off your left nostril with the index finger of your right hand and exhale for the count of four. Breathe in through your right nostril, and then out through your left, closing off your right nostril with your thumb. Repeat half a dozen times. This is great for relaxing you at any time of the day.

If possible, do this outside, facing the sun, first thing. Failing that, your bedroom's fine. Stand straight and tall, feet bare and about a foot apart. Hold your hands, pointing upwards, in front of your chest as if you were praying.

1   *Inhale* and lift your arms straight above your head, stretching backwards a few centimetres so that you feel a stretch across your front.
2   *Exhale.* At the same time, bend forwards from your hips so that your hands are on each side of your feet. You may have to bend your legs slightly at the knee until you get more flexible.
3   *Inhale.* At the same time, place your right foot behind you as far as you can. Then place your left foot there too, so that your hands and feet are supporting your body.
4   *Exhale.* At the same time, lower your knees to the floor, then your chest, then your chin. You should look as if you are about to do a press up.

Defining idea...
'I got into yoga late, when I was 38 or 39. I wish I'd started earlier.' – STING

5 *Inhale.* At the same time, slowly straighten your
arms and arch your back from the waist so your chest is lifted off the floor.
6 *Exhale.* At the same time, push back onto your knees, tuck your toes in, then
straighten your arms and legs so that you make an inverted V, standing on your toes.
7 *Inhale* and step between your hands with your left foot.
8 *Exhale* and step between your hands with your right foot.
9 *Inhale.* At the same time, slowly return to the standing position.

Now repeat. Take your time to learn how to do this properly. The breathing is
important. But with practice you should be able to do this between 10 and 20 times
in a minute. The more you do it, the more energy you gain. Once you've got the hang
of it, swap the leg you lead with from stage 3 (right first, then left) – but I found it
helped to get the hang of it one way before I started mixing it up.

One result of all the upward and downward movements, say yoga adherents, is
that they strengthen the adrenals, those glands that we depend on for energy and
which are overworked by stress. The 'Salute to the Sun' is a marvellous,
instant tonic but taking up a regular class and beginning your own
practice, as it's called, will benefit you more.

Does yoga deliver? I've met some yoga practitioners who weren't
as relaxed, enlightened and serene as they thought they were.
But I've never met one who didn't look fabulous. So that's a nice
secondary benefit.

5 ways yoga slows down ageing

Research studies have shown that yoga...

1. Slows weight gain. Yoga practitioners over the age of 45 were 8lbs lighter than those who didn't do yoga.

2. Ease pain – it's been shown to relieve back pain.

3. Induces sleep. After three months yogis sleep better.

4. Decreases stress. One class a week reduces the stress hormone, cortisol.

5. Keeps skin elastic. Ten days of yoga reduces the 'oxidative stress' that results the breakdown of the skin's framework, collagen.

See *idea 54* for the easiest yoga routine that slows you down and revs you up simultaneously.

55. How to start exercising when you really don't want to

Exercise is the one thing that will boost your energy levels faster than anything else. But what if you just can't get started?

Research shows that when life gets busy, exercise is one of the first things to get bumped off the schedule. But before you berate yourself for your lack of sticking power, it's good to remember that, even for professionally fit people like personal trainers, exercise is cyclical. There will be times when it gets pushed to the sidelines. However, for those who have learned how much exercise helps them cope with a busy life, the gaps before they start exercising again are likely to be shorter than for your average Joe. If you've never exercised at all, this idea aims to get you to a stage where you too know that the benefits are so great, it isn't worth going without it for too long.

This idea is equally suitable for those who have never exercised regularly, and those who used to, but have lapsed. If it's too easy for you, ratchet up a gear, or jump some steps – but beware. Research has shown that there are two reasons that exercise programmes fail:

- we don't see the results we want (that's dealt with below); or
- we set our expectations too high.

It's far better to do a little and stick to it until you have the exercise habit than go nuts, join a gym, write an ambitious exercise programme and then give up completely after a couple of weeks of failure to keep to it.

Here's an idea for you...

When you're drawing up your plan, remember the acronym FIT: frequency, intensity, time per session. First work on frequency – aim to do some form of exercise five or six times a week. Then work on 'T' – the time you spend at it each time you do it. Then move on to the intensity – use hills to make you work harder, or go faster, or try a more difficult stroke if you're swimming.

DECIDE ON YOUR GOAL

If you've never exercised before, or haven't for a long time, please start with a modest goal. If it's ten minutes of activity a day – that's brilliant, as long as you are confident you will do it. Aim to visit your local pool once a week, then three times a week. Aim to swim once a week, and walk round the park once a week. Aim to do a yoga class on a Saturday morning.

YOU GOTTA HAVE A PLAN

You need to make a schedule where every week you are aiming to do a little more, a little more frequently until you are exercising for around three to four hours a week – enough to get you out of breath for most of the time. That could take a year, but don't think about that now. Stick your monthly schedule on the fridge. At first your goal should be just to stick to your weekly plan. Once you've got the hang of it, you can make your goal bigger, such as: run round the park, undertake your local fun run, cycle to the next town then cycle back.

If you are very exhausted, very unfit, have been ill or are very overweight, all you might be able to manage is walking up the stairs. Fine. Make that your goal: to walk up stairs three times a week, then five times a week, and so on from there. Aim for cardiovascular exercise to begin with, that gets your heart beating, because that's the type that will give you energy fastest.

When I've not exercised for a while, here is my programme.

Defining idea...
'Exercise is labour without weariness.' – **SAMUEL JOHNSON, English writer**

- *Week 1.* Walk slowly for five minutes, walk briskly for five minutes, walk slowly for five minutes. Aim to do that for three days a week.
- *Week 2.* Aim to do the same five times a week.
- *Week 3.* Walk slowly for ten minutes, walk briskly for ten minutes, walk slowly for ten minutes. Aim for four times a week.
- *Week 4.* Walk slowly for five minutes, walk briskly for twenty minutes, walk slowly for five minutes. Aim for five times a week.

Then I start running for blocks of time. Eventually, I'm running for most of the time and I'm doing it every second day.

56. Get in the raw

Eating more raw food – we're talking carrots rather than chicken – is a well-documented route to raising energy levels.

The most famous raw food proponent was Dr Max Gerson. He started off by using a raw-food diet to cure his own migraines, then other people's migraines. Then he moved on 'up' the disease ladder until he became famous for his treatment of cancer. Gerson believed that the starting point of all illness is an imbalance between sodium and potassium. His theory was that eating raw fruit and veg (which are loaded with potassium) increases oxygen uptake by the cells and mobilises white blood cells to fight disease. This results in better health and vastly improved energy.

Most doctors wouldn't agree with this, but then they wouldn't disagree that, as a nation, we'd benefit from upping our fruit and vegetable consumptions. Personally, I once followed a 100% raw food diet for a month and felt marvellous on it after just a few days. I had energy to burn and seemed to achieve much more completely effortlessly. But it is a huge faff at first and can take over your life. I once read a fascinating account by a journalist of living on raw juices for a few weeks in an attempt to reverse the genetic condition that would mean she'd be blind in her thirties. To her amazement, and that of her ophthalmologist, her sight improved during her experiment, but she found the effort of juicing vast quantities of vegetables every day too high a price to pay. She couldn't leave her home, shackled as she was to her juicer.

Here's an idea for you...
What puts people off juicing is that the preparation and clean-up after takes longer than drinking the juice. The secret is to gather all the ingredients of your juice together and fill your sink with soapy water before you start. Chop and clean in one shot. When the juice is made, pop the dirty bits straight into hot water to soak while you sip your juice slowly. Soaking immediately makes clearing up much quicker.

The writer and alternative-health guru, Leslie Kenton, is a devotee of raw food. Her realistic recommendation is for a diet that is 75% raw and 25% good-quality cooked wholegrains (brown rice, wholemeal, organic bread). At this level of raw food intake, she believes you get all the health benefits, including an increase in vitality. She has written extensively on how to transfer to a raw-food diet.

You would have to be very motivated to move over onto even a 75% raw-food diet. Another option is to gradually introduce more raw foods into your normal diet. What you will probably find is that, as you eat more raw food, you will enjoy the 'clean' taste and find that you are gradually including more healthy, less processed foods. It goes without saying that the gurus of raw food insist on organic: where that's not possible, scrub all produce thoroughly under running water.

Defining idea...

'Everyone has a doctor in him or her; we just have to help it in its work. The natural healing force within each one of us is the greatest force in getting well. Our food should be our medicine. Our medicine should be our food.' – HIPPOCRATES

SOME IDEAS THAT ARE EASY TO INSTIGATE

- Eat a bowl of salad leaves a day – rocket, lettuce, basil, parsley, watercress.

- Experiment with different types. Grate a little carrot or apple over your leaves, or add some homemade vinaigrette, balsamic vinegar or olive oil.

- Start every meal with raw food. For breakfast, fruit; for lunch, fruit or a salad; for dinner, salad again. It is an easy way to up your five fruit and veg, and as a side effect it should help you lose weight: research showed that those who ate a small salad before dinner ate less at the meal and lost weight effortlessly.

- Buy a juicer. Vegetable and fruit juices give a concentrated shot of vitamins and minerals, and they are easily digested. Recent research shows that drinking fruit and vegetable juice three times a week slashes the risk of Alzheimer's disease by 76%. (The Gerson Diet, incidentally, recommends ten huge glasses a day.)

- Make your own coleslaw. One of the very easiest ways of including more raw food is to grate half a cabbage, a couple of carrots and an apple into a bowl and mix up with a minimal amount of mayonnaise. Or better still, skip the mayonnaise and soften the slaw with your own homemade vinaigrette sweetened with a little honey. This tastes so good that commercial coleslaws will soon seem too cloying.

57. De-stress your morning: eat breakfast

If you don't, you're missing out on the number one trick for combating energy loss.

I'm evangelical about this one. If you're tired, and you don't eat breakfast – that's probably the reason.

I'm not a person who likes to eat in the morning, but years of talking to nutritional experts brainwashed me. They all said it was vital. I started. My energy levels soared, specifically my mental focus. The difference in concentration is so fundamental that now, no matter how frantic my morning, I won't drive unless I've eaten breakfast.

This has turned me into a breakfast fascist. If I were an employer, I wouldn't care about the standard of a potential employee's CV if they wouldn't promise to eat breakfast each morning. They may not realise it, but they are certainly not performing to their full potential, even if they think they are.

The best fuel combination is a carbohydrate and protein breakfast. Carbohydrate releases energy quickly (it gives you the boost to run for the bus), but protein releases energy for longer (it will help you clinch the deal during that tricky pre-lunch conference call). If you eat carbs alone in the morning or nothing at all, your body may well crave more carbs at 11 a.m. – hence the dreaded doughnut run that wreaks such havoc with your figure and your idea of yourself as a person in control of their life. So remember. Carbs good, bit of protein essential.
Here are some ideas:

Here's an idea for you...
Try this heart-boosting smoothie, which fulfils all the criteria. Mix half a pint of ice-cold semi-skimmed or soya milk with a banana, a pinch of cinnamon and two teaspoons of fish or flaxseed oil. Throw in a handful of soft fruits such as raspberries, blueberries or strawberries. (Out of season, you can buy frozen packets of these in supermarkets.) Sip, with a handful of nuts.

OK BREAKFAST
Bowl of non-sugary cereal (Shreddies, All-Bran) with semi-skimmed or skimmed milk. Piece of fruit or good-quality juice.

How to make it better
The milk provides some protein, but not much. Nibble on a little hard cheese or cottage cheese, or have a slice of cheese on wholewheat toast to get some more protein in there.

BETTER BREAKFAST
Porridge with plain yogurt and a handful of seeds and dried fruit and/or a teaspoon of honey to sweeten.

How to make it better
Again, try the cheese thing, or a handful of nuts on top of the porridge. You may find that the yogurt does enough to fill you up. It does sometimes for me. But not always. Which is why you should build up to the ...

BEST BREAKFAST
- Scrambled eggs on wholegrain toast.
- Mackerel or kippers on wholegrain toast.
- Smoked salmon and cream cheese on wholegrain toast or bagel.
- Omelette with cheese, tomato and mushrooms.

Defining idea...
'To eat well in England, you should have breakfast three times a day.'
– SOMERSET MAUGHAM

How to make it better
Add a piece of fruit and you're set to go.

MY FAVOURITE BREAKFAST
My friend Lynn Osborne, a gifted acupuncturist, gave me two
nutritional tips – green tea and drinking chicken soup for breakfast.
A bowl of homemade chicken soup is a marvellous breakfast on a cold morning –
on any morning. Protein, vegetables (for carbohydrate) and filling without being
fattening. You can throw in some noodles if you feel like it. You feel light and full of
energy. Use your own recipe or try this one. This makes enough for five bowls. Keep
half in the fridge and freeze the other half until later on in the week.

Buy yourself a special breakfast bowl. Enjoy your soup as you drink it. Think of China –
calm and peace (which is, of course, where Lynn picked up the habit during her training).

Sauté one chopped leek and one chopped onion in a little olive oil, then add a
minced garlic clove and cook until they are transparent. Add three chopped
potatoes, one chopped carrot and 1½ litres of chicken or vegetable stock, plus a
handful or two of cooked, shredded organic chicken. Throw in a pinch of nutmeg,
grated ginger or horseradish if you like. Bring to the boil and then turn down the
heat and simmer for fifteen minutes or until the potatoes are cooked. Add a
handful of greens – pak choi, spinach leaves, curly kale, watercress – and continue
to simmer until these are just cooked. I like mine chunky but you could liquidise
yours if you prefer. Add pepper. I don't use salt, and if you do, try to cut down.

58. Take time to shop well

Turn your supermarket shop into an energy-boosting adventure.

Live a little – eat more! Choosing from a wide variety of foods will boost your energy. (And changing your variety of crisps doesn't count.)

The average person eats only around twenty different foods. How dull is that? Nutritionists say we should eat from the widest variety of foods possible because, unsurprisingly, that will result in getting the optimal number of nutrients. You should be looking to make your choice from between 60 to 70 different foods on a regular basis!

There are two advantages when it comes to your energy levels in mixing it up.

1   You will be eating a cornucopia of energy-boosting nutrients.
2   You will render your shopping trips a lot more interesting.

The nutrients that are vital for energy are the B vitamins, vitamin C, magnesium, iron and chromium. Shopping with the following lists in mind will ensure you're topped up with all of them.

Here's an idea for you...
Stick to the perimeter of your supermarket like glue. Almost always, the 'real' food is focused on the outside of the store, the junk in the middle aisles. Leave your trolley at the end of the aisle when you go to buy cleaning fluids and pet food. Having to carry junk food back to your trolley makes it less likely that you'll pick them up in the first place as it's a lot harder than just tossing them in.

THE TOP 10 MULTI-TASKERS

To make it really easy when you're shopping *add three of these a week* to your shopping trolley and mix it up: select another three next week. They have been chosen to supply a good mix of B vitamins, magnesium, iron and chromium – the nutrients especially crucial for energy release.

- Bran flakes – packed with iron, B vitamins and vitamin C.
- Beef – iron, chromium. (Liver is another good food for supplying the energy nutrients.)
- Wholegrain rice and bread – B vitamins and magnesium.
- Chick peas – magnesium and iron.
- Oats – vitamin B and magnesium.
- Sardines – magnesium and iron.
- Quorn – loaded with one of the key B vitamins.
- Turkey – vitamin B12 and iron.
- Nuts and seeds – mix and match different types for 'broad spectrum' cover. Pumpkin seeds are a particularly good source of iron.
- Rye bread – good for iron and B vitamins.

TWELVE CRACKING VITAMIN C SOURCES

Choose three a week, on top of your usual foodstuffs. Mix them up. These all supply more than 20mg per 100g of food: blackcurrants, bran flakes, Brussels sprouts, cabbage (raw has double), cauliflower, citrus fruits, kiwi fruit, mango, raw red and orange peppers, raspberries, strawberries and watercress.

205

Defining idea...

'There is no love sincerer than the love of food.' – GEORGE BERNARD SHAW

SIX TOP SNACKS

These combine the all-important energy combo: protein with carbohydrate. Stock up with enough of these so that when you need a between-meal pick-up, you can reach for a snack that will fill you up without sending your blood sugar soaring (which leads to a slump in energy later). Some of these are a bit odd at first, but just try eating one of these snacks mid-morning and mid-afternoon, and you'll be amazed at how satisfying they are.

- Two oatcakes with peanut butter
- Nuts – a good handful maybe with a few raisins or sultanas
- A stick of celery spread with cream or cottage cheese
- Slices of apple spread thinly with peanut or other nut butter
- A vegetable juice with a few nuts on the side
- A boiled egg and a couple of rye crispbreads or a slice of rye bread.

OTHER GREAT ENERGY FOODS TO ADD TO YOUR SHOPPING LIST ON A REGULAR BASIS

Eggs (protein/vitamin B); pumpkin seeds (a great source of zinc); mackerel (best source of omega-3, which is the wonder nutrient of the moment, and also a great source of protein); bulgur (a good source of slow-releasing carbohydrate for long-lasting energy); Marmite (good for B vitamins); basil (beloved by herbalists for its uplifting qualities); artichoke (rich in vitamin C and magnesium); beetroot (high in vitamin C, magnesium, iron and B vitamins); kale (packed with iron and B vitamins); lentils (loaded with magnesium); celery (has special phytochemicals that are good for energy and improving mood).

6 ways slowing down can make you healthier by tomorrow

1. Take the stairs rather than the lift.

2. Take 10 minutes off every hour of your working day.

3. Chew your food slowly and thoroughly – it aids digestion.

4. Cut noise – your own as well as other people's. Wear earphones that cancel out noise if necessary. Noise levels are rising and they have been found to increase heart rate, blood pressure and irritability.

5. Swap to natural cleaning products – and less of them. You may need more elbow grease which slows you down but it reduces the amount of chemicals you're exposed to.

6. Aim to sleep around seven and half hours a night. Eight is the top end of what has been shown to be the optimum amount of sleep. Less (or more) is linked with higher mortality.

59. Just a minute ...

One-minute bursts of energy cunningly slipped into your usual routine will revolutionise your energy levels.

And if you combine these with the latest research on 'activity' rather than exercise, you'll get fit too, without even trying ...

Just about the fastest way of feeling instantly more energetic is to get the blood pounding in your ears and the breath whizzing in and out of your lungs. A quick burst of activity is also great for dissipating stress hormones. Learning how to navigate through your day, building in little pockets of activity is one of the surest ways of becoming more stress-resilient and better prepared to cope with the demands of your life.

This idea offers a blueprint of how to slot one-minute bursts of activity and slightly longer sessions throughout your day. Your energy levels will soar, but there's an added bonus. You can also feel smug that you're looking after your body as well as those who exercise. Research from an exercise research centre in Dallas shows that those who are active for 30 minutes three times a week are as healthy as those who exercise at a gym for 30 minutes three times a week. This idea has been accepted by our own Health Education Authority, and they recommend being active for 20–30 minutes every day as being a reasonable goal for staying healthy. Activity means gardening, walking briskly to work, climbing stairs rather than using lifts, playing football with the kids, stretching to dust on a high shelf. The easiest way to do this, I find, is to build in some 10-minute-or-so activity sessions and, every hour or so, do a minute's exercise for its energy-boosting effects.

Here's an idea for you...
Here's a physical and a mental energiser. March on the spot for one minute.
According to self-esteem expert Gael Lindenfield, marching on the spot for one
minute not only gets your heart beating fast, it has mental benefits too. The
left–right action stimulates the connections between your brain's hemispheres
and speeds up your thinking.

If you want more energy. Cast your eye over the following programme and look for
one-minute boosters. Try these or something similar and feel the difference in your
energy levels.

If you want to get fit too. You do need a plan. You need to know that you're doing
your 30 minutes or else you end up climbing one flight of stairs and kidding
yourself it's enough. Here is a sample timetable of how you could build in enough
activity.

RE-ENERGISE YOUR DAY

- *7 a.m. – One-minute booster.* Here's a trick. Place your alarm clock at the bottom
  of the bed. Stretch to reach it. Now you've started, don't stop. Spend a minute
  stretching in bed. Children stretch when they wake up. So do animals.
  Movement stimulates the waking part of the brain and makes getting up
  easier.

- *7.15 a.m. – Ten minutes 'being active'.* Do some yoga stretches such as the sun
  salutation or some resistance training with some light weights. Increasing
  blood flow and raising your body temperature will help wake you up.

- *8 a.m. – One-minute booster.* While you're waiting for the kettle to boil, do star
  jumps for one minute.

Defining idea...
'The best effect of any book is that it excites the reader to self-activity.'
– THOMAS CARLYLE

- *9 a.m. – Ten minutes 'being active'.* Walk to a newsagent five minutes from your home or desk for your morning paper. There and back equals ten minutes' activity.

- *11.30 a.m. – One-minute booster.* While sitting at your desk do some abdominal 'pull-ins'. Sit straight in your chair. Breathe in and pull your navel in and up, hold and let out. Each one should take a second. Aim for 60 in the morning (and fit in another 60 in the afternoon).

- *1 p.m. – Lunch.* If you were going to be really good, you could fit in a quick walk, gym visit or run up and down the stairs a few times. But hey! You're doing so well, you can head straight for the pub.

- *3 p.m. – One-minute booster.* Stretch out the tension in your shoulders by standing straight and clasping your hands behind your back.

- *5 p.m. – One-minute booster.* Get a refreshing drink, say, a green tea. While you're waiting for the kettle, run up and down stairs for one minute.

- *6 p.m. – Ten minutes 'being active'.* If you're going to exercise properly this is a good time to do it. If not, do some activity when you get home – gardening or running up and down stairs.

Congratulations. Not only are you more energetic – you're an exerciser, too!

60. What are you drinking?

Slowing down to drink enough calms and energises. Dehydration is a major cause of loss of energy.

Only a lamentable one in ten of us are drinking the 1.5 litres a day of fluid that we should be (and when it's hot, when we exercise and we're ill, that should be two litres). Are you drinking enough? Water is the best hydrator of all, mainly because it's got nothing in it that needs to be processed by your body so it supplies the fluid without any stress on your hardworking organs. The simplest way of ensuring that you're drinking enough is to check your urine from mid-morning onwards. It should be straw-coloured.

If you don't drink enough, you get very tired. You may also overeat as we often mistake thirst for hunger. Try drinking a cup of water every hour and you might find your appetite for snacks decreases. You should also find that your need for tea and coffee reduces automatically.

Which brings us to caffeine. Tea and coffee have the benefit of supplying caffeine, which makes us more alert. Except it doesn't. A recent study has discovered that caffeine doesn't actually work to make us more alert if we drink it regularly. It only has an effect on occasional users. People like me who don't feel they can function without coffee first thing are merely suffering from withdrawal effects. What isn't in dispute (yet) is the effect that caffeine can have on physical performance. Sip an espresso or energy drink half an hour before exercising and you're likely to push harder and achieve more.

Here's an idea for you...
Want an amazing mid-afternoon pick-up? Take one dessertspoonful of Sea Buckthorn cordial (from health food stores or www.weleda.com) in a cup of boiling water. You might want to add a little honey to begin with until you get used to the taste. Sea Buckthorn has ten times the vitamin C content of lemons (three dessertspoons gives you your daily intake) and vitamin C acts like your usual espresso – it wakes you up. Don't drink it before bedtime or it may keep you awake.

Coffee and tea are no longer the 'bogies' they were once thought to be when it comes to hydration. For years we've heard that they are diuretic, causing us to lose fluid. But now that advice has been changed. The water in tea and coffee actually does contribute to hydration unless you really overdo it. In summary: the story on caffeine changes every month, but drinking around four cups of ordinary strength coffee or six cups of ordinary strength tea, doesn't appear to do any harm, and may do some good.

My own line is to drink a cup of strong coffee in the morning and then go onto water-based drinks. Caffeine does overwork your adrenal gland which can lead to energy slumps, and too much makes you jittery. Personally, I could drink a lot more than one cup a day and function OK, and so could most people. But if I have more than one cup a day, then I don't get that delicious buzz in the morning from my morning hit.

Defining idea...
'Reminds me of my safari in Africa. Somebody forgot the corkscrew and for several days we had to live on nothing but food and water.' – W.C. FIELDS

So for you, me and everyone else, it's a balancing act. Just don't go over the limits set above or you could be robbing your energy bank.

I think it's much easier to get enough good quality fluid if you stop seeing it as a chore and start seeing it as an opportunity. Each glass is its own little ritual, giving your wellbeing and energy levels a fillip. Below is my plan. I stop, I sip, I savour.

THE MAGNIFICENT EIGHT

- *7 a.m.* – Glass of hot water with the juice of a quarter **lemon** on waking – said to aid your liver. Works for me.
- *8 a.m.* – Glass of water to wash down your **multivitamin** and daily fish-oil supplement taken after breakfast.
- *11 a.m.* – A cup of **Rooibus tea**. This red bush tea from South Africa is loaded with antioxidants and its distinctive taste makes it a great substitute for coffee addicts.
- *1 p.m.* – Cup of **green tea** after lunch. It helps rev up your metabolism, and those who drink four cups a day are less likely to suffer from brain ageing.
- *3 p.m.* – Glass of water with an effervescent **vitamin C** tablet – vitamin C wakes you up.
- *5 p.m.* – A glass of **sparkling mineral water cut with fruit juice**. Think of it as a cocktail – the effervescence will get your evening off to a sparkling start.
- *7 p.m.* – A cup of **mint tea** after dinner – try crushing your own mint leaves in a glass of water or bung in a teabag – either way, great for helping your digestion.
- *9 p.m.* – A cup of **chamomile tea** to soothe you off to sleep.

61. How to get enough sleep

The answer's simple, make like a great big baby.

Lack of sleep is a growing problem, and like all health writers I've written thousands of words on the subject of getting a good night's sleep. I've interviewed most of the country's top sleep specialists. And what did I learn? That possibly treating yourself like a baby is the best thing you can do. Babies have to learn to go to sleep themselves. Most of us (but not all of us) learn this – but some of us (many of us) forget.

How much sleep is enough? The standard advice is that there is no 'right' or 'wrong'– it's what's right for you. So when people like Madonna say they can get by on four hours sleep, it's possible, but not desirable.

For the great majority of us who have normal working hours, aiming to get to bed by midnight and sleeping for at least six to seven hours is the bare minimum we need simply to restore our bodies after a hard day. Most of us would do better getting to bed significantly earlier and aiming for eight solid hours. Latest research is nudging towards nine hours a night as optimum. So if you're in the Madonna camp, thinking that you're doing pretty well on four or five, it's worth re-examining.

Here's an idea for you...
If you can't sleep, don't lie in bed for more than twenty minutes, becoming increasingly frustrated. Get up, read for twenty minutes, then try again. Don't put on a bright light, a TV or a computer. The idea is that you don't let your bed become associated with misery.

Here are four lessons we can learn from babies:

BABIES NEED A LOT OF SLEEP
And so do most grown-ups, whether they like it or not.

Are you shaking your head and thinking you'd love to sleep more, if only you didn't keep waking in the middle of the night? Most people I know who can't sleep have tried everything that their pharmacist and doctor can suggest. Or they are self-medicating with alcohol. But that's doing nothing to deal with the original problem. Are you working long hours (and that includes housework)? Under huge mental strain? For the record, stress is the number one reason according to The American Psychological Association for short-term sleep problems such as frequent middle-of-the-night waking and insomnia. If you know that something is keeping you awake at night, your only solution is to resolve the stress in some way.

BABIES ARE GOOD AT RECOGNISING WHAT'S KEEPING THEM AWAKE AND GETTING IT DEALT WITH SO THAT THEY CAN GET BACK TO SLEEP
Most grown ups aren't. But without resolving stress, and cutting the strain they're under, they'll never get enough sleep.

Then there are stimulants. Research shows that caffeine drunk before midday can still affect your sleep that evening. All of us, ideally, should be having our last cup by noon, and those who are sensitive should cut it out altogether or limit themselves to one cup of caffeine at breakfast. Alcohol knocks you out and then causes you to wake up in the early hours of the morning. Any sort of screen can

Defining idea...

'There are two types of people in this world: good and bad. The good sleep better, but the bad seem to enjoy the waking hours much more.' – WOODY ALLEN

knock you off your sleep pattern. I know one woman who was chronically sleep deprived for two years before she made the connection between checking her emails just before she went to bed and waking up worrying about work at 3 a.m.

BABIES NEED A RESTFUL ROUTINE, LIKE A WARM BATH AND A BEDTIME STORY BEFORE BED

And grown-ups like a warm bath and a bedtime story before bed too. Grown-ups who are drinking, partying, emailing, watching TV, chatting with their mates on the phone or in other ways keeping their brains active could well get too stimulated to sleep. What they need is a relaxing ten minutes in the tub and a nice, quiet read.

BABIES SLEEP BEST IN A DARK ROOM

So do grown-ups. We evolved as a species to sleep in almost total darkness. Even a small amount of brightness can be strong enough to enter our retina even when our eyes are closed. This sends a signal to the brain that upsets the internal clock. Light in the hallway, shouldn't enter your room, turn the digital alarm clock to the wall, don't fall asleep with the TV on. Blackout curtains are recommended if your streetlights are bright.

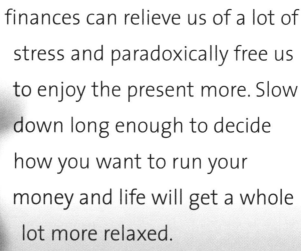

Prioritise your peace of mind...

Some wise Eastern dude said that money itself isn't important. It is just a metaphor for how we choose to make our mark on on the world. If we are tight; we're tight with our emotions and how close we let people get to us; if we're careless of our money, we don't value ourselves and life can get very stressful.

Taking the time to sort out our finances can relieve us of a lot of stress and paradoxically free us to enjoy the present more. Slow down long enough to decide how you want to run your money and life will get a whole lot more relaxed.

62. Love your money

And it will love you right back. When that happens life gets a lot less stressful.

Quickly, without thinking too much about it, write down three phrases that come into your head when you think about your finances.

(Hint: unless your three words are 'abundant, balanced, life-enhancing', then you need this idea.)

This idea is about respect. If you're disrespectful of your money, I'm prepared to bet that money is a stressor in your life. If you don't take care of your money, the chances are that, just like a neglected teenager, it's never going to amount to much. Worse, the relationship will probably deteriorate further. One day your money is going to do the equivalent of coming home pregnant with a crack cocaine habit.

HERE'S A QUICK TEST
Get out your wallet or purse. Check out how it

Here's an idea for you...
Go treasure hunting. Look for money down the side of sofas, in pockets, in foreign currency. How much money have you got stuffed in books. Or unrealised in gift tokens. How much of your money are you ignoring?

looks. Is it neat with bills folded, receipts tucked away. Or is everything stuffed in higgledy-piggledy?

HERE'S A QUICKER ONE
How much money have you got in your wallet right now? If you're out by more than the price of a coffee, you need this idea badly. Your money is your friend. You should love it like a member of the family. You wouldn't go to the shops and forget to bring home one of the kids. Well, why the hell would you misplace your money?

LOOK FOR YOUR LATTE FACTOR
Make a list of everything you spend in a day. Keep a notebook with you and write down how often you take money out of the 'hole in the wall' and what you spend it on. Every cheque you write. Every card you swipe. Every time you spend a penny. Literally. Keep it up for a week, preferably for a month. Now multiply (by 52 or 12). That's what it costs to run your life. Go through and highlight the big essentials – the mortgage, the essential bills. Now get out a calculator and work out what you spend on lunches, clothes, magazines, newspapers.

You're looking for what has been called 'the latte factor', those items that are completely expendable and add very little to your life but cost a fortune. It will frighten the bejasus out of you. My latte factor was £472. I needed that money a whole lot more than Starbucks. You also realise how much it costs to run your life. The very first day I practised this exercise I spent £197.45. All I came home with was a pound of cherries. The rest was debt I couldn't remember accruing. Shocking.

Defining idea...

'The safest way to double your money is to fold it over and put it in your pocket.'
– KIN HUBBARD, American humorist

We're not going to talk about debt here but if you've got personal debt, do this for a month and you are going to work out exactly why.

Writing down what you spend is a fantastically useful exercise whether you're overspending or not. It sure as hell won't destress you in the short term but it will in the long term. It allows you to see almost instantly who or what you're spending your money on and then decide if you're happy with that. It allows you to take control, and every way you can find to foster the illusion of control is helpful if you want to be less stressed. Spiritual teachers tell us that money is neither bad nor good, it's simply a way we register our presence on the world. If you fritter away money as a distraction, you'll never focus long enough to work out what's really important to you. If you spend what you don't have, your spirit as well as your bank balance is going to be overstretched. Your bank balance isn't important. Your spirit is. Respect it, protect it – and you're going to make someone very happy and that someone isn't your bank manager.

63. Red is the new black

Awash in credit card debt? Here are some strong pointers for how you can manage your way out of financial trouble.

Health experts are bemoaning the fact that we're fast becoming a nation of fatties. The thing about the population carrying a few extra kilos is that it's pretty obvious to the most untrained of eyes. Take a walk down your local high street and watch people waddle.

Our readiness to take on previously unheard of levels of debt is a different story. Barring a spectacular fall from monetary grace, our financial health is our secret. How could the couple two doors along afford to have that conservatory built? Who knows? How can the neighbours manage to put all three of their children through private education? How can the office administrator go on quite so many expensive holidays?

What we *do* know is that collectively we are carrying more on our credit cards and mortgages than any previous generation. The average household has debts of around £38,000, with many of us owing between *six and twelve times our household's annual income.*

DEBT'S THE WAY TO DO IT
We're debt junkies. Go to college and come out with a qualification and a pile of bills. You've chanced on a bargain in the sales but you're a bit short this month? No problem – stick it on the credit card. Whether it's buying a house or a car or just paying for Christmas, resistance to debt has never been lower.

Here's an idea for you...
When Marlon Brando cries out 'The horror, the horror' towards the end of *Apocalypse Now*, he hadn't, to the best of my recollection, just opened his latest credit card statement. When the statements for your cards turn up over the next few weeks, make a note of the interest charged in each case, tot up the total interest you pay each month and multiply it by 12. That will give you a ballpark figure for the year. If that doesn't make you cry out in anguish, you may be beyond redemption.

Somewhere along the line, we've succumbed to the delusion that owing money is sophisticated. We look on that elderly uncle who'll only buy something when there's cash in the bank to pay for it as some kind of financial *ingénue* rather than as a model of financial prudence.

And, of course, it's getting ever easier to pile up the debt. Credit card companies seem to fall over themselves in their haste to bump up our credit limits, and then send us a letter telling us the 'good news' that our capacity for debt is now that much greater. Damn their eyes.

Even worse, they're now sending us blank cheques every few weeks. Aside from the fraud risks posed by these unsolicited letters falling into the wrong hands, these cheques usually have punitive conditions – no interest-free period, a transaction fee and often less than attractive interest rates.

Don't get me wrong. Used sensibly, credit cards can be a neat budgeting tool, which can provide a bit of financial flexibility. And borrowing money via your credit card can be extremely positive if you use it to buy smartly. If, for example, you had used your credit card to buy some tickets for a big theatrical or sporting event and then

Defining idea...
'I don't borrow on credit cards because it is too expensive. There's no question that a credit card is an expensive way to do borrowing. I would not recommend to anyone that they chronically borrow on a credit card.'
– MATTHEW BARRETT, chief executive of Barclays Bank

put them up for sale on eBay, you can make a tidy profit. Part of the trouble is that most of our credit card spend tends to go on buying liabilities rather than assets. Borrowing money to buy things that go down in value is a very bad habit to develop.

According to some estimates, most households in the UK have at least five active credit cards, including store cards, at any given time. Do you know what your total credit card debt is? Do you know what rates of interest you're paying on the cards you use? Chances are they vary quite widely.

TARGET YOUR MOST EXPENSIVE CARDS
Here's my advice. Find the card that's charging the highest rate of interest and focus on paying that off as soon as you can. Don't add to your woes by using it to buy anything else. All those other cards? Just send them the minimum payment until you've cleared public enemy number one. Once that's done, turn your financial firepower onto the card with the next highest rate of interest. And so on.

You might be thinking at this point that a suggestion to clear off your credit card debt is hardly ground-breaking advice. Maybe it isn't, but I do know that poorly managed credit cards are the source of many a mate's financial woes. Also, there's a world of difference between people that understand the concept of good credit card management and those of us who adopt an active strategy. As the wise old Chinese proverb says (although thinking about it, maybe it's a Klingon *bon mot*), *'Thought without action is sterile.'*

64. I think therefore iPod

If you've ever bought something and then regretted it almost immediately then this idea is for you. You'll learn how to save money by avoiding impulse purchases.

There's a Marx Brothers' film – I think it's 'A Night in Casablanca' – where Groucho is hired to run a hotel. On arrival, he makes an announcement to staff, which goes something like this: 'There are going to have to be some changes around here. From now on, if guests ask for a three-minute egg, give them a two-minute egg; if they ask for a two-minute egg, give them a one-minute egg; and if they ask for a one-minute egg, give them the chicken and tell them to work it out for themselves.'

Maybe Groucho's motives are questionable but he did manage to hint at today's retail world in which speed of delivery and instant gratification have become the norm. There's an episode of *The Simpsons* where a gigantic new deep fryer is being installed. Perhaps you remember the following exchange:

Shop owner: It can fry a whole buffalo in 40 seconds.
Homer: (wailing voice) Oh, I want it now!

As ever more demanding customers, we want better quality, we want cheaper prices and, above all, we want it more or less immediately. The bookshop owner who tells us that it will take two weeks to order the book we want is seeing

Here's an idea for you...
Part of the intention of having a 28-day list is to introduce a cooling-off period into the purchasing process. Another way to give yourself pause for thought is to try an experiment along these lines: work out how much you put on your cards last month and draw that sum out in cash. For the next month, try paying for everything with that money. Turning barely noticed credit card spend into extremely visible cash-burn can be quite a shocking way to discover just how much you get through. Alternatively, you may find that using real rather than virtual money inhibits your spending impulses.

increasing volumes of business going to internet booksellers. 'Now' is becoming the only acceptable delivery time.

There's physiological evidence to suggest that going on a spending spree gives us a short-term high. We actually enjoy buying stuff. Just as we're prone to comfort eat to cheer ourselves up and to allay anxiety, so comfort spending is a path to retail orgasm.

Let's be honest, it's probably something we've all experienced. There we are, wandering through a department store and we see *it*. It could be a TV, a cool top, a DVD... but it's a must-have. Chances are that until you saw it, you didn't even know that it existed. But now you've seen it and you want it – badly. You know you're a bit short this month really, but you reach for your plastic chum and it's yours.

Feels good, doesn't it? The weird thing is, of course, that a few weeks down the line, that must-have doesn't always seem quite so necessary to your life. If you've ever thought to yourself that you have a wardrobe full of clothes and nothing to wear, chances are that you've been a victim of premature retail ejaculation.

Incidentally, don't imagine that you're only at risk when you're out shopping. It won't be long before most retail accidents happen at home. Shopping online is just as dangerous when gratification is only a mouse click away.

Defining idea...

'When you look at the buying habits that have taken hold in our culture over the past 30 years or so, you can see that we made the decision somewhere along the line to work longer hours so we could acquire more things. We've exchanged our leisure time for stuff.' – ELAINE ST JAMES, *50 Ways to Simplify your Life*

So here's an idea that will save you money and help reduce the clutter in your home. From now on, every time you come across an item that you would normally be tempted to splash out on and which costs a significant amount (you decide what counts as significant), hold back from buying it. Go home and put it on your 28-day list. Make a note of the item, the date you saw it and the cost. If after 28 days you revisit your list and still think it would be a good buy, then consider acquiring it. If you do buy it, the heightened anticipation of finally getting your hands on it after a wait of 28 days and more is quite something.

(A friend of mine calls this tantric shopping. The method works particularly well with singles and albums made by contestants in reality TV programmes. That amusing version of 'Jungle Rock' produced by early rejects from *I'm a Celebrity, Get Me Out of Here* seems less essential six months down the track.)

If after four weeks you're still unsure about the merits of buying a particular item, put it back on the list for another four weeks. Apart from keeping your home a bit freer from clutter, this will save you a fortune. Not a bad return for a *soupçon* of discipline.

65. Manage your credit

credit limits are not virtual income, they simply reflect our capacity for debt. It's well worth exploring how well you use credit. We'll also look at the value of credit as a means of smoothing over short-term cashflow issues.

George Orwell's book '1984' introduced us to the concept of doublespeak, i.e. language that is deliberately constructed to disguise or distort its actual meaning. When it comes to the language deployed by credit card companies and banks to 'help' us manage our personal finances, we hit the gold standard of weasel words.

So here's the reality behind some financial doublespeak. *Credit is simply another word for debt.*

As linguistic sleights of hand go, it's pretty good. After all, think of the connotations that the word 'credit' has: phrases like 'to their credit' or 'creditworthy' or a 'creditable performance' makes the word seem like a desirable thing to have. But substitute our likeable chum 'credit' with its ugly alter ego 'debt' and it's a whole new ball-game. Imagine getting a letter from a credit card company saying 'Good news! We've decided to increase your debt limit.' Or picture a shop that offers 'interest-free debt for six months'. Doesn't seem quite so tasty does it?

When a credit card company increases your credit limit, what it's really saying is that you are considered to be a reliable payer of the extortionate rates of interest they charge.

Here's an idea for you...

There are some nifty offers out there encouraging you to transfer outstanding balances from one credit card to another. Often, these offers come with low or no interest charged for maybe six or nine months or – if you're in luck – until the transferred amount has been repaid. Be careful not to spend on these cards. If you make any purchases, the credit card company will almost certainly clear the cheapest debt first, leaving you to accumulate interest at the higher rate on any subsequent purchases.

So just reflect for a moment on how you tend to use your credit, sorry debt card. Unless you are some kind of credit card paragon who uses it purely as a convenient alternative to carrying around a wad of cash drawn from the plentiful reserves residing in your current account, the chances are you're using it when you can't afford to buy something outright, and so you buy the item on credit.

A question: when you don't have the money in your current account this month to pay for the item in question, does it occur to you to consider whether you're any more likely to have the money next month to pay off this new debt? If you have a bonus coming through next month, then fine – a month or two's interest may be a small price to pay for the benefits of having something now rather than later. But the chances are that you are going to be equally strapped for cash next month, in which case you're in danger of heading inexorably into a world where it will take you an age to clear the core debt. And even that assumes that you're not continuing to purchase new stuff from time to time.

Don't get me wrong. I'm not saying that credit cards are the devil's spawn (although if you're using them to spend money you don't have on things you don't really need, there's something unholy going on), but they can tempt us into spending habits that are beyond our real means.

Defining idea...
'A check or credit card, a Gucci bag strap, anything of value will do. Give as you live.'
– JESSE JACKSON, preacher and politician

However, it doesn't have to be like this. It's possible to use credit cards so that they work to our advantage and not the other way around. Here are some tips for making best use of them:

- If you can pay outright without using a card, do so.

- Always try to pay off 10 per cent of your balance every month on your credit cards – if you only pay the minimum it will cost you loads and take an age to clear.

- Do not, whatever you do, build up the amount you owe on store cards. With one or two exceptions, their annual interest rates are extremely high.

- Used intelligently, credit cards can be useful sources of free credit. Used rashly, they can bring about an imperceptible slide into long-term debt.

66. Manage your debt

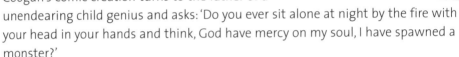

I suspect we've all been there. Don't despair. Here are some positive techniques for getting out of debt.

I always smile when I think of that interview on an episode of the Alan Partridge show in which Steve Coogan's comic creation turns to the father of a unendearing child genius and asks: 'Do you ever sit alone at night by the fire with your head in your hands and think, God have mercy on my soul, I have spawned a monster?'

Although 'spawning a monster' may be putting it a bit too strongly, it would be nice to think that the banks, building societies and credit card providers who have fuelled the current spending binge are suffering at least one or two pangs of guilt.

Many of us have been making the most of historically low interest rates to borrow money and to rack up debt on our credit cards. Our level of collective debt is unprecedented. It's reckoned that around an average 12 per cent of our income is eaten up by servicing debts.

And that figure is based on current interest rate levels. How would we cope if our bills suddenly went up by 20 per cent? It only takes interest rates to rise a few percentage points and it could happen.

Here's an idea for you...
This is strong medicine but if you're not convinced that you have a problem, try producing a consolidated debt statement. Every three months, compile details of all the money you owe anybody, including credit card debt, the outstanding balance on any loans you have, overdrafts, even the tenner you owe your best mate. This will give you an all too clear picture of the state of your finances.

Part of the trouble is that the older of us have forgotten the years of double-digit rates, and the younger of us have no real experience of the cost of borrowing rearing up. OK, we can bang on about how the credit card providers should be more responsible about unsecured lending. We can criticise them for setting low minimum repayments which can tempt customers to repay little more than the interest on the amount owed and so never pay off the debt. Ultimately, though, we are the ones who have to dig our way out of the debt hole. Waiting for a lottery win, or for a bequest from a distant relative, is no strategy.

TECHNIQUES FOR GETTING OUT OF DEBT

- **Stop the rot.** If you have multiple credit cards, identify which one has the most draconian interest rate and shred it. Don't tuck it in a drawer and rely on your willpower not to use it. History suggests this is not a great tactic. If you can, consider transferring the debt on this card to the one carrying least interest.

- **Talk to your creditors.** Let them know you're having problems. Depending on the extent of your debt, you may want to agree a strategy for clearing the debt. Work out how much you can realistically afford to pay. Focus on the most important monthly payments – mortgage/rent, council tax, gas, electricity, etc.

Defining idea...
'I can get no remedy against this consumption of the purse: borrowing only lingers and lingers it out, but the disease is incurable.' – **WILLIAM SHAKESPEARE**

- **Don't panic but don't ignore the problem.** You may have seen nature programmes where creatures stay very, very still in order to evade predators. Your debt won't go away; in fact, ignoring it guarantees that it will get worse as the interest builds up and your creditors start to hound you. Don't ignore court papers.

- **Don't pay for advice.** There are plenty of sources of free help and counselling. Talk to your bank, ask your employer for advice, try the Citizens' Advice Bureau.

Getting into severe debt is horrible – I know, I've been there (it happens when you write for a living!). The crucial first step back to solvency is to face up to the fact that you're in debt and to recognise that you need to adopt a conscious strategy to get out of it.

67. How to deal with severe debt

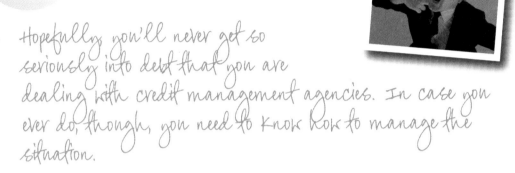

Hopefully you'll never get so seriously into debt that you are dealing with credit management agencies. In case you ever do, though, you need to know how to manage the situation.

Most of us have been strapped for cash from time to time. Generally we are able to dig ourselves out of trouble with a bit of financial belt-tightening or some creative use of credit cards. It's not always that easy.

Remember the character played by Kevin Costner in the movie *Field of Dreams* who felt impelled to build a baseball stadium in the middle of nowhere on the basis of advice from a mystical friend that 'If you build it, they will come'? There's a variation on this that applies to many people who get deep into debt and are unable to extricate themselves: if you owe it, they will come. The 'they' in question are either the people who are owed money or their appointed debt collectors.

KNOW WHAT YOU'RE SIGNING UP TO
If you should fall into serious debt, here are a few tips on how to handle the situation:

- Don't panic or ignore the problem: unopened bills won't go away.

- Decide which debts take priority – like mortgage or rent – and which cost you the most through penalties or higher interest rates.

Here's an idea for you...
The days when lenders would send the boys around armed with baseball bats are largely the stuff of fiction and these days are confined to the extreme fringes of society. But watch out for the dodgy practices given above. They still happen from time to time.

- Only agree to pay off debts at a rate you can keep up. Don't offer more than you can afford.

- Contact those who you owe money to as soon as possible to let them know you're having problems.

- Remember that's it's better to make a small payment than send nothing at all.

- Keep copies of *all* correspondence. You will need them if you want to seek help and advice from a third party.

- Seek advice if organisations won't accept your repayment offers.

LENDERS HAVE RESPONSIBILITIES TOO
Lenders and debt management companies have to behave properly. Examples of their (illegal) deficiencies include:

- Failing to investigate or provide proper details/records when a debt is queried or disputed.

- Failing to deal with appointed third parties such as Citizens' Advice Bureaux or independent advice centres.

- Pursuing third parties for payment when they are not liable.

Defining idea...
'It is very iniquitous to make me pay my debts. You have no idea of the pain it gives one.' **– LORD BYRON**

- Falsely implying or claiming authority – such as claiming to be working on court authority.

- Contacting debtors at unreasonable times and/or intervals.

- Claiming a right of entry when no court order has been obtained.

- Misleading debtors by the use of official-looking documents such as letters made to resemble court claims.

Lenders aren't allowed to ignore the dodgy practices of debt collectors acting on their behalf. If they do, their fitness to hold a credit licence can be called into question. Generally though, according to the Office of Fair Trading (OFT), complaints about debt management companies have dropped substantially in recent years.

So if you do get into debt, at least you shouldn't be unreasonably treated by the people you owe money to. Which leaves you free to concentrate on the task in hand, namely rebuilding your financial reputation.

68. First save, then spend

If you find it difficult or impossible to save money here's an approach that will enable you to divert some of your monthly discretionary spend into a savings account.

Let's be clear – building up your savings is a very good thing to do and an excellent habit to get into. Not least of all because we all find our wallets or purses ambushed at short notice by sizeable bills coming out of left field at us. You know the sort of thing: the central heating breaks down this evening, the roof springs a leak or the car starts making a noise like a Tuvan throat singer.

As well as warding off emergencies, savings can enable us to plan for the future. It might be something coming up relatively soon – your next holiday, upgrading the computer or replacing the car (that Tuvan throat singer thing is not good news, believe me). Or there may be a more distant blot on your financial landscape – children going to university perhaps.

When these things happen, you have three basic options: (a) draw on your savings; (b) go into debt; (c) write a snappy begging letter. If option (a) isn't available because you have little or no savings, you're left with unpleasant option (b) or unlikely option (c).

You might be thinking at this point: OK, obviously having savings is a 'good thing' but what if there isn't anything left over at the end of the month to put into a savings account.

Here's an idea for you...
Set up a standing order from your current to your savings account, and make sure it goes out early in the month. (Wait until the end and you may well find that you've no money left.) Make it a reasonable amount but critically one that you can afford. To help avoid any temptation to dip into your savings, set up the savings account so that the money you've saved isn't too readily accessible. Use the building society across town rather than the one around the corner, and consider going for an account where you have to give notice before you can make a withdrawal.

Don't get suckered into a 'not today, maybe tomorrow' attitude to saving. This may be an accurate description of your current situation but what I'd suggest is you could be experiencing a monetary version of Parkinson's Law (you know the one – it states that work expands to fill the time available for its completion). Most of us spend what we earn; if our pay goes up, we upgrade our lifestyle and we're soon spending what we earn again.

Against this backdrop, you can see the flaw in looking to save whatever is left over in your account at the end of each month. Chances are the sum involved will always be a big fat zero (and that's in a good month).

So spending and then saving what's left over will get you next to nowhere. Here's an alternative: try saving and then spending. In other words, set aside a certain amount each month as savings, and then make the remainder your budget for the month.

It's Parkinson's Law in reverse: reduce the amount of money you have available to spend each month and then adjust your lifestyle accordingly.

Defining idea...

'Accumulating three months' income won't happen overnight. For most people who embark on a serious saving programme, it will take four to five years to reach this target.' **– ALVIN HALL, psychologist and presenter of the TV programme** *Your Money or Your Life*

Is this possible? Well yes, when you consider that, on average, around 20 per cent of household expenditure goes on leisure. Think of the thousands a year that we can fritter away on lattes, newspapers and magazines, pricey sandwiches, DVDs, chocolate and so on.

If you don't have a savings mentality, try setting yourself a goal. It might be to have three to six months' salary set aside for emergencies, or maybe to get hold of a plasma monitor in the next twelve months. Whatever you plump for, having a goal gives a bit of meaning and purpose to the idea of saving. It comes in handy when you next walk past Starbucks to remind yourself that passing up a take-out coffee is not just wilful self-denial, it's helping to bring that 42-inch screen just a bit closer.

10 sweat-free ways to save while keeping it simple

1. Cook from scratch – eschew fast food and processed meals.

2. Take a list when you go shopping and stick to it. Avoid impulse trolley moments.

3. Buy your own drinks in the pub – don't let others include you in their round, you'll lose friends.

4. Make your own lunch sandwiches.

5. Find cheaper hobbies Go running, visit museums, join a reading club.

6. Grow your own vegetables.

7. Spend less time with big-spending chums.

8. Share car journeys and taxis.

9. Let others pay their share of expenses – question why you need to be the one picking up the tab.

10. Stop buying clothes for a time. We only wear 20% of what we own. The other 80% is festering.

69. Destroy your piggybank

What will I learn here? When interest rates are low, putting money into a savings account generates dismal returns. But used intelligently that money can generate far better returns for you.

As you may have read elsewhere, there's no doubt that saving is 'a good thing'. We're not doing as much of it as we might – these days people are saving just 5.4 per cent of their disposable income, compared with a high of 12.4 per cent in 1980 and a long-term average of 8.9 per cent – but just about all of us see the merit in saving.

The trouble with the notion of saving is that, well, it's just a little bit dull. Remember those kids we went to school with who used to put some of their pocket money away each week? They generally weren't the ones in our gang. (If you're thinking, 'Hey, that was me,' at this point, I do apologise – I'm sure you've blossomed into an interesting person in the intervening years.)

When my parents encouraged me to save, it generally seemed to involve putting coins of small denomination into a brightly coloured plastic piggybank only to open it some time later to find exactly the same amount there. Barely enough to buy a Mars Bar, and zero growth to boot.

Here's an idea for you...
If you do have a savings account, remember to keep an eye on interest rates. One of the very worst things you can do to your finances is to put money away and forget about it. If you open a savings account and take your eye off the interest rate it pays, you often end up being stitched up good and proper.

Now I've grown up (allegedly), the thought of saving still fails to excite my senses. And with interest rates at such a low level, it's next to impossible to get excited about salting a few bob away every month into a building society account.

There is, I think, a real problem here. Apparently, 44 per cent of people have no savings at all. I appreciate that some of those 44 per cent have no choice in the matter, but a tidy chunk of people don't save but could if they really wanted.

Perhaps you need to bring to the savings party the sense of risk and excitement that exists in the world of investing. So, instead of putting a set amount away every month into a low-interest (in every sense of the phrase) savings account, let's start speculating to accumulate.

I'm not necessarily talking about investing in the stock market, even though we've all seen those figures that get trotted out regularly to show that – in the medium to long term – investing in the market has consistently outperformed a building society account.

There are plenty of other ways to build a better return. I know a number of people who wouldn't dream of dabbling in stocks and shares, but who use their knowledge of a particular market to build their savings.

Defining idea...
'Risk comes from not knowing what you're doing.'
– WARREN BUFFETT, probably the world's most famous and influential investor

One chap I know has an expert knowledge of brass instruments. Instead of putting a set amount into a savings account every month, he uses that money to buy instruments, which he refurbishes and then sells on at a tidy profit. I know somebody else who buys books from second-hand bookshops and then sells them on eBay or Amazon – again at a profit. In both case, the profits they're making far outstrip the interest rates available. Just as importantly, they're both really enjoying turning a hobby into an income stream.

Of course, there is a level of risk to this – just as there is in playing the markets. But in the case of my two chums, and I suspect thousands of people like them, they have confidence in their knowledge of their particular niche market, and they see real merit in using their savings to fund an enjoyable pastime with the prospect of gaining returns on investment that puts more traditional saving methods into the shade.

70. Make your decisions and then move on

Managing our personal finances to good effect necessarily involves us in making decisions. How can you best make decisions in a financial world that's full of choice?

If you live in the UK, you can choose between around 8,000 mortgages, 1,300 or so credit cards, and over 1,000 savings accounts.

You might be thinking that it's fantastic to have so much choice. In a competitive marketplace, that must mean that there are some sensational deals out there if only you could find a way of tracking down the best ones.

Psychologist Barry Schwartz, author of *The Paradox of Choice*, believes that having so much choice isn't necessarily good for us. Because of the growing number of options we are presented with, we don't always have the time to look at all the information out there to make the best choice.

Dr Schwartz asks us to think about the difference between the best and good enough. He suggests that there are two types of decision-makers: one group he calls *maximisers*, people who want the absolute best, and so have to examine minutely every choice for fear they'll miss out on getting the best. However, looking at all the choices is usually frustrating and takes too much time. He calls people in the second category *satisficers*: these are people who look at the options and choose an option that is good enough.

243

> **Here's an idea for you…**
> Another decision-making strategy is for us to cede all or part of the decision to somebody else. In the healthcare field, for example, we expect the doctor to tell us what kind of treatment we need. When it comes to making big financial decisions, perhaps we should leave it to experts who can filter the available choices and recommend one option to us or perhaps offer a shortlist of choices.

Generally speaking, we should strive to be satisficers because a satisficer is usually happy with their choice. In contrast, a maximiser isn't normally happy and often regrets what he or she bought.

Of course, some decisions are more significant than others. A typical supermarket carries more than 30,000 items. When we go to do the weekly shop, we are visiting a repository for non-durable goods, i.e. goods that are quickly used and replenished. Buying the wrong brand of biscuits doesn't have huge emotional or financial consequences, because we can buy the right brand next time. But in many other settings, we are out to buy things that cost more money, and that are meant to last. And here, as the number of options increases, the psychological stakes rise accordingly.

Schwartz recounts an amusing tale about attempting to buy a pair of jeans. The choices befuddle him: relaxed fit, acid-washed, button-fly? While he doesn't place much importance on the pants he wears, he moves on to more serious questions, such as choosing the right retirement fund or healthcare programme where penury or death can result from an ill-advised selection.

So how can we make the best possible decision about something as important as our personal finances when we know that there's no such thing as the best possible decision?

Defining idea...

'The fact that some choice is good doesn't necessarily mean that more choice is better... There is a cost to having an overload of choice. As a culture, we are enamoured of freedom, self-determination, and variety, and we are reluctant to give up any of our options. But clinging tenaciously to all the choices available to us contributes to bad decisions, to anxiety, stress, and dissatisfaction — even to clinical depression.' **– BARRY SCHWARTZ,** *The Paradox of Choice*

The trick of it seems to be for us to sift through as many options as we can and then take our time to make the best decision we can considering all the available options we are aware of *at the time*. Having decided, we act. Then, for the sake of our mental well-being as much as anything, we choose to live with our choice – for a period of time anyway. We might consciously decide to review the decision at some point in the future but we won't beat ourselves up in the meantime if it looks like better options have become available.

The important thing is to recognise that there is no such thing as a perfect, long-lasting product offering in the financial services field. So let's get used to the idea. As Clint Eastwood famously said in one of his Dirty Harry movies, 'a man's got to know his limitations'.

245

71. Track your outgoings

It's time to look at the implications of not knowing how much you've spending month by month. We'll also consider the benefits of keeping a daily spending diary.

I have a friend who's an adviser to small businesses and he has a pet theory that many businesses that go bust do so not as a result of a major investment decision – renting a shop, a big marketing campaign, upgrading computers, etc. – turning sour, but rather on the back of small, almost invisible, but bank-balance-sapping expenditures.

The same can be true of our personal finances. Not many of us go out every month and spend £500 on the likes of a new TV, or kitchen table or a motorised lawnmower. On the other hand, we can regularly find ourselves forking out for a round of drinks here, a DVD there, maybe a magazine, a taxi home, a sandwich for lunch and so on. And it's often the cumulative effect of these here-and-there micro-spends that tilts our bank balance into the red or puts one of our credit cards onto a life support system.

Realistically, it's not easy to keep track of what we spend, particularly as we often use credit cards for day-to-day expenditure like the supermarket shop. Credit cards can be helpful additions to our financial armoury but they can all too easily blur our sense of what we're spending. Not so long ago, we would withdraw some cash from the bank and that would be our weekly budget. We had no obvious other source to draw on and so we had to make do with the cash we had to hand.

Here's an idea for you...
One word of caution about this exercise. You'll need to ask yourself how typical your income and expenditure patterns have been for the month you were keeping your diary. There will be seasonal patterns to your spending – going on holiday, Christmas, car insurance, etc., on top of which you will find your wallet or purse ambushed occasionally by bills coming out of left field at you. If you've been to the dentist or opticians recently, you may know what I mean.

So here's the crunch question: do you have any idea how much you've spent over the past month? I'm betting that only a handful of people could tell me to the nearest pound. OK, so maybe that handful needs to loosen up a bit, but if you produce an estimate of your monthly expenditure that's out by say 10 per cent or 25 per cent or even 50 per cent, the signs are that you may have a money management problem. Alternatively, you may be the possessor of wealth so vast that you really don't need to be reading this book at all (you're welcome to stay by the way, it's just that you're not the market segment I'm currently addressing).

Of course, you can't know how accurate your estimate is without having the actual expenditure figure available. To this end, and also to provide a base for a budgeting system for the future, I'd like to encourage you to keep a comprehensive daily diary of expenditure for one month. Yes, write *everything* down – bus fares, coffees, magazines, dry cleaning, supermarket shopping, direct debits, phone bills, car fuel, dog food, everything else. Don't rely on memory: you'll inevitably understate the true figure.

Defining idea...

'Don't fall into the trap of convincing yourself that the bad habits uncovered...are just a one month aberration.' – **ALVIN HALL, psychologist and presenter of the TV programme** *Your Money or Your Life*

When you've gathered a month's data, see what your reaction is. Pleased? Horrified? Then try categorising what you have spent under the headings 'fixed costs' and 'discretionary spend'. The point is that once you're armed with some quality data, you're in a position to respond and take any necessary action.

72. Choose the best people to advise you

CONTRACT

If your financial circumstances can justify it, you may need to look for a financial adviser and perhaps an accountant as well to help you manage your finances as effectively as possible. Here's how to choose a good 'un.

Some combinations just don't work: red wine and fish; juggernauts and country lanes; Rod Stewart and just about anyone on the planet. You might think that accountants and beauty competitions are similar misfits.

So you may be surprised that I recommend that anybody looking for an accountant should always hold some kind of competitive selection process. Never pick an accountant from a field of one.

If you need an accountant, it's probably wise to get a qualified accountant. This is not to say that there are not good unqualifieds around. They may have plenty of experience, and they generally charge less. Where a qualified accountant scores is that he or she will be insured against negligence or advice or work going wrong.

Before you hold your beauty parade, speak with friends and colleagues to see if they are happy to recommend someone. This is much better than just ploughing through the *Yellow Pages*. Try and meet up with at least three contenders for your business.

Here's an idea for you...

If you're looking to select an independent financial adviser (IFA), rather than an accountant, you can still use many of the same questions from your accountant quiz sheet. Here are some additional areas worth probing.

Charging. Ask your IFA to explain the differences between fees and commission when you first meet. Increasingly people prefer to pay fees.

Qualifications. Do they have a relevant qualification? In the UK, for example, the benchmark qualification is the Financial Planning Certificate (FPC), and a competent adviser must hold all three components of this certificate or equivalent. Some advisers also have advanced level qualifications in their specialist areas, e.g. pensions.

Access to the company providing the product. An adviser should feel totally confident and be willing for you to talk directly with the product provider involved.

Degree of specialism. Many IFAs are all-rounders, but some may specialise in mortgages, for instance. However, some may not advise on certain areas at all. You may prefer to deal with an IFA who will not provide advice but will set up your investment, protection, pension or other financial product on your behalf, often on a more cost-effective basis than you could arrange yourself.

Regulation. Advisers must be regulated by a recognised authority.

When you meet up (and by the way, these initial meetings ought to be free of charge), here are some of the questions you might want to ask:

- How long have they been in business? You may feel more comfortable with someone who has several years' experience.

- How much do they charge? Hourly fees are most common but a fixed fee for the first 12 months can often be arranged. What are the charges if the tax authorities decide to investigate your tax affairs?

Defining idea...

Q What's the definition of a good tax accountant?
A Someone who has a loophole named after him. – **ANONYMOUS**

● Are they a member of a recognised professional body where you can seek redress if things go wrong?

● Does their tax return service include advice or merely helping with form filling?

● If your affairs are of a specialised nature, do they have the expertise to handle your case?

● Can they provide other clients as references? A good accountant should be happy to put you in touch with other customers.

● Will your affairs be handled by them personally or by one of their staff? In the larger firms you could easily find a less qualified junior dealing with your affairs.

● How effectively does the practice work? Ask for estimated response times. How long does it take to speak with a partner? Will the practice contact you with, for example, news about tax changes?

And there's one critical, final question. This one you need to ask yourself: do you think you could get on with your accountant? It's not a matter of whether you would want to go on a skiing holiday with her and her family, but if you feel uncomfortable in her presence, it's unlikely to be the most productive of relationships.

73. Facing retirement: be a lion, not a lemming

There's a lot of doom and gloom surrounding the financial plight of pensioners. However, it is possible to manage the financial implications of retirement, and the sooner we start to think about this, the better. Here are some tips for ensuring that our senior years are as comfortable as possible.

According to Mintel, the market research group, hundreds of thousands of people are heading into retirement still burdened by mortgages that have a number of years to run and owing thousands of pounds on their credit cards.

The situation is only likely to get worse as people find that their endowment mortgages aren't stumping up the money needed to pay off the debt, and as the baby-boomers, in effect the first credit card generation, carry unprecedented levels of personal debt into their twilight years.

Add into the recipe the ballooning cost of care for the old folks in their retirement homes and the inheritance implications of that. Mix in the spectre of a possible steep fall in house prices as a glut of baby boomer family houses come onto the market. Season with the diminishing likelihood of any of us making it to

Here's an idea for you...
One problem with all of these options is that they are based on juggling what you have. One further option is to consider joining the ranks of the 'newly unretired', a growing number of people who, whether through choice or financial necessity, look to work on beyond retirement. Traditional retirement dates hark back to an era when most work involved physical effort and we were clapped-out husks by the time we reached our sixties. In the era of knowledge work, there's no reason why we shouldn't continue working well into our seventies or eighties

retirement without at least one change of employer (and the impact that might have on our pensions). Add a dash of reduced pensions in the light of disappearing final salary schemes. *Et voilà,* there's no cake so we can't eat it!

And that's not to mention growing numbers of people who are remortgaging their homes to give their children a deposit for a house or to pay university costs.

Look, I'm sorry if you're now feeling like you've just emerged from a trendy cinema that had no air-conditioning and the standard uncomfortable seats, having endured a particularly depressing subtitled trilogy by a Polish film director with a cheerless world-view and an unpronounceable name. (I know what you're thinking, and yes, my ability to tap into the emotional *Zeitgeist* is uncanny.)

Before you mentally move me from the file marked 'purveyor of brilliant ideas' into one called something like 'self-deluding gloom-meister and writer of books you regret buying', take heart: there are steps you can take to ward off the future depicted above. When it comes to facing retirement, forewarned is forearmed. So if you are still some way off of retirement, make a note in your diary to look at your finances at least five years before retirement and, if you can, start a serious campaign to pay off as many debts as you can.

Defining idea...

'I expect it will become increasingly common over the next 15 to 20 years for people to reach retirement without having paid off their mortgage. Inflation can no longer be relied upon to reduce debts and many people don't fully appreciate how much other debt they have taken on.'
– DAVID BITNER, Bradford & Bingley Building Society

By the way, you might want to start thinking about inheritance tax implications, especially if you are one of the fortunate few who could deliberately increase their mortgage in retirement because you want lots of debt to put against the value of their estate for inheritance tax purposes.

74. Invest rationally

Here we're going to explore how Nobel Prize-winning work in the field of behavioural economics can teach us a thing or two about managing our own finances.

Here's a quick general knowledge quiz:
- How long did the Hundred Years War last?
- Which country makes Panama hats?
- In which month do Russians celebrate the October Revolution?
- What was King George VI's first name?
- What is the colour of the black box in a commercial airplane?

To check the answers, have a look at the end of this idea. For now, though, I hope you won't mind taking my word that things are not always as they seem. The trouble is that it's one thing for us to recognise and smile at these quirks of illogicality and irrationality when questions like these pop up in pub quizzes, quite another for us to accept that we ourselves are prone to irrational acts. After all, everybody's behaviour is entirely logical from their own point of view.

Princeton professor Daniel Kahneman shared the 2002 Nobel Prize for economics for his work in the fields of behavioural finance and behavioural economics. What Kahneman and his colleagues uncovered was just how irrationally we behave when it comes to making investment decisions.

Here's an idea for you...
When you are making your investment decisions, make sure you have enough data. Rather than leaping to conclusions based on scant data, look at as many numbers as possible. Don't rely just on recent performance; look over a longer period. 'It doesn't take many observations to think you've spotted a trend,' warns Kahneman, 'and it's probably not a trend at all.'

According to Kahneman, a trap that professional and amateur investors alike tend to fall into is to have what he calls an 'optimistic bias'. Research shows that our forecasts of future stock-market movements are far more optimistic than past long-term returns would justify. The same goes for our hopes of ever-rising house prices or of doing well in games of fortune. Here are a couple of examples of irrational investment decision-making that Kahneman has uncovered:

- **Believing the sure-fire tip.** We tend to put undue weight on 'inside information'. Whether it's a financial pundit in the weekend press or somebody down the pub telling us about a certain winner in an upcoming horse race, we fail to recognise that they're offering educated guesses at best.

- **Focusing on short-term gain and over-managing our decisions.** Kahneman reports that when an investor sells one stock and immediately buys another, the one that was sold does better by an average of 3.4 per cent in the following year. In other words, we would be better investors if we just made fewer decisions. Apparently, this tendency to over-trade is in part due to counterproductive regret; we trade far too frequently because we're chasing the returns on shares we wish we had bought earlier.

Answers: 116 years, Ecuador, November, Albert, Orange

Defining idea...
'People tend to fear losses more than they value gains. A $1 loss is more painful than the pleasure of a $1 gain... As a consequence, they will take a greater risk and gamble in a losing situation, holding on to the position in hope that prices will recover.'
– **JOHAN GINYARD, Uppsala University, Department of Psychology**

The key to making good investment decisions, then, is to rely more on our analytical powers and less on our emotions. The trouble is that it's not at all easy for us to remember this when we're facing a significant loss on those shares that we had such high hopes for. Perhaps the thing to do is to sell the shares in an analytical spirit and then go for some emotional retribution by lambasting the bloke down the pub who told us they were a sure-fire thing.

75. Learn the power of 12 (and 52): annualise your savings

I'm now going to outline a way in which you can save decent sums of money without too much pain. It's the financial equivalent of 'large oaks from little acorns grow'.

Imagine that you've just been given some bad news by your garage, or your builder, or your dentist. For example, your shower's causing a major damp problem in your master bedroom and it really needs attention soon (how your dentist knows this is another matter).

The upshot is that you're going to have to find £1,500 to sort out the problem.

How are you going to find this money? You could put it on the credit card but that's just shuffling the debt around. Or maybe you could dip into your emergency savings fund, but you were hoping to put that towards the cost of buying a new car. Or perhaps you could cancel the holiday you had planned for the summer, but that would be such a drag because you really could do with a break.

Or you could give up eating Snickers for a bit.

Here's an idea for you...
Of course, you don't necessarily have to keep this going for a year. A 2004 survey suggested that abstaining from chocolate, alcohol, coffee, crisps and cigarettes during Lent could net savers around £660. The bank calculated that giving up a daily latte between Ash Wednesday and Easter can leave savers £86 better off, while foregoing a daily pint of lager could save £92. Smokers who buy a packet of cigarettes a day could save over £200.

OK, so that's a bit of an exaggeration for dramatic effect, but the point is that our cash has a habit of dribbling away in lots of small amounts here and there, and that if we could harness a whole bunch of small (and probably relatively painless) savings, we can quickly build up a healthy financial stockpile.

Psychologically, pocketing 40 pence on the back of a Snickers unconsumed doesn't seem like a saving worth having. What can reinforce the impact of a bit of confectionery-related restraint is to try multiplying out the saving over a 12-month period. Imagine that Snicker is one of five you eat each week; that makes the saving £2 a week, or a starting-to-get-impressive £104 a year.

259

Defining idea…
'If you want to appreciate the cumulative effect of saving, think of Nassau in the Bahamas: Note All Small Savings Adding Up.' – JOHN VILLIS, writer and educator

When I was faced with a unexpected £1,500 bill a little while back, this is how I raised the money over a 12-month period:

Item given up	Annualised saving
A bottle of wine a week	£260
Sunday newspaper	£73
A Mars Bar a week	£22
Packet of crisps a day	£75
Coffee on way into work	£480
Evening paper on way home	£100
A DVD a month	£195
A CD a month	£140
A paperback a month	£85
A bottle of lager a week	£75
Total saving	**£1,505**

These numbers get even more significant when you bear in mind that they come out of our take-home pay. Try working out what proportion of your annual salary is needed to fund these items. If you're on the average wage, for example, this little lot above are broadly equivalent to one month's pay.

I have a friend who describes this focus on realising a series of small savings as moving from 'penny profligate to pound proud'. Mind you, he works in marketing.

76. Sod the Joneses

It's not wise to pursue ever bigger pay cheques to fuel ostentatious displays of wealth. As Lily Tomlin put it: 'The trouble with the rat race is that, even if you win, you're still a rat.'

Curse those high-livin', debt-ridden Joneses. If they get a new car, then we have to get a new car. If they get a conservatory built onto their kitchen, then so must we. If they go for an around-the-world holiday, we feel bound to follow in their footsteps. The more they spend, the deeper we're prepared to dig into our own pockets.

Keeping up with the Joneses was originally the title of a comic strip by Arthur R. ("Pop") Morand that ran in many US newspapers from 1914 to 1958. The strip chronicled his experiences living in suburbia, where neighbours were fiercely competitive, and continually tried to have the nicest house, lawn, etc. So the phrase has come to describe the practice of competing to maintain an appearance of affluence and wealth for the benefit of others.

One thing's for sure, keeping up with the Joneses has never been so expensive. There are more and more things that we can spend our money on, especially when we are bombarded every day with thousands of 'buy me, buy me' marketing messages. There are even magazines whose sole purpose is to tell us about this year's must-have 'stuff'. These days, to paraphrase Marshall McLuhan, the advertising is the editorial.

relax and enjoy life

> **Here's an idea for you...**
> When it comes to deciding specifically how much money we want to earn to have
> 'enough', we need to take stock of every aspect of our lives – the home we want,
> the work we do, the lifestyle we're after, etc. Each of us will have our own answers
> to these questions, but I'd advise you to be sure that you've take into account the
> long term. After all, none of us wants to outlive our money.

Perhaps it's part of the deification of celebrity that seems to be a feature of early
21st century living, or maybe we've always put wealthy people onto a pedestal.
Whichever might be the case, wallet envy has become the deadly *sin du jour.*

THE PRICE OF KEEPING UP
There's an exercise I run as part of a personal finance workshop in which I ask the
participants to brainstorm the implications of trying to keep up with the Joneses.
Here are some of the items they come up with:

- Always looking to move up the property ladder
- Bigger mortgages
- A new car every three years
- Private education for the children
- A better holiday than last year's
- Credit card debt
- Multiple credit card debt
- Exercise equipment we don't use.
- Books we don't read, CDs we never get round to playing
- Wardrobes full of clothes and nothing to wear
- Feeling tired
- Never being satisfied

Defining idea...

'We can manage our time. We can sày no. We can give less priority, or more, to homework or to paid work. Money is essential but more money is not always essential. Enough can be enough.' **– CHARLES HANDY,** *The Age of Unreason*

TO KEEP UP OR NOT TO KEEP UP

It's not a cheery list, is it? The good news is that there is an alternative. We can choose to decouple from everything Jonesian. We can declare that we will move the focus of our lives from 'excess' to 'enough', and we can re-gear our finances accordingly.

The reality is that, unless you're one of only two people in the world, there will always be people who are better off than you and people who are worse off than you. You had better get used to it.

77. Review, monitor and act

The biggest enemy of financial well-being is inertia.

In early 2004, it was announced that David Beckham, the England and Real Madrid footballer, had chosen the Queen's stockbroker to look after his fortune and that of his wife Victoria, the former Spice Girl. Beckham, the world's best-paid footballer, signed a deal for Cazenove to manage around £40m of the couple's wealth.

We don't need to have Beckham's level of wealth to recognise the principle that our finances don't manage themselves. They need to be monitored and reviewed on a regular basis.

Trouble is, all too often, our idea of a financial review is to check whether we have enough cash on us to fund this evening's drinking and maybe a taxi home. In other words, we fall into the trap of concentrating on the here and now at the expense of planning for the future. On the bright side, the fact that you're reading this idea suggests that you'd prefer your financial future to unfold with intent rather than by accident.

So this idea is about taking active charge so that you can manage your finances and they don't manage you. You might take advice from others but ultimately it is your job to make sure you make it financially and no one else's.

There are three fundamental activities that anybody wishing to optimise their finances needs to undertake on a regular basis: namely to review, to monitor, and – critically – to act.

Here's an idea for you...
We can probably all improve our ability to review, monitor and act if we choose to do so. Try browsing the financial sections of the weekend papers, attending a money management course, or taking up opportunities for annual reviews of your mortgage and bank accounts. It can also be helpful to build the financial literacy of those around us – why not pass this idea onto somebody you think might benefit from reading it.

Here's an incomplete list of some of the things you might care to consider under these categories:

REVIEW
- Undertake a root and branch review of your financial position at least once a year.

- Start to think five, ten and fifteen years – maybe even longer – into the future. What are your financial goals? How are you going to make them happen?

MONITOR
- Know where your money goes every month.

- Check the accuracy of your bank statements and tax notices – everybody makes mistakes.

ACT
- Avoid the loyalty trap. If your research shows that you're not getting the best deal from your bank, credit card company, life insurer, be prepared to move elsewhere. Remember that in the UK alone, you can choose between around 8,000 mortgages, 1,300 or so credit cards, and over 1,000 savings accounts.

Defining idea...
'Action may not always bring happiness, but there is no happiness without action.'
– BENJAMIN DISRAELI

- Try and save something every month – set up a standing order and then try to forget about it. Aim to have 9–12 months of your expenditure tucked away to protect you against unplanned events – surprise babies, job loss.

- Remember the 28-day list – don't spend without thinking.

- If you can pay outright for something, do so. Don't be tempted into a credit arrangement unless it is cheaper. Remember that putting something on your credit card, particularly if it is a store card, is one of the most expensive forms of borrowing around.

- Always try to pay off 10 per cent of your balance every month on your credit cards. If you only pay the minimum it will cost you a small fortune and take ages to clear.

The real point about taking control is that it involves a mixture of reflection and action. You need both – reflection without action is sterile, action without reflection lacks direction and mindfulness. To tweak a cliché: today is the first day of the rest of your financial life. So what are you going to do about it?

3

Part three

Look outward – find time for who and what is important

Relationships and creativity – two hugely satisfying areas of life that all too often we put on the back burner because we perceive them as being drains on our precious time. We should prioritise them as the life-enhancing wonders that they are.

One of the great tricks of life is to take time for family, friends and working towards your personal goals no matter how busy you are. Automatically, you'll feel life is not just slowing down but becoming deeper and more satisfying.

QUIZ: **Are you there for those who care?**

Taking the time to reduce your stress levels nearly always means improved relationships with the people you care about.

You have forgotten a good friend's birthday (score 1)

You have forgotten your mother's birthday or needed prompting (score 2)

You have forgotten your partner's birthday or needed prompting (score 3)

You have forgotten your child's birthday or needed prompting (score 4)

In the last year, you've cancelled a personal lunch or dinner appointment at less than 24 hours notice because you're too busy (score 1)

You nearly always cancel personal appointments because you're too busy (score 2)

You have significantly cut down on socialising to the point that it is nearly non-existent because there was never the time (score 3)

In the last year, a good friend has said she or he would like to see more of you but you always seem too busy (score 1)

In the last year, more than one good friend has said they'd like to see more of you but you are never around (score 2)

In the last year, your partner has said that he or she feels you're never around (score 3)

You feel you have more in common with work colleagues than friends (score 1)

You often feel a little bored in the company of your friends (score 1)

You feel you have more in common with people you work with than people at home (score 2)

You feel distant from those at home (score 2)

You sometimes feel guilty about how little you are involved in your family's life (score 3)

Scoring

A score of 0. Well done. You may be busy but the busy-ness of your life doesn't seem to be affecting the quality of your relationships.

A score of even 1 in this quiz means that you need to slow down and take time to nurture your relationships. The questions are grouped so you can see areas where you can immediately make improvements. The first section is a litmus test for 'caretaking' relationships – the very nuts and bolts of connection. The second is about prioritising relationships. The third and fourth are about social isolation. (Hint: when we find other people boring it's usually a clue that we've become so wrapped up in our world that we have grown really boring.)

All of the ideas in the relationship section should be relevant if you scored high (over 8) but if you feel distant from children try *idea 78*, from your partner try *idea 79* and from everyone else try *idea 81*.

Relax and relish your relationships

78. Short cuts to great parenting

Modern life means we often don't make time for those we love most.

You need focused parental skills. Calm parents usually lead to calm kids, but when you're frazzled, they reflect it and have a horrible tendency to get bad tempered, argumentative, clingy and sick.

That's because stress is contagious. You get stressed, your kids get tetchy – at best. At worst, they get ill. Most parents know the rule of 'reverse serendipity' that guarantees it's on the days when your car gets broken into and your job depends on you delivering a fabulous (and as yet unprepared) presentation that your youngest will throw a wobbly and hide under his bed refusing to go to school because he's dying.

It's not mere coincidence. Research shows that even when they're tiny, children pick up on their stressed parents' frowns, tense jaws, averted eyes and other physical signs of stress. In turn, they cry or become withdrawn.

Up to the age of about ten, children think their parents' stress is their fault. After that, they're less egocentric and recognise that outside factors cause it, but still, they can feel it's their responsibility to sort out the problem for mum or dad. Parents often applaud this 'caretaker role' that children take on because they see it as a sign that their children are growing up responsible and caring. But since your twelve year old can't possibly stop your boss firing you or your mother's less than endearing habit of reeling around Sainsbury's drunk at 3 p.m., his efforts to lighten your load, although laudable, will only be a partial success. Children discover that their efforts aren't making you happy and that can transfer into adult feelings of guilt and low self-esteem.

Here's an idea for you...
Next time you talk to a child get on their level, eye to eye. They respond better.
Kneel when they're toddlers. Stand on a stool when they're teenagers.

SHORT-TERM ANSWER
Explain that you're stressed out, tell them why, but also show them that you're
working out a way to handle it. Your competence in the face of a stressful day is an
invaluable lesson for later life. Saying 'I'm stressed, here's what I'm doing about it',
and giving them a timescale of when they can expect you to be back to normal
goes a long way to reassuring them.

And on those days when it's all going pear-shaped, your kids are being unbearable
and not letting you get on with what you have to do, then the best advice is to give
them what they want – your time. This piece of advice was taught to me by a

275

Defining idea...
'There is no way to be a perfect parent, but thousands of ways of being a great one.'
– ANON.

grandmother and I've been stunned at how well it works. Pleading for an hour of peace won't work, but ten minutes of concentrating on them – a quick game, a chat, a cuddle and a story – calms them down and they tend to wander off and let you alone.

LONG-TERM SOLUTION

Besides demonstrating your competence in handling stress, the other side of stress proofing your kids is to make them feel secure. The more secure your child is, the better he'll be able to handle stress – even the stress that's caused by you. And the better he'll be at handling stress for the rest of his life.

More than all the myriad advice I've had on childcare from child behavioural experts, the most useful was from a taxi-driver who told me that since his three children were born he'd always made a point during the working week of spending ten minutes a day with each one of them. Ten minutes a day sounds meagre but it's enough – if you actually do it. It's better to be realistic and consistent than to aim for an hour and achieve it only once a week. Even worse is to keep interrupting your time together to take a call from the office. Chat, wash their dolly's hair, read a story (hint: older children still like being read to) – but treat that ten minutes as sacred.

79. Take the stress out of your relationship

Too busy to talk? Remember, divorce is pretty stressful too.

Stress proof your relationship and everything else will fall into place – eventually. There is absolutely no point in reading on until you put this idea to improve your relationship into action: it is the *sine qua non* of relationships. Once a week minimum, you and your partner have a 'date' where you focus completely on each other and nothing else. It may only be for a few hours. It doesn't have to involve a lot of money. You don't even have to go out – although I strongly recommend it. (Couples who spend too much time sloping around the same small space tend to lose that loving feeling.) Seeing your love in a new environment helps keep love alive, even if it's only your local park. But whatever you do, you must spend at least a couple of hours a week talking to each other or you are taking a mighty big gamble with your love.

IF YOU WANT SOMETHING – ASK FOR IT

Second guessing what your partner thinks or feels is such a waste of time. You're nearly always wrong, and your assumptions lead to fights. You might assume your partner can see that you spending five hours a night on housework is unfair. On the other hand you might assume your partner can see that sex once a month isn't going to win you any prizes in a 'red-hot couple of the year' competition. (The two may well be related, by the way.) However, you could well be assuming wrong. Do the work yourself first. Work out what you want to make you happy. Then let your partner know. It might end up a compromise, but you've at least got a chance of getting it this way.

Here's an idea for you...
Get into bed. Whichever one is feeling emotionally stronger should 'spoon' around the other. Hold your hands entwined resting on the recipient's heart. Regularise your breathing so you exhale and inhale at the same time. Lie there and breathe in unison.

KEEP SURPRISING EACH OTHER

No, not with the news of your affair with Geoff in accounts. To recreate the passion of your first romance, you have to see each other through new eyes. To do that you have to be passionate, engaged in your life, interested in the world. If you're not fascinated by your life, you can hardly expect anyone else to be. And remember the power of spontaneity. Plan to be spontaneous. Take it in turns to surprise each other, even if it's only with a curry – although the occasional weekend in Paris would be better.

CONSTANTLY PLAN AND DREAM

A relationship that doesn't move forward will die. You have to dream big. Whether it's planning your next holiday, your fantasy house, another child, a downsize to the country. Not all these plans have to come to fruition, but you have to build common dreams and turn some of them into goals that you're working towards as a team.

HAVE SEX

Call me old-fashioned, but I think this is important. Lots of couples don't of course, but I would say that unless you're both absolutely happy with this (are you sure? See first item on this list), then you're sitting on a potentially huge stressor.

Defining idea...
'My wife and I were happy for twenty years. Then we met.'
– **RODNEY DANGERFIELD, American comedian**

GIVE YOUR LOVER WHAT THEY NEED TO FEEL LOVED

This can melt away stress in a relationship. Find out what your partner needs to feel loved – meals out, compliments, sex, praise in front of your friends, jammy dodgers on demand. Ask. Then give it. Often. There is absolutely no use in you saying you love your partner, or showing them that you love them *in your way*, if they don't feel loved at the end of it. When your home life is stressed, ask your partner 'Do you feel loved?' And if the answer's no, do something about it.

80. Out of your head

A way of slowing down that could improve your sex life too. Result.

If you want to win the battle against speed and stress, pay attention – to everything except what's going on in your head. Just about everything else you'll read on stress will tell you to meditate to beat it. Good idea. Meditation is incredibly effective. Hundreds of research studies prove that it reduces hypertension, cholesterol and a load of other markers of stress-induced illness. It gives more energy, a happier disposition and a better sex life.

I want to be a meditator. God knows, I've tried. Like Vienna and elasticated trousers it's something I'm looking forward to in my later years. In the meantime, I will use an idea that delivers much of the benefits without all the spiritual expectations, and is easy to bring into play whenever you need it. A sort of meditation-lite, if you like.

Mindfulness came out of the work of Jon Kabat-Zinn (author of the fabulously titled *Full Catastrophe Living*), a scientist who runs stress-reduction programmes at the University of Massachusetts Medical Centre. Kabat-Zinn wanted to find a way of teaching patients how to kick-start their own healing powers. Like meditation, mindfulness gives control by helping you to listen to your body.

Lie down (although you can do this sitting if it is more convenient). It helps at first to close your eyes. Become aware of your breathing. Don't force deep breaths but 'see' in your mind your breath entering through your nostrils and flooding your

Here's an idea for you...
Make your morning shower a mini-meditation session through the power of mindfulness. Listen to the sound of the water, and the sensation of the water on your skin. Let thoughts float down the plughole, concentrate only on what your body can feel, see and hear.

lungs. Listen to the sounds of your breath. Concentrate on nothing else. When your mind wanders, let these thoughts float away, imagine them as little white clouds and return to the breath.

(That's it.)

It's recommended you be mindful for 45 minutes a day for best results. If you can manage just 5 minutes (which is all I fit in most days), you will find it helps immensely. This keeps you calm when things gets hairy and seems to work especially well for maintaining your sense of humour when life seems dire. It appears to have all sorts of health benefits too – aiding healing and lowering blood pressure.

It is also not necessarily as easy as it sounds. Stopping and listening and just being allows you to access great joy and happiness, but it also makes it hard to ignore feelings of grief and anger and disappointment that surface when you stop whirling around in a frantic rush long enough to listen to them. If these feelings arise for you, pay attention. Kabat-Zinn says that practising mindfulness helps his patients learn what they really want from life and after it becomes second nature to become still and focused, he recommends that you ask yourself questions during your mindfulness sessions such as 'What do I truly love?' and 'Where am I going?'

Defining idea...
'Now's the day and now's the hour.' – **ROBERT BURNS**

The point of this is to make you more aware of the here and now. It is quite shocking when you realise how often your mind is occupied with running over what has happened in the past and fantasising about what might happen in the future (and fantasy is all it is: none of us can know what's going to happen). The here and now is a great place to be – because nearly always in the here and now you are absolutely fine. Mindfulness transports you away from fear and towards self-reliance and self-confidence. You can use it when you're brushing your teeth. You can use it when you're having sex. It will automatically make any activity more profound and you more calm.

With practice you will find yourself falling into the mindfulness state at odd times – making dinner, crossing the road, in the middle of a conversation with your bank. This is the best way of turning 'space' into 'useful experiences'.

81. Slow down long enough to listen

If you better your communication skills you'll also improve your relationships, enhance your performance at work and create more enjoyment in your social life.

We're inclined to believe that the important thing in life is what we say, how we say it and what we contribute to a conversation. All of that's important, but the real skill in communicating is how well we listen.

LISTENING IS AN ART FORM
I used to find it virtually impossible to keep my mouth shut! Partly because I care passionately about people and I want to use the wisdom I've acquired from all my life experiences to help people. I was so excited that I hardly ever waited for people to finish their sentences before leaping in with my thoughts. Teaching personal leadership showed me that many people do the same thing, often for the best reasons in the world. When I finally truly learned about the power of listening, I was shocked beyond belief at how I'd continually interrupted others and not listened. I'd always thought that I was a good listener!

It's crazy because we'd like to be sure that we're making the best decisions possible in all aspects of our lives. How can we possibly do this if we never let people finish their sentences? Unless we listen to people, we won't fully understand what they're saying. Often when we probably don't have the full picture we leap ahead and make a decision, and then spend an enormous amount of time sorting the problems we've helped to create.

Here's an idea for you...
At your next meeting or family discussion, listen to people and don't interrupt. Observe what's happening. How much real listening is going on? What opportunities are being missed due to interruptions? How many people can't get a word in edgeways? Whose ideas are being driven through? Consider how useful this behaviour is and how you can share what you have learned. What changes can be made to achieve better outcomes? Remember that people asked to change their behaviour will need to see the benefits of doing so.

I recently read an amazing magazine article discussing the space shuttles *Columbia* and *Challenger*. The overall conclusion was that the accidents should never have happened because there were people further down the organisation who realised what the problems were. However, nobody was listening to them.

THE YELLOW BRICK ROAD
Imagine that you're walking down a yellow brick road to get to a beautiful castle. You can't see the castle clearly because it's hidden by mist, but you know you really want to get there and explore it. While you're walking, you meet a large group of people who you think will pass either side of you. They don't. They knock you over, trample all over you and kick you. Once they've gone, you get up and start heading towards the castle again. Soon you meet two great friends. They're going off on another path and, after lots of chat, persuade you to go with them before you go to the castle. You enjoy your trip with them but then return to the path to where you wanted to go in the first place – the castle. Next, you meet someone who knows exactly where you're going and doesn't want you to go there. That person becomes violent and eventually drags you off to somewhere else. In reality, if there had been some police officers standing around they may well have arrested some of those people for physical violence.

Defining idea...

'The reason we have two ears and only one mouth is that we may listen the more and talk the less.' – **ZENO, Greek philosopher**

Now imagine this scenario. You're in a meeting and you have an idea that isn't totally clear but you want to share it nevertheless. However, every time you try to open your mouth you find that everyone else is so busy talking about their ideas that you can't get a word in edgeways. Or they want you to look at their ideas first. Or you're told that your idea can't be considered because a decision has already been made.

What is the difference between these two pictures? I would like to suggest that there isn't one. One is physical violence; the other is mental. Every time you interrupt someone else it is in fact mental violence.

82. What will become of us?

In a relationship, life is apt to take over and we can begin to drift apart without realising that it's happening. Suddenly we can find that we don't actually know each other any more.

Setting aside time to develop a relationship, no matter how long we've been in it, is one of the most important things that we can do if we value this partnership as a lifelong commitment.

WHERE IS THE PROBLEM?

Let's look at a work situation first. There are two types of work activities: maintenance and development. Maintenance activities cover things that you do on a daily basis just to get your job done and include selling, taking orders, answering the phone, opening the mail, etc. Development activities are different in that they are one-off tasks and may include designing a new product, launching a new computer system, reorganising the office so that it operates more smoothly, and so on. Maintenance activities are things that we measure (*have we reached our sales target?*), are highly visible (*we haven't and everybody sees the figures*), affect the here and now (*how are we going to pay the salaries this month?*) and are low risk. Development activities, on the other hand, are the complete opposite. So, not surprisingly, everyone is drawn towards maintenance activities. Yet an organisation that doesn't invest time in development activities is liable to be overtaken quickly by its competitors and go bust.

Here's an idea for you...
Sit down with your partner and agree that you want your relationship to be special. Then commit to the time that you're going to put into it, even if it means some rearranging of other activities. Ask each other what you really want from this relationship. How, ideally, do you want it to be? What needs to change for it to be that way? Don't just ask yourself what you really want. Ask the question, 'What do we really want?'

A relationship is the same. When we first fall in love it's all about development activities – getting to know each other, exploring each others' hobbies, finding new hobbies that you could do together, and so much more. Then we move in together and perhaps get married. And what takes over? Maintenance activities like cleaning the house, working all hours to pay the mortgage, shopping and cooking.

And then children come along and the problem escalates! The cost of living rises, we become full-time chauffeurs and household chores double. And what now happens to the time that we used to spend together developing our relationship and getting to know each other even better? That comes somewhere near the bottom of our priorities.

TAKE THE TIME

The things that always seem to suffer most are our relationships. How often do you find yourself writing in a Christmas card, 'We really must get together this year'? Worse, you then find yourself writing the same thing in next year's card. I have three activities that I do consistently at work. One is delivering workshops or fulfilling speaking engagements because if I don't do this I'm not earning enough money to pay the salaries today. One is selling and marketing because if I'm not doing that I may not be able to pay the salaries tomorrow. The other is developing my people. Which do I end up doing all the time? The first two, of course. Which is the most important? The last one, without question. So, now think about how important your special relationship is. Does it deserve the time to continually develop so that you can become closer and closer?

83. Search for the hero

We know the score. You fell in love with a hero and now your relationship isn't as wonderful as when you first met. We'll help you track down your partner's lost appeal.

Do you miss the good old days, when your lover listened spellbound to your stories, treated you like the sexiest creature on earth and made you feel warm and fuzzy?

Have you heard that after the initial glow of romance, you're left with something deeper, more mature, that's, well, a bit boring really? That, once you've settled with your mate, spontaneity, romance and heroics are just for high days and holidays? It's just not true.

Of course relationships change with time. As we get to know our partners better, we often love them more deeply and feel a closer bond. But this new companionship should be an add-on to the old intensity, not an instead-of. In the drudgery of our daily grind, it's often far easier to look for problems than solutions. At times it might feel as if the hero or heroine you fell in love with has sneaked off, leaving behind a dull git or crone. We believe the hero is still there, waiting in the wings to be rediscovered and nurtured back to health.

It takes a bit of effort to root out your partner's inner hero and you might have to look quite hard. We know that when you're in a rut of working, shopping, cooking, bringing up kids, cleaning, watching television, arguing and worrying, it can be hard to believe there's a hero inside your tired, sniping partner. If that sounds

> **Here's an idea for you...**
> Time for a little live experiment. Spend a day noticing and appreciating all your partner's mini heroics. Try to make at least twelve comments, like: 'I love the way that even though you've been up half the night with the baby, you still look gorgeous.' At the end of the day, spend a little time alone evaluating your partner's responses. We hope you're pleasantly surprised.

familiar, we suggest you ring-fence half an hour to yourself, grab a sheet of paper and answers the following questions:

1. Why do I love my partner?
2. What would I miss if we weren't together?

The tricky part is to then share your answers with your partner. Instead of attaching your list to the fridge, sneak your responses into conversations. For example, if you love your partner's sense of humour, instead of just guffawing at her jokes, try making a comment like, 'I like it when you make me laugh. Nobody makes me laugh like you do.' Or, if you appreciate hubby getting your kids to stick to bedtime, say something like, 'I love the way you're a really hands-on dad. I couldn't have got the kids to bed without your help.'

PEEL OFF THE LABEL
Everyone, your partner included, lives up or down to others' expectations. Try to avoid labelling your partner. If you think 'he's not romantic' or 'she's always late', you're less likely to notice the times when he does buy roses or when she arrives ahead of you.

If your girlfriend usually leaves you to do the laundry but one day does the ironing on a whim, resist the temptation to make a sarcastic comment like 'Are we expecting the Queen round for tea?' and instead try 'I really like it when you iron the shirts' (and don't tell her she's missed a bit).

Defining idea...

'I remember a lovely New Yorker cartoon, so poignant I cried. The drawing was of an obviously poor, overweight and exhausted couple sitting at their kitchen table. The husband, in his t-shirt, had not shaved. The wife had curlers in her hair. Dirty dishes and nappies hung on a makeshift clothesline strung from a pipe to the fridge. They were drinking coffee out of chipped old mugs. The caption was the man smiling at his wife, saying, "I just love the way you wrinkle your nose when you laugh".'
– LEIL LOWNDES, relationship expert and author

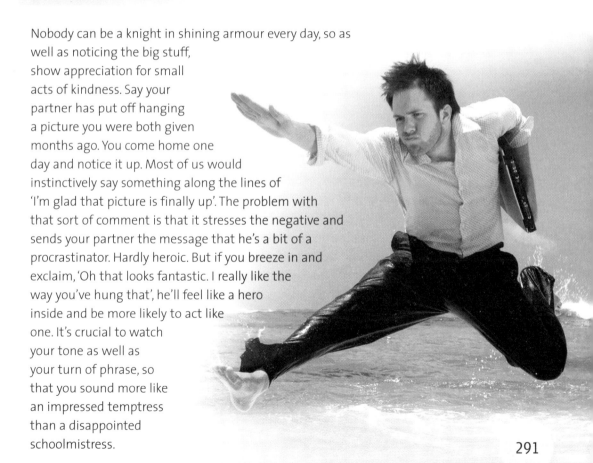

Nobody can be a knight in shining armour every day, so as well as noticing the big stuff, show appreciation for small acts of kindness. Say your partner has put off hanging a picture you were both given months ago. You come home one day and notice it up. Most of us would instinctively say something along the lines of 'I'm glad that picture is finally up'. The problem with that sort of comment is that it stresses the negative and sends your partner the message that he's a bit of a procrastinator. Hardly heroic. But if you breeze in and exclaim, 'Oh that looks fantastic. I really like the way you've hung that', he'll feel like a hero inside and be more likely to act like one. It's crucial to watch your tone as well as your turn of phrase, so that you sound more like an impressed temptress than a disappointed schoolmistress.

291

84. A walk on the wild side

Whether you saunter in companionable silence or amble in animated conversation, nothing quite matches a daily constitutional. It's an escape from domesticity and a chance to reconnect with the person who matters.

Unless you live in an offshore lighthouse, there is always somewhere to walk. The sort of journey we're talking about does not need to have a specific purpose or destination, though it might involve the collection of a newspaper or be broken up by a pint in a local pub; the real reason is to have a change of environment and a change of air. Open spaces have mind-expanding properties which help you to think more clearly; all of a sudden, difficulties become more doable and problems less problematic. Walking boosts your level of serotonin, the feel-good chemical in our brains. It also releases the body's natural opiates, endorphins, giving you a buzz. When we walk with our partner we associate feeling high with him or her.

As we know all too well, small spaces can be constricting and close down creative processes. Perhaps you could try to take a walk most days, or even take them more frequently if you are working from home. In the countryside, by the sea, in every village and town there is always something to see, hear, touch and feel. If you really think there's nothing worth looking at in your local area take a short drive, park up and walk from there. Life is different on foot, the pace is slower, there are fewer distractions and you don't have to worry about parking, drink driving or one-way streets.

Here's an idea for you...
Next time you find yourself getting into an argument, why not suggest you go for a walk together to take time out and regain your composure? You might agree not to discuss the contested subject, or do so only after an interval of, say, half an hour.

If one of you feels like walking out, go for a walk together. It will clear your heads of clutter and put problems into perspective, and the chances are that you'll walk out with a problem and home with a solution. Walks give couples a chance to talk and think. And on warm summer evenings a chance to stop and drink. And it goes without saying that a walk will make any meal eaten afterwards all the more enjoyable.

If fitness is an issue for one or both of you then start gradually, walking a bit further every day until you can complete a short circular walk of your neighbourhood. Give it three months and you'll soon be looking for longer, more challenging walks to stride out on. And remember that the increased fitness from these companionable walks will benefit your love life in other ways too.

Walking can perk up your relationship in different ways. Perhaps, like many couples, you went for more walks in your 'courting days'. Going for walks, years or even

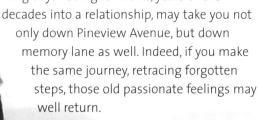

decades into a relationship, may take you not only down Pineview Avenue, but down memory lane as well. Indeed, if you make the same journey, retracing forgotten steps, those old passionate feelings may well return.

relax and enjoy life

Defining idea...
'I have two doctors – my left leg and my right.' **– Anonymous**

Many couples find that joining a walking club gives them a sharper focus and opportunities to meet like-minded saunterers or strollers. If there isn't a club within a short walking distance from your home, why not start one?

But if you want a definitive reason for taking walks, one word comes to mind: serendipity – the faculty of making happy and unexpected accidental discoveries. Sometimes it is what you discover in the environment: a new building site to spy on, a skip to raid, an unexpectedly lovely garden, a humorous ad in a shop window. Or the happy discovery might be something one of you says, triggered by something you've seen.

A walk is a journey into your partner's head and heart.

85. Snap, cackle and print

Want a picture-perfect relationship? Slowing down long enough to take up photography can put your relationship back into sharp focus. Give it your best shot.

Camera shy or just shy with cameras? We'll show you how to feel comfortable either side of a lens. Couples who shoot together stay together, as they share a developing interest.

LIFE THRU' A LENS

We live in a visual age, where pictures or images rather than words are the major means of telling stories. Most of us own a camera. Sadly, most cameras are used thoughtlessly (if at all), hastily pointed at family reunions, resulting in drab snaps. But your humble camera can help you develop a vivid, vibrant relationship. Photography helps you see and interpret circumstances differently. It enhances communication as you'll develop new ways of enlightening, informing, amusing and persuading each other. Pack a couple of disposable cameras next time you go out. As you document special moments or record unforgettable experiences, you'll make images that are personal and special to the love of your life.

SNAP YOUR ART OUT

Photography is perhaps the most accessible ways of producing personalised art. Most of us haven't the time, talent or inclination to take up watercolour painting, learn to blow a trumpet or throw a pot (except in anger); yet becoming an arty photographer is within everyone's grasp. We suggest you set out to create photo-art that stimulates you both emotionally as well as visually. Whether you want to become monochrome magicians, specialising in moody black and white portraits,

295

Here's an idea for you...
Celebrate your good times with an album of firsts. Leave spaces next to photos of your first date, first Christmas, first holiday, first time white water rafting and first anniversary to add poems, prose, letters and other memories.

or focus on composing stunning landscapes using saturated colours, there are people, books, camera clubs and gear to get you there.

PICTURE THIS

Many people fantasise about being cover stars. Take some dramatic portraits of your partner to rediscover subtle curves and textures of his face and skin. Pros say the relationship between photographer and model is a crucial component of a completed work of art. So poor rapport means poor pics. If your partner feels ill at ease or overexposed, take time to unwind together and persuade him to let his personality shine. If you stimulate poise at a photo shoot, it will build trust in other areas. Time taken here isn't wasted. The sensitivity and perception you show will spill over into the rest of your relationship. Find something about your partner that you love and focus on it. It might be her long hair, bedroom eyes or that look. Take it in turns to be sitter and snapper, or snuggle up for some couple shots taken with a timer.

PRIVATE VIEWS

Of course, your interest in your partner is more than merely aesthetic. Taking 'glamour' shots, exploring and capturing images of each other's bodies from interesting angles, is a clandestine yet sensual pleasure. If, photographically speaking, you're going all the way, you might need to go digital or set up a home darkroom to develop your indecent exposures.

Defining idea...
'A photo is a reprieve, an act of suspension, a charm. If you see something terrible or wonderful, that you can't take in or focus on, take a picture of it, hold the camera to it. Look again when it's safe.' **– GRAHAM SWIFT, author**

CLUB TOGETHER
Camera clubs are great places for couples to improve skills; you can learn how to use your flash new equipment and look at the world from alternative angles. The ones we've been to are full of helpful enthusiasts keen to pass on a lifetime's experience (sometimes overly keen!). One club we know is held in a rugby clubhouse and the social side thrives. Socialising with other couples who share your passion is a surefire way of making friends.

PIN UPS
Albums are great, but we never look at them often enough. Why not surround yourself with a few of your memories? Try a photo wall where you re-hang regularly, gallery style, or peg a few new prints along a simple clothes line pulled taut across a bare wall.

OFFSHOOTS
By printing photos onto special computer paper, you can transfer your favourites onto T-shirts, mugs, mouse mats and other household items. Imagine your partner's face when he discovers you've snuck a personalised T-shirts into his luggage when he's on a business trip. That way he can still go to bed with you, even if you're apart.

86. Sowing the seeds of love

Put some spring into the autumn years of your relationship. We'll help you sow, hoe and prune your way to blossoming passion. Nurture your garden and nurture your love life.

Does your closeness with your lover wax and wane? Relationships have seasons, and a bit of joint gardening can teach you how to make the most of Love's summer and weather the worst.

SECRET GARDEN
A bit of joint gardening is time together well spent: you might think it's about achieving a common goal, but gardening is so much more than that. Like many couples, your garden may well be used by the whole family, with different areas for entertaining, growing edibles and playing. We recommend you select a spot that you both can convert into a hideaway from the rest of the world – a backdrop for midday musings, moonlight picnics and tussling behind the bushes.

Lovers' gardens should ooze serenity. Your perfect spot will be secluded, but also soft and soothing. You might opt for a wild flower meadow with poppies and grasses, or something more formal with lawn and borders. Talk to each other about colours. Do you want something bright and bold, or would you prefer romantic hues like pinks, violets and muted blues? Plants with intense fragrance, like lilies, rose, jasmine and honeysuckle, are relaxing and can send you to sleep. If you'd prefer a love garden that energises and refreshes, plant herbs like lemon thyme, peppermint and rosemary.

Here's an idea for you...
Hammocks are a great place to hang out in, but for the ultimate sensual seat, you need a camomile bed. It's easy to grow one by planting camomile in a low raised bed made with railway sleepers. Fill your bed with soil mixed with ericaceous compost. We suggest you plant pot-grown camomile plants about 10 cm apart, in March to May. Once your bed has filled out a bit, just add a couple of pillows. The camomile will released its fragrance every time you use your bed. Keep it well watered in summer and trim with a strimmer.

HEDGE YOUR BETS
Surround your area with hedges, fencing, trellis or other screens. It can be particularly effective to paint trellis before growing climbing roses and passion flowers up it. Accessorise with wind chimes, water features and hammocks, or hang a swing from a tree. If you're feeling adventurous, why not build a tree house with turrets and a drawbridge? If you have children, you might have to build two; otherwise your love-nest will soon be their play-den.

SPRING
In the spring of your romance, you probably felt high on love. You may even have lost your appetite. This is because the appetite-suppressing chemical phenylethylamine is released when we fall in love. Spring is also a good time for romance in your garden. Recall your early heady days as you bask in sweet smells of lavender, rose or lily-of-the-valley. Feast on an outdoor picnic under a rose arch. Or get raunchy behind the rhododendrons. Focus on the structures underpinning your relationship as you build structures in your garden, like an arbour or loving seats.

SUMMER

In the summer of love, we produce higher levels of two other hormones, called oxytocin and vasopresin. Both bring out your nesting instinct. A radical garden makeover at this time could give you both a joint focus. Oxytocin has been called the touch hormone. Increase oxytocin levels by touching each other and your plants. Textures have never been more important in your corner of paradise. Include plants you can stroke, like pussy willow and pampas grasses, which have sensual feathery fronds. Poppies are papery and delicate. Lilies feel silky smooth and sexy.

AUTUMN

In your garden, as in your relationship, autumn is a time of change. Traditionally the time of the so-called seven-year itch, maybe you're longing for a bit of instant gratification. Sometimes love can't wait, and gardens are no different. There's not much point planning a garden that will be a sensual Eden in a couple of years but a barren desert until then. So, don't be tempted to grow everything from seed. And while you're waiting for the passion flowers to climb, enjoy some pink and red annuals.

WINTER

Relationships often suffer from winter blues: times when everything feels dormant and the world looks bleak. The winter of love can make your relationship feel a little sloth-like. So get out there. Gardening lowers blood pressure and makes you feel upbeat. Browse junk shops for alternative garden accessories. Could that rusty colander be painted and turned into a hanging basket? Share plans and joint visions. Growing together will help you get that spring honeymoon feeling back, but like composted soil, it'll be deeper and richer.

6 ways to get your message across*

1. Use 'I' and 'me' not 'you'.

2. Check your assumptions – they are probably wrong.

3. Have one argument at a time. Stick to the present, don't bring up old stuff.

4. Aim for a 'win-win' which means both of you get something. Give to get.

5. For a 'win-win' you have to know what you want. What do you want to achieve?

6. Try requesting rather than criticising or complaining.

* Thanks to www.shrinkwrap.com.
Find more ideas on clear
communication there.

87. The PERT solution

Relationships, like books, films or plays, have a beginning, a middle and an end. Need a hand navigating your way through the middle in the middle?

30% of marriages split up when couples are between 40 and 60. Why? Midlife crisis, male menopause, empty nest syndrome, career catastrophes, wandering bifocals – Old Father Time has plenty of ways.

Too old for clubbing, too young for meals-on-wheels? All couples face times of turbulence: changes at home, at work, in our bodies and in our minds. The middle years, of your life or your relationship, don't have to be heartbreaking or alarming. Use them as a catalyst. They're the power for change. Finally free from childcare, you're free to be what you want to be and probably have more disposable income than ever.

A mid-relationship crisis is a multifarious beast. Perhaps you've been dissatisfied with your relationship for a long time, and it feels like make or break time. Forty-seven-year-old Neil was kept awake at night fretting over missed opportunities, wondering what might have been if he'd accepted that job offer or married his ex-girlfriend. He would brood silently for hours and gave his wife Elaine the cold shoulder. She shared his sadness and felt she'd never done what she wanted to either. Disappointment could have destroyed them, but they were able to turn it around. They moved out of

Here's an idea for you...
Next time you feel threatened or ground down by mid-life or mid-relationship blues, try to see them as mid-life opportunities. Challenge beliefs like 'I'm no good for anything now our children have all started school'. Turn them into new openings, like 'Now I have time to be what I've always wanted to be'.

the city, Elaine is re-training as a careers counsellor and Neil has taken a year's sabbatical to write the novel he's dreamt about for a decade. They're poorer financially, but pursuing their different life courses has made their relationship richer.

You don't have to be middle aged to have a mid-life crisis. Former Spice Girl Mel C has spoken about her mid-twenties crisis and university students are blaming their relationship break-ups on mid-university crises.

KEEP YOUR RELATIONSHIP PERT
Mid-relationship is a superb time for assessing and appraising your relationship. A friend of mine calls it 'keeping it PERT'. PERT is a project management technique he

Defining idea...
'The greatest potential for growth and self-realisation exists in the second half of life.' **– CARL JUNG, psychoanalyst**

was taught years ago as a young accountant, but he swears it's the secret to his long and happy marriage. The original PERT was developed in the late fifties for the US Navy's Polaris project. This one is adapted for relationship rejuvenation and works like this:

Plan
So you woke up this morning and wanted to throw in the towel? It's surprisingly common to feel the need to destroy or give up all we've worked for. Many people think that if they just had a better, more understanding partner, all would be well again. But wait. Before you post that resignation letter, call in the divorce lawyers or book a one-way ticket out of town, make a plan together. It sounds clichéd, but write down where you both want to be a year from now. Put it somewhere obvious, where you'll see it often – like stuck to your computer monitor or in your wallet. Now write twelve monthly targets which need to be done to meet your plan. Divide each into four weekly steps and set a weekly meeting to evaluate how things are going.

Evaluate
Mid-life provides a unique focus for change. As you look at your weekly plan, evaluate the progress you've made over the week and your relationship in general. You might find yourselves discovering aspects of your personalities you'd forgotten. By working together to achieve your plans, your relationship becomes richer and more satisfying.

Review Technique
Review your methods for reaching your year plan in the light of your evaluation. Are they working? Do they fit in with the relationship you want? What alternatives are there?

It can work for you. And if you feel discouraged sometimes, remember that PERT can also stand for Problems Eventually Resolve Themselves.

88. Skill up to get loved-up

Remember your first romance? Slipping secret love notes under the desk to your heartthrob of a schoolgirl crush? Even though school's out, you can recapture the excitement of those times.

In many relationships, most of the time one person does something and the other partner hears about it later. Attending an evening class can be a joint activity, to be done together.

LESSONS IN LOVE

So how can adult education teach you to get on better? Whatever class you pick, you'll see your partner in a new light: mingling, mixing, grappling with a new activity or trying to assimilate new knowledge. Throwing pots together in pottery class may stop you from throwing them at each other at home. You'll be working together a lot of the time, mastering new tasks and finding out stuff you both wish you'd known before. At best, you'll become a wise and wonderful couple with a host of shared skills and memories. At the very least, it should give you some laughs on the bus home.

TRANSFERABLE SKILLS

Going back to school together has spin-offs for other areas of your relationship. After attending Adventures in Advanced Accountancy, Leif and Enid found they were much better at analysing different situations and reaching creative but mutually acceptable solutions. Chuck and Martha studied counselling. Their joint work helped them distinguish between important and trivial matters in their fifteen-year relationship. Heleni and Ethel had been arguing almost every

relax and enjoy life

Here's an idea for you...
Not sure what evening class to join or what would suit you both? Many centres have open days or short taster courses which give you the chance to see if you both like fire-eating, information technology with business information systems, Japanese watercolour or synchronised swimming. You'll also be able to see the tutor in action and decide whether he or she is right for you.

evening. At intermediate sugarcraft they had to establish an effective working partnership. Their domestic relationship has been sweeter since.

ON COURSE

Taking courses or classes together won't turn you into a motivated, enthusiastic and hard-working couple overnight. Three weeks is more like it. But seriously, when did you two last share the sheer joy of learning for its own sake? Not to gain a certificate, not to brighten up an otherwise lacklustre CV, not to get that promotion, but learning something because the subject turns you both on?

Classes provide lots of things to laugh and gossip about – and gossip is an important social lubricant in long-term relationships. Evening classes are an especially rich source: the tutor's awfulness or brilliance. Then there are the other students, a godsend for people watchers. All human life goes to evening classes: full-time mums, skiving students, the pushy and the meek, the bright and the stupid. Sharing some sly in-jokes and politically incorrect observations with your partner instead of just watching these diverse groups interact or fight over the one remaining computer terminal helps the two of you to bond.

Defining idea...

'Soap and education are not as sudden as a massacre, but they are more deadly in the long run.' – **MARK TWAIN**

HOMEWORK

The skills and knowledge acquired in adult classes need not and should not stay there. Couples who attend a Thai cookery class can feast on exotic flavours at their next romantic dinner in. Other couples who, like us, have gone on a course to learn how to use a sewing machine could make over their homes with home-made soft furnishings. And if you choose courses with less tangible end products – assertiveness training or conversational Dutch – encourage each other to use your new expertise in other ways, like returning faulty items to their faulty retailer, or going on holiday to Amsterdam.

89. The biggest turn off

Looking for a quick fix for a dwindling relationship? This one's fast, free and fantastically simple. Unplug your telly and plug in to an amazing life together.

When did you last watch something on TV that transformed your relationship for the better? Time for some home truths: it's big, it's ugly and it rots relationships.

NOT TONIGHT, JOSEPH

Are you sick of your partner hogging the remote control? Do you continually fall asleep over soaps, reality shows or celebrity snowboarding? Most of us recognise the damaging effect that television has on our children, but what about our love lives? We think the hold television has on society is scary. Yet the role it plays in people's lives is rarely questioned. Decades ago, broadcasts only took place in the evenings and weekend afternoons. The service closed down at midnight and what telly there was, was watched on one machine in a communal area by whole families. Not any more. The telly is taking up more and more of lovers' free time and energy. Most couples watch around four hours of television a day. Television, like a baby cuckoo, insidiously pushes everything else out of the love nest. And at what cost? Is that manic machine in the corner interrupting your conversations, preventing candlelit

Here's an idea for you...
Getting rid of the telly seems too radical? Why not have a telly-free month? Put the box, or boxes, in the attic tonight and in four weeks time see how you've got on. Both keep a journal of your thoughts and feelings, and write down how you spent all that time.

dinners or maybe even stopping you trying out other ideas in this book? Whether you're channel hopping, station surfing or really engrossed in episode 307 of that sexy sitcom, you're missing four hours a day of prime time real life.

UNPLUG THE BOX AND PLUG INTO A WONDERFUL LIFE

If you tell people you haven't got a television, they think you're eccentric, mad or seriously weird. They might even wink and ask you what you do in your evenings. You can do a lot: mooch around markets, cruise on the river, see old movies on the big screen, snoop about in galleries, visit exhibitions, comedy clubs, musicals, quirky fringe plays and a lot of other fun stuff. You and your partner won't have to be joined at the hip and you can use your bonus four hours to do lots of things on your

own or with other friends. We're not saying you need to do all of these things, or any of them – you need to choose the activities that would suit you. How could you recharge your relationship in a few extra hours a day? Maybe you'd like to have time to go running together, make your partner a sculpture, become part-time puppeteers or join the local choir. Flick the off switch, get your life back and your relationship will prosper. Whatever you do, it's better than being passive voyeurs of other peoples' lives.

Defining idea...

'Stare into each others eyes, or at a piece of electrical equipment? Television eats up half the time you are not working or sleeping – ten years for the average person. All those things you want to be: a lover, a parent, a scholar, a wild teenager or a pillar of the community – when are you going to do all that? TV takes away your real life.'
– DAVID BURKE and JEAN LOTUS, authors of *White Dot*

90. Stop having sex

Bored with sex? Then take a break.

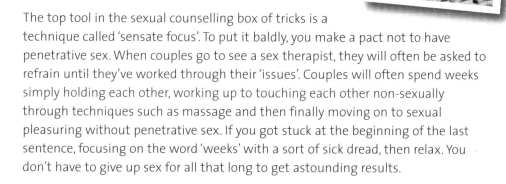

Focusing on sensuality rather than sex can remind you why sex is worth bothering with in the first place.

The top tool in the sexual counselling box of tricks is a technique called 'sensate focus'. To put it baldly, you make a pact not to have penetrative sex. When couples go to see a sex therapist, they will often be asked to refrain until they've worked through their 'issues'. Couples will often spend weeks simply holding each other, working up to touching each other non-sexually through techniques such as massage and then finally moving on to sexual pleasuring without penetrative sex. If you got stuck at the beginning of the last sentence, focusing on the word 'weeks' with a sort of sick dread, then relax. You don't have to give up sex for all that long to get astounding results.

Giving up sex completely sounds extreme, but couples find that taking a holiday from disappointed expectations and performance pressure – instead spending time getting to know each other again through strictly non-penetrative contact – works wonders when they want to regain their passion. Ripping apart old patterns of relating to each other means couples get back to basics. Simply spending time with each other trying to make your partner feel good is powerful. You'll remember what all the fuss was about in the first place.

Sex expert Tracey Cox says sex is like chocolate – if we get too much of a good thing we go off it. Think how much better chocolate tastes after you've given it up for Lent. It's the same thing with sex. Too much and we get jaded and take it for granted.

Here's an idea for you...
Don't focus on the outcome. Don't consciously try to arouse your partner.
Concentrate only on touch. The person being touched should try to dissolve into it
and concentrate on the sensations. This is a sort of meditation for both of you and
should at the very least help you to relax when you're frazzled.

You might be far from needing sex therapy, but there are very few couples who
wouldn't benefit from a spot of sensate focus. It encourages better communication
and sparks libido.

Choose a week when you both decide that you won't have penetrative sex.

Day 1 On the first night you cuddle up together on the couch.

Day 2 Go to bed an hour early. Naked. Lie in bed stroking and touching each
other. Talk about your lives. Reconnect.

Day 3 Take a shower or bath together with sensual oils.

Day 4 She gives him a long all-over massage.

Day 5 He gives her a long all-over massage.

Day 6 She massages him, including touching him sexually but not to the point
where he has an orgasm. She can explore his reactions to various kinds of
touching and ask for feedback.

Day 7 He does the same for her.

Day 8 By now the sexual tension between you should be causing visible sparks!

Defining idea...

'He was the kind of guy who could kiss you behind your ear and make you feel like you'd just had kinky sex.' – JULIA ALVAREZ, American writer

313

91. The least you need to do...

to keep your relationship minty fresh.

Read, digest and ponder. Then get your diary, a big red pen and start prioritising your relationship.

This chapter contains the three golden rules of a healthy relationship – the *sine qua non* of sexual happiness. All the technique and creativity in the world isn't going to fix the sex in a relationship where the couple is together but not together. On the other hand, couples that spend time together, and anticipate and plan for those times, find it hard to lose interest in one another.

RULE 1: DAILY...
How is your partner feeling right now? What's happening at work? How are their relationships with friends, colleagues, siblings, parents? Carve out fifteen minutes of every day to talk. If you find yourselves getting into a rut of busy-ness, when you pass like ships in the night for several days in a row without touching base, either go to bed before your usual time or get up earlier and have a coffee together so you can touch base.

Kiss each other every morning before you get out of bed. Take the time for a swift cuddle. Breathe deeply. Hold tight. Do the same at night. Never take your physical intimacy for granted. In this Vale of Tears we call life, you found each other. Pretty amazing. Worth acknowledging that with at least a daily hug, methinks.

Here's an idea for you...
Look for easy ways to cheer your partner up. Pick up a tub of her favourite ice-cream on the way home from work. Run him a bath and bring him a beer. Sappy gestures work – they build up a huge bank of goodwill that couples can draw on when life gets stressful.

RULE 2: WEEKLY...
Go out with each other once a week where humanly possible. Once a fortnight is the bare minimum. According to the experts, this is the most important thing you can do. Couples who keep dating, keep mating. Spending too long sloping around the same house does something to a couple's sexual interest in each other and what it does generally isn't good. So get out, preferably after making some small effort to tart yourself up so you're visually pleasing to your partner. Let them see why they bothered with you in the first place. (No, I never said this chapter was rocket science. I just said that it worked.)

RULE 3: MONTHLY...
Go for a mini-adventure – shared memories cement your relationship. Make your adventure as mad or staid as you like, but at the least make sure it's something that you haven't done since the beginning of your relationship. It really doesn't matter what it is, as long as it's not your usual 'date'.

What's the point? You see your partner coping with new environments and new skills and that keeps you interested in them. And them in you. Simple.

If you're shaking your head and tutting 'how banal', I'd get that smug look off your face, pronto. Research shows quite clearly that one of the defining differences between strong couples and 'drifting' couples is the amount of effort and time they spend on their shared pursuits. All of us have heard the advice, 'Spend more time with each other being as interesting as possible.' But how many couples do you know who actually do it? I'm prepared to bet that those who do seem happiest.

Defining idea...
'Good sex begins when your clothes are still on.'
– MASTERS and JOHNSON, sex research pione

92. Tantric sex

Not just a load of old joss sticks.

If you've absolutely had it with your partner's idea of foreplay being a quick tap on your shoulder and a hopeful expression, then it's time to slow down.

To the student of Tantra, sex is sacred, a means of accessing your spirituality and a way to meditate, transcend your problems and reach a happier more blissful state. For those of us who don't have the time or inclination to study Tantric sex in any great depth, it can still add a lot. It teaches sex is important, and by clearing time to undergo a few of the simpler rituals you declare to each other 'Hey, our sex life is a priority.'

Tantric sex teaches you to concentrate on your lover and on the sensations that you're feeling. Forget the orgasm. The journey not the arrival is what's important. And for that reason alone, Tantra can be liberating and mind-altering, even if you don't get into it the whole way.

RITUAL ONE: CREATE A 'TEMPLE OF LOVE'
A really simple method of foreplay is to make your bedroom a sensual haven quite different from the rest of your home. You don't have to opt for lurid leopard prints and black walls – unless you like that, of course – but take a long look at your bedroom as if seeing it for the first time. Does is say 'love', 'passion', 'excitement'? Is it a room devoted to the two of you?

First, think about what's in the room. Would you say that the television contributed to improving your love life? Unless you mainly use it to watch porn, probably not. Perhaps you spend more time watching it than talking to each other. If you want to keep the TV, find a scarf to cover it as a mental signal that you're switching off

Here's an idea for you...
Try dreaming of rainforests, droning music, an overflowing bank account...once you're out of Sting-world though, Google 'Tantric', but set your porn filter to 'Kill'.

from the outside world. Similarly, ban work paraphernalia – piles of clothes waiting to be ironed, family photographs, anything that takes your attention away from each other and onto your responsibilities. Repair and clean tatty or old furnishings. Clear away clutter. Throw open the windows and let some fresh air circulate. This room is a reflection of your relationship – it's where you spend the most time with each other. It should sparkle.

Finally, create a love altar. Find a picture of you both together that symbolises the best of your relationship. When you look at it, you should feel warm and compassionate towards your partner and strong as a couple. Place it in a nice frame where you can see it easily every day. Keep fresh flowers next to the photograph and candles – anything that you have to tend regularly and pay attention to – as a physical reminder that your relationship needs similar care and tending. Make sure

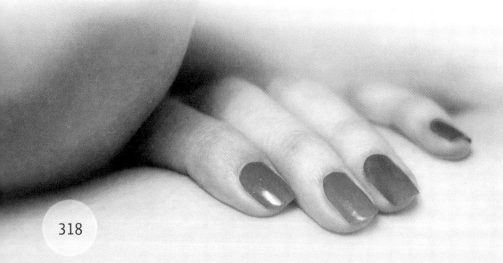

Defining idea...
'The relation of man to a woman is the flowing of two rivers side by side, sometimes mingling, then separating again, and travelling on. The relationship is a life-long change and life-long travelling.' **– D. H. LAWRENCE**

there are soft lights in your bedroom and soft music to hand, comfortable cushions or duvets that you can sink into, and a bedroom should always be comfortably warm so hanging around with few clothes on doesn't make you shudder.

None of this is genius level, but think of your and your friends' bedrooms. How many have been designed with sensuality, luxury, comfort and *sex* in mind? Your bedroom should be a place that's welcoming to both of you, so that you look forward to hanging out in the only place where most couples can be truly intimate and private with each other.

RITUAL TWO: THINK YOURSELF IN LOVE

Tantric sex depends on visualisation to build sexual energy. As your lover begins to caress you, feel how much they love you. Imagine their love for you flowing from their fingers and hands and nurturing you. Melt into their embrace. When they kiss you, feel that with each kiss they are showing how much they love you. Imagine the sexual energy that you are creating between you is visible as a red or pink light emanating from your genitals and surrounding you like a force field of love. As your partner touches you, imagine that your arousal is growing like a great wave of light. See it as fire or energy emerging from your deep pelvis and adding to the force field surrounding and supporting you. As you begin to have sex, imagine the energy passing upwards from the base of your spine to your heart and feel this energy as love around your heart – feel it as joy – and imagine it reaching out and surrounding your partner's heart. Then, as you get more excited, imagine the energy being drawn upwards and flowing out through the top of your head.

That's the way to enlightenment, but it takes a bit of practice. Look on the bright side, with all that visualising going on at least you won't be thinking about who's doing the school run tomorrow.

93. Walk the talk

When all else has failed, where can you turn? You could call in the pros who know what makes couples tick, willing to work wonders for you.

Couple therapy might seem extreme, but a little expert help can fuel your own efforts to re-ignite that elusive spark.

We know that re-energising your relationship can feel like hard work sometimes. Perhaps when you first met you were both full of hopes and expectations. Often, when we get to know our partners a bit better, we feel massively disappointed that they are not the combined sex goddess, gourmet-chef and superbrain all-in-one that we took them for.

While we'd agree that arguments and differences are part of all relationships, we'd also concur that when couples get stuck facing the same problems over and over, therapy can be a first-class opportunity.

IT'S GOOD TO TALK
Ask yourself if any of these ring true for you:

- We don't talk anymore
- He/she doesn't listen to me
- We argue all the time
- I'm not getting what I want from this relationship any more
- We can't agree on how to bring up the children
- We disagree a lot about money

Here's an idea for you...
Unsure whether couple therapy will help you? Why not investigate and ask for an assessment session? This'll give you a flavour of what to expect and you'll have an idea about whether you and your partner will be able to trust and get on with the therapist.

Most of these statements will resonate with anyone in a relationship. But if you've been struggling to sort them out and are getting more and more frustrated or unhappy, a good therapist could have a profound effect on your relationship, salvaging treasures from what seemed a wreck. They do this by helping you talk and, perhaps more importantly, listen to each other. Therapists working with couples know your relationship is intricate and complicated. They aren't like football referees or high-court judges. Pros won't take sides or try to blame one or other of you. They'll chip in so that you can understand yourself and each other better.

WHAT GOES ON?
Forget all those images of men in white coats and padded cells. You won't have to lie on a couch or look for strange images in inkblots either. Instead you'll meet a skilled professional to chat about both your opinions and feelings. Be prepared for a lot of questions, though. Therapists will ask you probing questions to establish what problems you're facing and how you both see them. They'll need to know about how you met and the story of your relationship so far, and they'll also ask about the previous relationships you've both had. Sounds really nosey, doesn't it?

They need to know this stuff to really understand what makes you both tick, individually and as a couple. Once they've got their head around it, they'll be able to help you understand yourself and partner better, decide what you'd both like to change and discuss how you can both make it happen.

Defining idea...

'When David [Arquette] and I got engaged we started therapy together. I'd heard that the first year of marriage is the hardest, so we decided to work through all that stuff early. – **COURTENEY COX**

TIME AND PLACE

Do you ever catch yourself mid-argument and think, 'What are we actually fighting about?' It's common. The reason behind your door slamming or plate smashing might not be obvious. Pros can lend a hand by helping you both spot core problems and deal with them. Matt and Elaine spent months arguing about who's turn it was to take out the bin, wash up, do the laundry or feed the cat. In therapy they discovered that the real reason they were fighting so much was over money. Matt felt insecure as he earned a lot less than Elaine, who was fed up with supporting him and envious of her better-off friends.

If you're not sure why you and your partner quarrel all the time or get on each other's nerves, it might be time to call the experts. Therapy offers ring-fenced time in a place away from the normal stresses of daily living, giving you a chance to sit back and unpick what has really been going on and what you need to tackle. He or she (and often one of each) will bring fresh ears and eyes to your relationship, as well as a wealth of expertise about what makes couples tick. Top themes in couple therapy are communication, finances, sex and parenting. That said, you don't have to be in trouble to call in an expert. Lots of couples use time with a pro to improve their relationship.

94. Who loves ya?

You've probably beginning to realise that life's too short to fall out with people you love. Is it too late to put things right? Of course not. It just takes a bit of know-how (and some courage).

Squabbles, particularly family squabbles, can get out of hand very quickly, and when you look back over the space of many years you can suddenly realise how trivial the whole thing was. Did it really matter that she had the pearls and you only got the garnet? Was what he said genuinely unforgivable? Are you suddenly wondering whether, through all the years of bitterness, you've got it all wrong? Do you miss her?

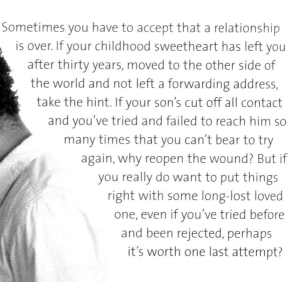

Sometimes you have to accept that a relationship is over. If your childhood sweetheart has left you after thirty years, moved to the other side of the world and not left a forwarding address, take the hint. If your son's cut off all contact and you've tried and failed to reach him so many times that you can't bear to try again, why reopen the wound? But if you really do want to put things right with some long-lost loved one, even if you've tried before and been rejected, perhaps it's worth one last attempt?

Here's an idea for you...
One of the best ways of re-establishing friendly relations with a long-lost friend or relative (especially if there was a falling-out) is to write a letter, because it doesn't put the receiver under any pressure. The letter needs to be short, simple and friendly, and if there was a row you shouldn't talk about forgiveness (which just says 'I was right and you were wrong'). Instead you should say that you regret that you're no longer in touch and would like to put the past behind and be friends again.

If you'd like to try but you're wondering whether it's worth the risk of being rejected, the best test is to examine the depth of your feelings. If you still feel mild irritation that your nephew backed his car into your front porch, or if you grit your teeth with exasperation every time you remember how your brother-in-law always got your name wrong, it rather suggests that you don't have much invested in the relationship – so you won't feel desperately hurt if your attempts at rekindling it don't work out.

But if you can't bear to touch the wound, and your stomach churns every time you think of your brother's name, it obviously goes much deeper. If you feel this is a nagging pain that's going to keep you awake at night for years to come you have two options.

You could bring the issue to the surface, perhaps by discussing it with a good friend or a counsellor, and try to find a way to work through the emotion and get it in a better perspective. This may well be the right course of action in some cases – if you were abused by a family member, why would you want to establish friendly relations again? Much better to come to terms with the issues, acknowledge your feelings and then put them behind you.

Your other option is to make contact – which means you've decided it's worth taking the risk of getting hurt. Making contact doesn't mean you have to grovel (despite the fact that you still think you were in the right). Neither does it mean

Defining idea...
'How much more grievous are the consequences of anger than the causes of it.'
– MARCUS AURELIUS

you have to make the other person put things right. You can change your own behaviour but you can't make someone else change theirs.

The key, therefore, is to act differently. Relegate the past to its proper place, forget about it, and begin the relationship again with kindness. If you're successful and you re-establish relationships, never ever refer to the quarrel.

Of course, if you've lost touch entirely with someone but would love to see them again you might have a bit of trouble finding them. Start by writing to their old address or phoning their old number. You might just get lucky and speak to them direct, or to someone who knows where they are now – they might even still have their post redirected. Try family members who could still have a contact address. But if the obvious sources don't work there are various ways of locating missing friends. The Friends Reunited website is an excellent resource for contacting old school-friends; the electoral roll is an interesting way of finding people again; telephone directories world-wide are now searchable via the internet.

Slow down and rekindle your passion

What happened to your creativity? Did you lose it somewhere between having the kids and paying the mortgage? We are all born creative creatures but as we get older we don't give our passion for ideas, images, words, pictures, music, dance, clog-carving – or whatever – the room to grow. Letting that part of ourselves out to play is inspiring, moving, changes us profoundly – and gives our life more meaning. It's 'serious fun'. Don't know where to start? Start here.

These ideas are about taking some time out to get a new perspective. They will throw a spanner into the usual pattern of your days, they will inspire you to start asking some questions – and then the magic will happen.

QUIZ: **Are you missing something?**

Recreation is just that. The chance to recreate yourself. But so many of us are so busy that we never take time out. And the result is a 'flattening' of life, a feeling that we're losing out. And we are: without the chance to recreate we risk losing our equilibrium, bounce and sparkle.

You take a 'breather' every few hours during your working day.   Yes ☐ No ☐

Your work doesn't impinge on your personal life.   Yes ☐ No ☐

You see plenty of the friends that matter.   Yes ☐ No ☐

You see plenty of the people that raise your spirit.   Yes ☐ No ☐

You have time at least once a week to act spontaneously – catch a movie, savour a cup of coffee at a pavement café, phone a friend just because they crossed your mind.   Yes ☐ No ☐

You read books as opposed to magazines, newspapers or work journals.   Yes ☐ No ☐

You leave work at a reasonable time each day.   Yes ☐ No ☐

You always take all of your holiday allowance.   Yes ☐ No ☐

You always take a full hour for lunch unless there's a real
emergency.   Yes ▨   No ▨

You always have time if a loved one needs half an hour.   Yes ▨   No ▨
☐

Score 1 for every 'yes', 0 for every 'no'.

7 or more. You do have time for yourself and you probably feel there is
enough time to follow your interests and come up with new ideas. But if
you feel you could be more creative see *idea 95*.

6 or less. You need to slow down a little more to give your brain space to
think. Try *ideas 1 and 9* to help you make a start.

95. Start anywhere, start now

How to start being creative with the things around you, right here, right now, no excuses, no prevarication.

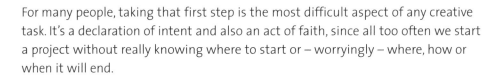

Not knowing when or how to begin is a problem we're all quite familiar with. It may well be the reason why you're reading this.

For many people, taking that first step is the most difficult aspect of any creative task. It's a declaration of intent and also an act of faith, since all too often we start a project without really knowing where to start or – worryingly – where, how or when it will end.

Sometimes, too, getting started can feel like the end of a lovely period of free and endless thinking. Giving shape and form to your ideas can feel like you're killing them a little, selling them short – or limiting them in some way that feels uncomfortable.

It's amazing, in fact, how creative one can be when it comes to finding ways of *not* starting. Some people feel the need to clear their desk of all distractions, to have gathered together all possible source materials close to hand, and possibly even to have installed all the latest software upgrades before they can do anything. Others might engross themselves in a series of seemingly urgent household chores, including laundry, washing up, gardening and supermarket shopping.

Here's an idea for you...
If you need proof of how pregnant with creative possibility 'found' objects can be, take a look at www.foundmagazine.com. You're almost bound to find something there that can become your jumping off point for a new idea.

These may look like avoidance techniques, but your supposed creativity experts (that's us, by the way) are here to tell you that a fair deal of vital mental and emotional preparation goes on during this time. A friend refers to this process (somewhat sardonically, it has to be admitted) as 'sharpening pencils'.

To some extent, how you delay and prepare yourself for the task ahead may well help reveal the best way in to your work. Sometimes you really do have to sneak up on your ideas and view them from several angles before deciding on your point of attack.

It is not always the best approach to start at the beginning. Quite often, you need to get to the point where you can see the whole of the project and understand the style of the piece before you can deliver an opening that really sets it all off.

Sometimes you tackle the most difficult and challenging problem first. Usually this is because you've already sussed out how to solve it, or you're so bursting with energy and excitement that you need something major to attack.

On the other hand, peripheral matters can often be good starting points, because they can be done easily and quickly. There's a lot to be said for getting something done, even if it's small.

relax and enjoy life

Quite *when* you start is a different matter – and usually depends on what your brief is. Much of the time, your creative work will be about addressing a specific problem within a specific time frame. That makes it easier to give yourself some deadlines to work to and a plan of action. But starting with a completely blank canvas and no particular brief changes the rules (a bit), and much depends on the resources you have to hand.

So pause from reading for a moment and take stock of all the things that are lying around you right now. If you're an organised person, you may well have a whole heap of really useful research material and tools ready and waiting. If you're not organised, you probably still have a whole heap of really useful research material and tools ready and waiting, but you just don't know it yet.

A lot of creativity is very much about looking at everyday things in a different light and putting them to use in unusual ways. So don't ever think that you have nothing to get started with. Just use what you can find.

96. Know your own history

If you can learn how to repeat good tricks and be aware of traditions in creativity you'll end up working faster and smarter.

To a large extent everything you ever do in your creative life can be seen as a reaction to the things you've done before. Sometimes it's a gentle refinement of previous ideas or working practices, sometimes it's a full-scale revolt against all that has gone before. Either way, if you're not aware of your past and the cultural heritage from which you are drawing, you'll be in severe danger of repeating mistakes endlessly, and never really developing your creative skills.

Every time you start a new project, try looking back over past work and picking key elements that reveal themselves as your standard working devices. Pick up, too, on key themes that keep coming back to haunt you. Ask yourself: 'What works for me about that? Why am I so interested in that kind of thing, those characters, objects, colours...?' If you inspect your past work like this regularly, you'll always be starting a new piece of work from a position of self-knowledge. And decisions about what to accept or reject from your creative past will be that much more solid.

One benefit of cataloguing and coming to terms with your own strengths and weaknesses is that you'll learn to achieve simple effects much more quickly. And if some of the standard elements of what you're doing are easily repeatable, you'll have more time to concentrate on the new. In this way, ideas can be like software libraries.

Here's an idea for you...
Replay the same scenes with different consequences. Shakespeare did this with similar characters in different plays (ambitious usurpers, jealous lovers, foolish kings, parted lovers), and the different consequences led to very different drama. Could you take four or five generic elements of your creative work and keep replaying them in different configurations like this?

Stand-up comedians do the same thing in building up libraries of jokes and stories. It's not that they're planning to do the same schtick every night (although some of them do). Rather, they want to have a broad range of material to draw upon when reacting to a specific situation, audience or heckler – and want to know than the material has been road-tested and works. Comedians also often have signature routines or catchphrases that their audience come to expect – or even demand – them to perform. For the successful stand-up the battle is to play with this familiarity, dropping in the catchphrase or joke at different points in the show, with a twist or in a slightly different context.

Some comedians are very good at understanding the deeper traditions of their craft and bone up on successful performers from previous generations. For example, Lee Evans in the 1990s owed a great debt to Norman Wisdom's routines from the 1950s – but was no less funny or contemporary because of that. Old wine in new bottles can still taste good.

Defining idea...
'Always dream and shoot higher than you know how to. Don't bother just to be better than your contemporaries or predecessors. Try to be better than yourself.'
– WILLIAM FAULKNER

People like Evans have broadened this lesson about knowing your own history and have benefited from knowing other people's. The key is to be comfortable with the idea of history repeating itself, but to remain critical about its value. Indeed, there can be something almost scientific about setting up the same parameters in a series of experiments and observing if the same outcomes occur. Very often they don't – or at least there are some fascinating variations and nuances. No two plants will grow exactly the same in the same soil. Think of Cézanne painting fruit or Rembrandt painting himself over and over again, each time revealing something different about the object they paint, as well as about themselves and their painting technique.

You could try doing this in your own life. Tomorrow, try and do exactly the same things as you did today at exactly the same time of day and for the same period of time. Note the similarities and differences in terms of how the day actually unfolds and the different feelings each day elicits. If you can get away with it, try repeating this for a whole week. By day seven, how do you think you'll feel? Terminally bored or creatively inspired? Probably a little bit of both, no?

97. Be organised

Keeping a tidy desk and writing out long neat to-do lists are all very well. But how can you be sure that you've going to end the day having really done something?

A big part of being creative is not simply about being 'inspired', it's about getting things done. So join the art and graft movement. Since we all became 'knowledge workers' of one kind or another – and increasingly time-poor as a result – time management has become a whole industry in itself. The world is infested with time-management devices, theories and techniques to make them work. But don't be fooled by this. Above all, don't panic-buy the latest newfangled kit and associated manuals that will ultimately do you no good. We're here to tell you that at the core of all of this time-management mumbo-jumbo lies just one essential device: the good old-fashioned to-do list.

Whatever you use to create your to-do list – be it a piece of scrap paper, post-it notes, a white board or a PDA – the basic principles are the same. You need to concentrate on three things.

1. smart and realistic prioritisation of the tasks

2. the breaking down of big tasks into smaller, more achievable ones

3. the making of a new list for every new day

Here's an idea for you...
Write a list of impossible tasks. Put it away somewhere safe and only get it out at the end of a day if you're completely overwhelmed, or you feel you haven't really achieved what you set out to do. Looking at it might help you regain a sense of perspective and become re-energised for tomorrow.

When it comes to prioritising, remember Pareto's principle, or the '80/20 rule': 80% of all results come from 20% of all efforts. This means that roughly one in five of the items on your list are truly essential and you should concentrate on completing these. Everything else may be useful, but the world won't end if they don't get done.

Don't confine yourself to simple A, B, C-style rankings of importance, however: you also need to recognise that some tasks take longer than others. For example, one 'A' category phone call might take just five minutes while an equivalent writing task could take as much as five hours.

If you have one big important thing that needs to be done by the end of the day ('Send hard copy of manuscript to publisher'), be aware that a dozen smaller tasks are hidden within that one bald statement ('Check the printer works, check there is enough paper, print out the manuscript, proof-read, make revisions, print out fresh copy, bind/staple, write covering letter, buy large envelopes and stamps, check and write address, check time of the last post...and send!'). Each one of these smaller tasks needs to be itemised and allocated time. If you don't do this, how can you ever be sure that your one big to-do item of the day is really achievable?

Sometimes, your list will become just too cluttered with tasks, big and small. To combat this, make two separate lists: one of things you *absolutely* need to do today and another of things you might get round to if you have the time or inclination. Don't even think about looking at the second list until the first has been dealt with.

The end of each working day is an important time. It's then that you should compile your lists for tomorrow. Don't wait until morning and find that the first task on your new to-do list is writing a to-do list. And don't just re-edit today's list – start afresh each time.

Quite often people use up the last half hour of their working day tidying up and 'clearing the decks' for the next day. Don't. It's much better to greet the new day with a messy desk and a clear head than the other way round.

98. Create arbitrary rules

By applying your own illogical constraints, you can quickly discover creative ways of bending the rules imposed on you by other people.

The simplest way to impose a constraint on your creativity is to give yourself a deadline. Sure, this isn't necessarily arbitrary, since there may be good reasons for finishing a piece of work within a fixed period of time – other people may be depending on you, and it's more than likely there's money riding on the job. But even when you don't have a strict deadline, it's tempting to give yourself one anyway.

When starting with a blank sheet (literally or figuratively) give yourself just 30 minutes to work up some ideas and then force yourself to go with what you've got at that point. This is a great way of stopping yourself from over-developing or over-refining (or over-indulging) your ideas – or trying to pack too much into one activity or framework. Just because you have lots of great ideas doesn't mean you have to deal with them all at the same time. Keep some back for later.

As well as rules for your outputs, think about silly regimes for absorbing new material. For example, Marshall McLuhan made it a rule to read only left-hand pages, but why not read only the first forty pages of any book you pick up? Or go one better and open two books at random, both at page 40, and force yourself to develop some new ideas based only on what you read on those two pages.

Rules are about patterns too. One definition of human intelligence could be our ability to detect patterns in everything we perceive. Equally, one could define

Here's an idea for you...

Play an arbitrary game of cards. Deal each other a random number of cards and then simply make up rules on the fly about when to discard, when to pick up, when to swap cards, what constitutes a winning hand, etc. Take it in turns to add one arbitrary rule at a time and see how long you can carry on playing without the whole thing collapsing or blows being exchanged. Call each other's bluff about seemingly invalid turns and transgressions. That way you'll have to explain the game to each other and – who knows – you may actually end up inventing something you can play again as a proper game!

human creativity as our ability to arbitrarily impose patterns on a seemingly disorderly world.

So this business of rule-making is really a very practical way of forcing yourself to think in cycles, to work with sequences, to record your own tendencies, to define behaviours and calculate probabilities – all key skills for the creative person.

It's also teaching you to be at home with the rules of randomness and gambling. The composer John Cage often used the rolling of a die to help make decisions about the composition of his music. (He also decided to become an expert in mushrooms, because 'mushroom' sat next to 'music' in the dictionary.)

Being arbitrary is a great way to kick-start processes generally. Quite often designers will choose the font for a new company's logo simply by taking the first letter of the company's name and then finding a font with a name that also starts with the same letter (though not many Z-companies use ZapfDingbats, oddly enough).

Defining idea…

Defining idea…
'*Read only Left-Hand Pages: Marshall McLuhan did this. By decreasing the amount of information, we leave room for what he called our "noodle".*'
– **BRUCE MAU, designer**

It can also be helpful to give yourself some kind of regular quirk or idiosyncratic rule that becomes your own trademark. For example, Alfred Hitchcock often made a cameo appearance in his films. The film editor Walter Murch does his editing standing up (and his thinking lying down).

99. Restrict your choices to broaden your possibilities

It's perfectly possible to produce recipes for success based on just a few ingredients. More bread, anyone?

Every now and then, try to immerse yourself in creative exercises that use only one colour, palette, font or sound. You may have read elsewhere that 'anything's possible' and there are 'no limits' to what you can do. If you work without limits, however, it's very easy to lose focus and for your projects to become sprawling, rambling efforts that require a huge amount of editing and refinement – either by you or by someone else.

Imposing just one silly rule about what you're not allowed to do can have interesting results – such as setting yourself the challenge of using only twenty-five letters of the alphabet to write with, as follows.

'You might think it silly to hamstring your output in such a way, and at first it looks impossibly hard to do – but it's still worth a go, if only to gain a bit of insight into how your writing might spiral off down tortuous paths as you try to avoid using a solitary non-consonant. Although now, as you look at this paragraph, you may think it's not that hard at all.'

We write with restrictions all the time anyway without really noticing it. (It's the letter 'e' by the way.) Every time you send someone a holiday postcard you're writing in a strict frame with a limited word count – and your writing style changes accordingly: 'Weather great. Wish you were here. Etc.'

Here's an idea for you...
The founding father of bossa nova, Jobim, was once criticised (by an idiot) for being only concerned with rhythm and lacking any facility with tune or melody. Jobim's creative response was a tune called 'One Note Samba', a fantastic example of restriction at work. Could you dream up a song that is based around one single note?

Even if you're not on holiday, try and use postcards for all your written communications rather than A4 stationery (and think of the trees you'll save). If you're feeling really keen, try using only the back of business cards.

If you need further inspiration in this area, pick up a book on one of the greatest examples of restriction: haiku poetry. Haiku is a seventeen-syllable verse form consisting of three metrical units of five, seven and five syllables. Each haiku always includes a 'kigo', a season word, such as blossom to indicate spring, mosquitoes to indicate summer, etc.

Restriction can be just as effective in fields other than writing, such as painting. Consider Picasso's famous blue period, or Turner's concentrated globs of orange or red. Some artists simply fall in love with one colour. Yves Klein went as far as to patent the ultramarine colour known as International Klein Blue, or IKB.

Film-maker Derek Jarman famously made a movie *Blue* that is just that – over an hour's worth of luminous blue and nothing else, accompanied by snippets of sound, music and Jarman's own voice talking about his own blindness and approaching death from AIDS-related illnesses. It is strangely affecting and effective.

Switching off a sense in this way can augment your understanding of the world around you. Try walking around the house for a while with your eyes closed (be careful!). If you want a good laugh, make a movie while you're doing it and see

343

Defining idea...
'I think people who are not artists often think artists are inspired. But if you work at your art you don't have time to be inspired. Out of the work comes the work.'
– JOHN CAGE, composer

how the resulting footage differs from what you'd film with your eyes open. Better still, play a game of blind man's buff with a few friends and get the person with the blindfold to film the experience (maybe have a few drinks first...). The bulk of the movie you make will undoubtedly be rubbish, but you may find a few frames of brilliance that make you think about filming in a different way. Taking this to its logical conclusion, you can always blindfold your audience...

Try cooking with only, say, three ingredients (best not do this blindfold). The more conservative among you will probably plump for eggs, flour and milk to make a pancake – very smart – but the real challenge is to use three quite disparate ingredients. 'Oysters, passion fruit and lavender', we can assure you, can be made into something really delicious.

11 ways to spark a genius idea

1. Take a walk online. Use random clicks to see where you end up.

2. Drive to get lost. Don't worry about destination.

3. Let the toss of a coin make all your decisions for the day.

4. Write three 'stream of consciousness' pages of A4 on waking every morning for a week.

5. Sit quietly for 10 minutes every morning and evening. Breathe in for four, out for four. Feel the space opening in your brain as you breathe in, the tension leaving your shoulders as you breathe out.

6. Do everything with the opposite hand for one day.

7. Go home by a different route.

8. Stay up all night and see what occurs to you in the 'wee small hours' and just before dawn.

9. Whenever possible take a 20 minute nap in the afternoon. (It worked for Einstein.)

10. Pay attention to the thoughts that you have just as you wake up.

11. Create a 'wish list' at www.amazon.co.uk. You don't have to buy but by adding everything that interests you, you'll see connections in your wishing and a roadmap to where your passion lies.

100. Make more mistakes, faster

Working at speed with a high level of error can help you 'fail better'. Which means you'll get to something good quicker, leaving more time to slow down.

This idea is often attributed to Andy Grove of Intel, the processor manufacturing company that helped revolutionise the computer industry in the 1980s and 1990s. When your business is about crashing out millions of bits of finely etched silicon, it's easy to see why you might be prepared to keep the production line rolling even if a few batches get screwed up along the way.

For the sculptor who spends six months working one piece in stone, it may be less easy to write the resulting work off as a failure and start again. Nevertheless, for most of us, Grove's principle is a sound one. You have to keep scribbling and sketching, modelling and planning and thinking, setting things up to knock them down, scrumpling up bits of paper and throwing them in the bin, crashing and rebooting your computer, working continuously with enthusiasm and energy and wit, and above all without any embarrassment about the obvious cock-ups along the way. If you do this intelligently and energetically, other people will almost certainly be affected by your positive spirit and join you on your journey. Those who write you off as foolish and annoying – well, maybe hanging out with them is just another mistake and it's time to move on.

Here's an idea for you...
This week, try and fire off at least a dozen ideas. In many cases, the first eleven ideas will be crap (so try to think of the twelfth one first to save time!). Don't see that as a waste of effort – see it more as a range-finder. Only by working through your early shortcomings will you hope to refine your processes on the fly – and your instincts.

Also remember that mistakes are not always mistakes. Look at them another way and they become happy accidents. According to movie director Robert Altman, 'Chance is another name that we give to our mistakes. And all of the best things in my films are mistakes.' Mistakes, he is saying, are the stuff of life. And for him, they are also the stuff of art. (And according to chaos theory, they are also the stuff of stuff.)

This is the same attitude to life that Oscar Wilde describes when he writes: 'Nowadays most people die of a sort of creeping common sense, and discover when it is too late that the only things one never regrets are one's mistakes.'

Probably the most famous blunderer of them all is Alexander Fleming. Not only did he discover penicillin by accidentally contaminating some Petri dish samples and then not bothering to wash them up for a few days, he also discovered lysozyme when he didn't bother using a handkerchief and his nose accidentally dripped into a dish of bacteria. Are you creative enough not to wipe your nose for a week just to see what accidents might happen?

347

Defining idea...
'If I had my life to live over I'd dare to make more mistakes next time.'
– NADINE STAIR, poet

The true moral of this story might be: if it ain't fixed, break it.

Certainly, one of the best ways to understand how some things work is to break them apart. For your family's sake, it's probably best if you work out how to put them back together again as well, although this isn't critical (unless it's grandma's Zimmer frame). And if it turns out that you've broken something irretrievably, try and find a new use for what you've got left. Look at kids: they rarely throw old broken toys away, but remodel, fuse and repurpose them for use in another game.

And talking of small kids, it's as well to remember that we only ever learn to walk after a lot of falling over. In fact, if you want to get technical about it, walking *is* falling over. If you don't believe us, get up now and lean forward like you are going to fall – then stick your leg out at the last minute. Almost inevitably, your other leg will kick in and you'll take not one step but two in order to break your fall.

So now you see that even something as basic as walking is really just a controlled way for your body to blunder around the place.

101. Take risks

Just what are you prepared to put on the line in order to be more creative?

Taking risks can radically change the way you live. We all have very different ideas about what risk actually is. For some, the potential embarrassment of singing in public is just too risky. For others, climbing a mountain with the possibility of losing a limb or even dying comes under the heading 'fun'.

In the field of creativity, it's unusual to find people willing to risk death or serious injury for their work – but they are out there. Magician and showman David Blaine, for example, incarcerated himself in a glass box with no food for forty days. Performance artist Chris Burden crucified himself on the bonnet of a car. William Burroughs wrote many of his most famous works, such as *The Naked Lunch*, while under the influence of powerful drugs.

Quite often artists work with the deliberate intent of confronting social taboos. Damien Hirst and his fellow 'Britartists' definitely succeeded in 'shocking the nation' in the 1990s by using animal carcasses and pseudo-pornographic images to grab our attention. Around the same time, musician and artist Bill Drummond set fire to a million pounds in cash – deliberately wasting the money. And Michael Landy went one step further, using an industrial shredder to destroy *all* his possessions.

We're not suggesting that you try anything like this (hmm, well maybe...), but you do need to ask yourself where you draw the line. For example, how politically active do you want to be in terms of your creativity? Throughout history, artists, writers and musicians have been thrown into prison or executed because their ideas were considered anti-social and subversive. Alexander Solzhenitsyn, for example, was exiled to Siberia for many years because of his writings. On the other hand, Ezra

Here's an idea for you...
Draw a square grid. Mark the left-hand side as 'Safe', the right as 'Dangerous', the bottom as 'Serious' and the top as 'Silly'. Now position your creative ideas on the grid by marking a dot with your pencil. Serious and safe ideas live somewhere in the bottom left corner. What would you have to do to them to push them into other areas?

Pound flirted dangerously with Fascist politics, tarnishing his reputation as a poet and critic, and instead of prison was carted off to a mental institution.

How conservative or radical you want to be with your ideas is very much a personal decision, but you do need to understand the scale by which you can measure those ideas. For example, think back to moments in your life when you have felt deeply embarrassed or exposed in public. What caused them, and how did you react to each situation? Did you deliberately put yourself in a risky situation or were you ambushed? Did you do something to retrieve the situation, or did you simply get angry – or run away? By looking back over these events, you should be able to get a closer reading of what your personal fears and inhibitions are. In many ways, you may well have already been very creative in managing to ignore or suppress them.

But you should also think of developing creative ideas that confront and expose your fears. At the most basic level, if you have a fear of heights, make yourself go to a very high place. If you don't like snakes, go to the zoo and spend an hour in the reptile house. Write down how you feel, dramatise it, tell people about it in such a way that they feel the 'buzz' you felt at the time.

Another important question regarding your 'risk assessment' is: what have you got to lose? Make an inventory of all the things in your life that you value, that define who you are, that make you happy – family, friends, home comforts, holidays, etc.

Defining idea...
'It is not because things are difficult that we do not dare; it is because we do not dare that they are difficult.' **– SENECA**

Now score the importance of each out of ten. Take your time: these are important to you.

Now, take all the things that have scored eight or less, and think of an action or a situation that would put each one in jeopardy. In fact, take each as the subject matter for your next creative project and see how you would cope with losing them – or at least exposing your own dependency on them in public. For example, how would you cope if you lost your house or flat because you failed to meet the mortgage payments or pay the rent; burnt it down; got kicked out by your partner; got hounded out by the community...

Follow through the consequences of some of these – what kind of creative work would lead to not paying the rent or falling out with your partner or being offered a new job?

Even if you don't take this line of thinking any further, you should now be more aware of what kind of creative risks you really are prepared to take. And what risks you're actively choosing to avoid.

351

102. Thinking inside the box

You've got more ideas and sparks of inspiration than you have time to deal with them. Find out where to store those ideas you haven't got round to yet.

The most obvious way to sort your ideas into categories and box them up is to institute a filing system. Problem is, filing – as we all know – is one of the most boring activities known to man.

A huge proportion of the stuff we put into filing cabinets never sees the light of day again. The main reason for this is we don't bother making notes about 'why' we're filing anything. And there's never an action point assigned to the things we squirrel away. We actively decide in most cases to do absolutely nothing about the things we thought were worth saving from the bin. If you're not careful, all you'll have to show for keeping a whole load of newspaper cuttings is a pile of newspaper cuttings and no new ideas.

The way out of this is to make the filing cabinet your playground. Crucially, your thinking about all the things you store up in little boxes needs to be associative; you need to develop tools and techniques for mixing and matching your clippings, organising them into thematic clusters or charting them on a map in some way.

Here's an idea for you...
If digital displays are not your thing, revert back to old-fashioned cabinets. Collectors of the past were very fond of display cabinets for showing off vast hordes of stones, shells, bugs and butterflies. Many of us still like to decorate our homes with this kind of stuff. Create your own display cabinet, containing whatever you consider to be interesting, beautiful or talismanic. Or start a collection of one particular type of thing.

Technology can help with this. There are some great tools out there – usually offering some kind of database structure that allows you to scan in items and then tag them with ratings, keywords or labels of some kind. At the click of a button you can then change your 'view' into the database, so that the things that might appeal to your current train of creative thought right now are closer to hand while the less interesting stuff is further away. Digital music tools like iTunes work exactly like this in that you can even get the computer to randomly generate playlists from your collection based on music type, your personal ratings, number of times a tune has been played recently, length of tune, etc. (Hmm. Not that random, then, but you can see what we're driving at.)

To make this kind of ongoing filing and retrieval system work really well, you have to get into the discipline of annotating and 'tagging' everything you come into contact with as you go along. A simple way to understand how this might work is to sign up to the Amazon online store (www.amazon.co.uk) and start adding items to your Wishlist section. You don't have to buy anything. You just log your interest and, as you do it, your Wishlist grows. You can annotate this with reasons 'why' you want this item.

353

Defining idea...

'Shadow boxes become poetic theatres or settings wherein are metamorphosed the element of a childhood pastime.' – **JOSEPH CORNELL**

Very quickly you will have created a list of things that interest you, all sat alongside each other. Connections and themes might grow as you sift back through this. And since your Wishlist is 'free to air', all your friends can quickly discover what to buy you for your birthday. The online phenomenon that is blogging is pretty much about this same process too.

At this point, you might be wondering what this has to do with boxes. But really, all we're talking about is collecting stuff and playing with it inside digital display panels rather than inside wooden or metal boxes.

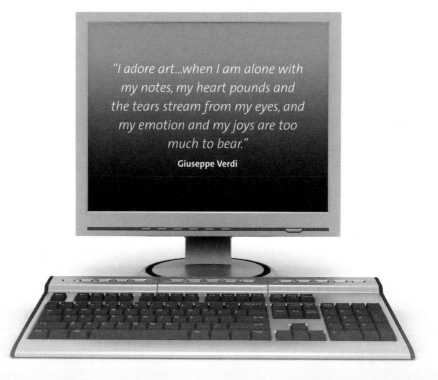

"*I adore art...when I am alone with my notes, my heart pounds and the tears stream from my eyes, and my emotion and my joys are too much to bear.*"

Giuseppe Verdi

103. Network near, network far

Learn to value friends, and appreciate enemies.

We speed up and lose friends. But it's much better to slow down long enough to stay in touch. It's official – having a wide network of people to talk to is good for your health. Japanese health experts claim that regular face-to-face contact with friends and neighbours reduces stress and thus lowers the risk of stress-related illnesses.

In the UK, recent research suggested that middle-aged men in particular are prone to becoming too solitary (in their sheds, presumably) and thus shortening their life expectancy. Statistically, it has been known for years that married men – in social family environments – live longer than bachelors. All this goes to prove that putting yourself about a bit, making sure you're achieving a high turnover of new acquaintances, will help you to be not only more creative, but more healthy with it!

Most of us have surprisingly few genuine friends. Sure, your address book and your email client may be stacked full of names, but how many of them are really friends? A BBC online survey revealed that on average people tended to have twenty friends in their address book, while during the week they only kept in contact with four to seven of these. (By the way, there was no significant difference between the figures for men and women.)

It's actually easier than ever to increase your circle of friends and acquaintances now that we live in a networked world, just by using your email. Go through your email inbox right now (assuming you have one – if you don't, sort it!). Perhaps you've already noticed how many times emails addressed to you have also been cc-

Here's an idea for you...
As well as playing games of 'Six Degrees of Separation', trying to connect two random people together based on who they know, why not indulge in a game of 'Six Degrees of Kevin Bacon', the game where you connect actors via films starring Kevin Bacon. Full rules at www.louisville.com/loumag/mar/bacon.htm

ed to other people. Now ask yourself – how many people on that cc-list have you communicated with in a meaningful way? Not that many, we'd wager. Well now's the time to start.

Don't worry, this isn't what they call 'spamming' because you've already been connected to these seeming strangers via a shared email. And this email also gives you something to talk about. So pick out someone you've never really talked to before and start an email correspondence. Start with a 'Don't I know you?' query or a 'Can you help me?' request, or similar. Keep it light, be helpful and friendly, don't be bothersome, and make yourself look like you're someone useful to know. Stay alert to replies and slowly build up a rapport.

Why do this? Well, any new contact you make will expand your knowledge of the world at large and could lead to new ideas or collaborations. According to the theory of 'six degrees of separation' (whereby any two people in the world can be connected via a chain of aquaintances that is never longer than six people), by making contact with just a few people in this way, you'll be getting yourself hooked into a much larger social network very quickly indeed.

As internet commentator and social software academic Clay Shirky points out:

'The social tools of the internet, lightweight though most of them are, have a kind of fluidity and ease of use that the conference call never attained: compare the effortlessness of cc:ing half a dozen friends to decide on a movie, versus trying to set up a conference call to accomplish the same task.'

Defining idea…
'My father said to me, many years ago, "Hang out with people who are brighter and smarter than you and they'll drag you up with them," and that has actually been the truth.' – **MICHAEL PATRICK CRONAN, designer**

Exploiting and managing your network in this way can also mean you stay alert for people who really don't like you or your work. 'Keep your friends close, and your enemies closer,' advised Machiavelli (not to us personally, you understand). The good news is that on a well-run network you can see exactly what those bastards are up to (they're usually pretty vocal) and you can pre-empt every possible criticism of your creative endeavour well before it actually happens.

104. Do absolutely nothing

Learn to just be. After all this creativity you probably need a rest.

It can actually be quite hard to do absolutely nothing. For a start, you have an inquisitive, creative mind that finds interest in everything around you. Even when you're just sitting in your back garden, or slobbing out on the couch, your brain is at work, taking in new stimuli and synthesising ideas. You are never at rest, even if other people think you are.

Sadly, creative people can do a very good impression of being useless layabouts. Because of this, other people can be a real problem when you're trying to get away from it all. As soon as you look like you're doing nothing, they will often step in and try to 'keep you busy'.

In these modern times, a lot of us work from home or exist in weird hybrid spaces between work and play – and we're none the worse for that. Trouble is, in this kind of setup, as soon as you look like you've officially stopped working, domestic responsibilities can quickly come crashing in: 'the lawn needs mowing'; 'there's a whole pile of laundry in the bathroom'; 'it's your turn to look after the kids'.

It's also hard sometimes to synchronise your 'nothing' time with everything else that's going on around you. You might want to just lie on the couch and snooze for a moment, or read a good book. Someone else might want to watch TV in the same space or play a noisy computer game. Don't put up with this. It's vitally important to find a space where you can literally do nothing and empty your head a bit – and if that means saying 'Bugger off. I was here first', then so be it.

Here's an idea for you...
Close your eyes if you want to, but try not to fall asleep. Empty your head of all worries and totally relax your muscles. Be at one with the sounds and smells around you. Keep your breathing shallow, but regular. Yes, what we're talking about here is a form of meditation – and any form of this you can get into is a good thing.

Creativity is a draining business and it's also a little bit 'Zen' (as we keep mentioning), so it's important that you enter and exit this world in a state of relative calm and peace. If you don't believe us, think about brainstorming sessions you've had in the past. We're willing to bet that the most effective ones happened when you were fresh and at ease, and your head was filled at first with, well, nothing. They will also probably have lasted less than two hours. Anything longer than that and things don't come easily. You get tired. You're head is probably spinning and you really do need a rest. You need to find a space where you can literally do nothing and...

God bless those people who can work creatively for more than, say, four hours at a stretch. But most of us will actually find that four hours of genuine creative endeavour is a good day's work. The rest of the day can be filled nicely with admin, basic grunt-work, socialising, new research – and resting (i.e. doing nothing).

Defining idea...

'You must have a room or a certain hour of the day or so where you do not know what was in the morning paper...a place where you can simply experience and bring forth what you are, and what you might be...At first you may find nothing's happening.' – **JOSEPH CAMPBELL**

Men of a certain age will probably think of this as 'shed time', and indeed it is helpful to ring-fence a space of your own. But sheds are usually about pottering, and even that is not allowed in this exercise. We really do want you to just sit or lie down in the sun and simply take in the world around you.

It doesn't matter where you are: if it's only twenty minutes in the steam room at the local gym, take the time to just sit there silently, with nothing whatsoever going on inside your head. Curiously this is actually a great way of generating fresh ideas, because for sure something strange will creep into your head at these moments anyway. Just don't be tempted to take those ideas any further straight away. Remember – you're busy doing nothing right now. And tomorrow is another day.

Live the good life

Imagine feeling as if you were really living. Imagine a life that was both richer and deeper than the one you're living now, with time to watch the seasons pass and a real sense of connection both to your loved ones and your environment. Imagine more rest, more laughter, more creativity, more fun. Imagine adding greater depth to your life and more meaning to your days.

Welcome to the next stage of slowing down. Either retirement or a real need for change means you're ready to discover what makes your heart sing – living simply, creatively, self-reliantly. This is where you finally take control of your life and do whatever you've dreamed of doing. For many of us, that's putting something back into the world for future generations. For others it could be writing a novel or simply slicing into a tomato that you've grown yourself.

Whatever your ideal, get set to step into adventure and the excitement of the new...

QUIZ: **Does your life thrill you?**

A strange question, but one that perhaps we don't ask ourselves often enough. This quiz may give you the shock you need to clear the decks and start prioritising what you love.

1   A friend calls to say he's just been presented with a couple of tickets for a concert he knows you'd enjoy – tonight. What's your reaction?
    a.   Terrific!
    b.   There's resistance – it means hassle – but you'd probably go.
    c.   There's no way you'd be able to do anything so spontaneous.

2   How do you feel first thing in the morning?
    a.   Ready for the day ahead.
    b.   Sluggish until you have that first cup of tea or coffee.
    c.   Exhausted.

3   If your partner is obviously keen to have sex, your immediate reaction even if you act differently is:
    a.   Ooh yes!
    b.   Oh no.
    c.   It's been so long it would be really unlikely that the situation would arise.

4 Imagine you had an hour or so free to relax on the sofa. What would you do?

    a.   Relish watching a favourite movie or reading a book.

    b.   Start reading or watching television but probably doze off.

    c.   You never seem to be able to do that for more than 10 minutes, there's always something else to fill the gap.

5 You would love to cut your working hours, study a subject you loved or have more time for your own interests. You know...

    a.   That it's only a matter of time.

    b.   That if you could just organise your life a little, it would all fall into place.

    c.   That it's never going to happen.

Mostly a)s

Your life appears to give you both enough excitement and enough time so that you remain energetic and enthusiastic. You are ready for another challenge. Look at *ideas 114, 125* and *131* to see if any of it tickles your fancy.

Mostly b)s

So far you are coping with a life that is busy and stimulating but there are first signs that it is moving at too fast a pace for you to really enjoy it. Go right back to *idea 1*. Then try idea 110. Motivating yourself to change your life may well start with realising you are not so dependent on maintaining your present lifestyle.

Mostly c)s

You are both frustrated and bored with certain aspects of your life. Turn to *ideas 26–36* to inspire a change of attitude. Then look through ideas *110–114* – could it be time to consider drastic measures?

105. Book the bungee jump

There's a growing trend for physically challenging sports. Well, why not? Let's see what gets your adrenaline pumping.

Even an hour's session at the gym, or a jog around the duck pond in the park will give you a bit of a high, but if you really want to inject some excitement there's a lot more to be had. You could well be in better physical shape than you were in your twenties, but even if you're creaking at the seams a little there's no reason why you can't decide to push the boundaries. One of the best ways of keeping young, having fun and feeling that life's worth living is to do something that gets those hormones racing around your body.

Now, what gives me a kick is probably very different from what gets you excited, so there's not much point in my sitting here telling you to climb up a waterfall if that's your idea of a boring day out, but I can give you some idea of how to find the activity that'll give you a buzz.

Pardon me for starting on a down note, but I think it's best to rule out the things that really give you the willies. If you throw up at the mere thought of standing on a cliff top, there's not much point in booking yourself a climbing holiday – at least until you've had some therapy to deal with your fear of heights. Terrified of drowning? Forget about deep sea diving or white water rafting (but you might want to consider swimming lessons).

Here's an idea for you...
Too nervous for daredevil sports? Book a lesson in a controlled environment, with an instructor watching your every move, lots of first-class equipment, and a handy defibrillator just in case you panic. I'm not sure there's a tame version of a bungee jump, but what about learning to ski on a dry ski slope, or practising scuba diving in the local pool?

At the other extreme, there's no real excitement in going for things you know you love because you've done them before. If you've climbed three mountains, well, yes, you'll probably still get a thrill out of climbing your fourth, but it's probably not the same thrill you get from tackling something entirely new is it? If you own a yacht and have spent every holiday for the past ten years sailing the Med, you probably still get a lot of pleasure from it, but the adrenalin won't be anywhere near the level it was on that first trip.

Choose what suits you best, whether it's one of those stomach-emptying rides at the theme park, a drive around the ring road at rush hour, or a plunge into the waters of Oz. It's easy to find scary sports. You can probably list a dozen without giving it too much thought (and you can try checking the Dangerless Aerial Sports Club website if you're stuck) but how do you draw the balance between terror and ennui? What would give you a thrill without doing you any physical or psychological harm? Work down this quick checklist:

Defining idea...
'You may be disappointed if you fail, but you are doomed if you don't try.'
– BEVERLY SILLS, singer

- Do you have any physical limitations? These may make some activities obvious no-no's.

- Are there things that genuinely terrify you, to the extent that you can have a serious panic attack when you face them (e.g enclosed spaces, wide open spaces, or spiders)? If so, unless you're prepared to get some therapy first, any activity that includes these things can be crossed off straight away.

- Are there things you've always avoided because they make you uncomfortable (e.g. large dogs, snakes, heights)? Now here's a rich vein of possibilities. One way we get our kicks is by feeling we're not quite in control, so if you can organise something for yourself that takes you into contact with the thing that gives you the shivers, you'll get a whopping thrill out of the experience.

Oh, by the way, it's important that I tell you this: get your doctor's OK before you seize this idea. Get yourself insured if necessary. Don't take risks if you're not prepared to take responsibility for them.

106. Living on less

If you've always spent your income (or even more than your income) and you can't imagine how you'd cope on less money this one's for you. It's all about managing the budget.

I once knew someone who was obviously worried about whether he'd cope on his pension, so one day I asked him whether he'd worked out a budget. He amazed me by saying that, no, he was putting off doing that because it was going to be so time-consuming to go through everything he'd spent over the past year or so.

I'm not sure I ever convinced him that he'd got it upside down, but if you're a big spender I hope I can convince you that what you spend now is, to a large extent, irrelevant. All that matters is what you will be spending in future, and you're going to have to go back to the days of your penurious youth and remember the basic facts about budgeting. It's simple – if a bit tedious – to work out.

Find yourself a large pad of paper, a pen and a calculator. Get out your bills, credit card statements, bank statements and receipts for the last year and work through them, identifying every payment that will still need to be made when you retire. Include only the necessities of life – things like utilities, taxes, car maintenance, food. Total 'em up and see how much you've got left from your expected pension income so you can see how much you can afford to set aside for unexpected expenses (the lawn mower packs up), holidays, gifts and clothes.

Here's an idea for you...
Even if you've got years to go, try living on your pension now, before you actually have to. Work out exactly what income you'll have (not forgetting that pensions are taxable). For the next six months, do your utmost to live on what you'll be getting.

If it's looking a bit tight, work back through your bills to see where you might be able to save some money. For example, it's usually cheaper to pay utilities by direct debit, and if you shop around you can save money on insurance premiums (never automatically accept a renewal quote – always check the rivals because you're almost bound to find a better deal).

As a priority, sort out any debts and if possible aim to clear them all before you retire. If you've got a wallet full of credit cards, cut most of them up and just stick to the ones that charge the least interest or, even better, use debit or charge cards from now on. Pay off the bills on the cards that charge the highest interest as fast as you can, and don't even consider consolidating all your debts unless you're one hundred percent sure you understand what it's going to cost you.

If you can afford it, stock up on basic household items in advance of your retirement. Instead of having another expensive restaurant meal, have a trip to town and use the cash you'd have spent on posh nosh to buy yourself a set of towels or some bed linen, or a spare iron. If you do this, you'll give yourself a breathing space when you retire, so you can get used to living on the reduced income without having to worry about affording the small but expensive necessities of life as they wear out.

Defining idea...
'Never spend your money before you have it.' **– THOMAS JEFFERSON**

No matter how prepared you are, your domestic appliances (the ones that are really essential but really boring to buy, like washing machines, kettles and vacuum cleaners) will break down in the month after their guarantees expire. And have you noticed how these things always seem to work together to make life hell? There appears to be some kind of law that if the iron blows up on Tuesday the washing machine will seize up (full of water, naturally) on Wednesday. This means you will definitely need some savings. Start getting canny about spending now, so you can have a bit of spare cash ready. Save by never paying full price – buy at sale time, check out eBay, car boot sales, charity shops, markets.

107. Don't act your age

Hey. This is going to be great. It'll be the first time since you were a child that you'll have the chance to have fun without feeling guilty. Can you even remember what fun is? Remind yourself of the things that make you laugh.

For most of us, the trouble with being a grown-up is that we've got ourselves trapped in the treadmill of responsibility and we've kept fun firmly in its place for years. If, like me, you have offspring you'll have had some fun when your kids were small (and that was pretty well balanced, what with the nappies and the chauffeuring duties). If we're lucky we've had the odd weekend away, an occasional night out, an annual holiday, even the dreaded office Christmas party. But these things have often been squished into a hectic diary and we've turned up grouchy, begrudging the time and effort we've had to make, when we could have been at home zonked out in front of the telly. We don't, generally, get real fun, and it's so sad that we think that's how it should be.

I know this is true for me, because when I see a grown-up having real fun I think to myself 'Stupid idiot. He needs to grow up.' And, yes, I know that sounds like blatant sexism, but it usually is a man. For years I've made jokes about some men not growing up, and now I find the joke's on me. They've got it right all along.

Here's an idea for you...
Today, and every day from now one, set aside a small period of time – anything from ten minutes to an hour – and do something you enjoy. It could be serious fun (roller-blading down the High Street?) or it could be something really small. It doesn't matter what it is – go window shopping; cuddle the cat; kick leaves – just try for something different every day and, when you do it, do it one hundred percent.

What's the secret to fun? I can hardly remember. What were the real fun times? For me, climbing Dunns River Falls was fun; getting lost in the music at rock concerts was fun; punting on the Cam on a hot summer's day was fun; trying to play tennis last year (after a forty-year break) was fun, if a trifle embarrassing.

What were the fun times for you? When you've remembered them, ask yourself what was it that made them fun? How did you feel? The common denominator for me is that these things were all different from the things I normally do – and sometimes even a bit scary. (Cynics amongst you, stop laughing. Punting on the Cam is a seriously dangerous activity unless, like me, you're lucky enough to have an expert handling the pole rather than some idiot undergraduate who wants to show off.)

Your idea of fun is bound to be quite different from mine. You may have had fun trudging through the mud and facing the portaloos at pop festivals; you might get your thrills from racing round a Caribbean bay on an old tyre, pulled by a motor boat (I'm told it's like high-speed colonic irrigation). Train spotting or chess might be the activities that got your adrenalin going over the years. But the common denominator must, surely, be laughter? (Which, equally surely, must rule out train spotting?) If we're not laughing – or at least smiling – we're not really having fun are we? Nor are we experiencing the massive physiological benefits of laughter, which floods our bodies with happy hormones, relieves stress and is a thoroughly healthy activity.

Now, how do we recapture that feeling without necessarily having to repeat the experience? Since my kicks come from trying something new, my plan is to find some activities that are different – things I'd never even thought of doing before. Hmm, learn to tango perhaps? What does it for you? Whatever it is, commit to it by building it into your life so you have lots to look forward to over the next few months. Booking lessons, arranging dates with friends and paying in advance are all good ways of making sure you won't chicken out in favour of the sofa.

Defining idea...
'I refuse to admit I'm more than fifty-two, even if that does make my sons illegitimate.' – **LADY ASTOR**

108. Only the lonely

There's nothing sadder than someone struggling alone, unnoticed. Unless it's two lonely people living yards away from each other and never speaking. Build yourself a network of new friends.

The expectation is that we should all have true love, lots of friends and a cracking social life, but this isn't always so. Perhaps you're divorced or bereaved, or maybe you've never found that perfect mate we all dream about. It could be that you've worked abroad all your life and left all your friends behind when you retired back home to an entirely new life. Whatever the reason, it's not too late to do something about it. There's no reason why anyone should be lonely.

It's common sense that if you live on a quiet remote island you're less likely to make new friends than if you live in a busy village but, oddly enough, the reverse isn't true. If you live in the centre of a busy big city it's going to be harder to meet new people than if you're out in the quiet suburbs. But, wherever you live, you won't meet anyone unless you're prepared to work at it.

First and foremost, you won't get anyone to be interested in knowing you if you don't make an effort to be an interesting person and you struggle to find something to say when a new acquaintance asks, 'So, what do you do then?' Do your prep. Be interested in what's going on in the world; have an opinion about current events; have lots of hobbies (even if they sit neglected in cupboards for the greater part of the year, you can still wheel them out if needs be).

Here's an idea for you...
If you're planning to use your hobby to play the mating game, find an activity that genuinely interests you – otherwise you'll give up before you even begin – but decide carefully. And have a preview session to see what the gender mix is.

Secondly, and I know this is going to sound corny but I have to say it, join a club. Or find something that you enjoy doing and book a course in it. Attend your neighbourhood social activities, or your local church, or get some voluntary work in a local charity shop. Get a job that'll get you into a new environment – it doesn't have to be full time, exciting or even permanent but if it's the right kind of job you'll meet new people.

Defining idea...
'The human heart, at whatever age, opens only to the heart that opens in return.'
– MARIE EDGEWORTH, writer

OK, those are the easy and obvious bits. Much harder, of course, is the actual friend-making bit. How do you make that first, crucial contact? Do you stumble over the first move in case you're rejected? If so, remember that it helps to ask an open question (one that needs more answer than a 'yes' or 'no'). Try something friendly and easy like 'How are you managing to look so cool in this heat?' If he or she likes the look of you they'll find something to say in response; if they don't, well, just tell yourself that rejection isn't life threatening, and move onto someone else.

When you come to think about it, what exactly is it that makes you warm to people? Of the friends you've had over the years, what was it that attracted you to them? They might have been fun, witty, clever or kind, but I'll bet the one thing they'll all had in common was that they were interested in you. They wanted to know about you – where you lived, what you did with your time, what you enjoyed, what you didn't enjoy.

We don't make friends with people who aren't interested in us, and that's the key to making new friends. Fair do's, you have to be prepared to tell them a bit about yourself, and you have to make sure you're doing those interesting things with your life, but what will really get their eyes alight is your interest in them. Find out what makes your new acquaintance tick, what they do, who they are, and what they think of the world we live in. Watch out though – there's a fine line between being really interested and being intense. Too much interest makes people feel a bit hunted and you don't want a reputation as a stalker!

109. Laughter is the best medicine

We choose how we think and don't have to be driven by our emotions.

Recognising that we can choose to be happy whenever we want is unbelievably empowering. I used to spend much of my life stressed and unhappy, always worrying about tomorrow and about things that I had or hadn't done yesterday.

HAPPINESS IS A CHOICE

So says the author and speaker Robert Holden and, guess what, he's right! When I first started on my path of real growth I had to do some very deep soul-searching. One of the things that I needed to ask was why I felt stressed or depressed so often. The answer became clear. It was because I was choosing to feel that way. After all, I choose my thoughts, no one else does. I couldn't walk away from this fact, however hard it was for me to accept it.

At this precise moment, I'm sitting here writing this book to a very tight deadline. The sun is shining outside, I'm exhausted from a ridiculous work schedule and my hot tub is calling me. It may not be easy for me to choose to be happy at this moment, and if I don't choose to be happy it'll be much harder and take much longer for me to write this chapter. I'm choosing happiness!

Here's an idea for you...

Think of a chore that you really don't like doing. It might be similar to one of my daily tasks that really isn't great – I have seven dogs, and every day there's a little garden job called 'poo patrol'! Now decide how you're going to feel about doing this job. You can focus on how great the garden will look when you've finished and how happy that'll make you. Or you could focus on the great joy and happiness that the dogs bring into you life. Whatever chore you pick, choose to be happy during each moment that you're doing it.

I clearly remember a friend and colleague phoning me to tell me how excited she was about a new job she'd just been offered in Brussels. She was beside herself with joy and then told me that she'd be really happy once she was out there and had left her present job. I asked her why she was choosing to put off happiness until she got to Brussels instead of having a little happiness right now. She went very quiet and then said, 'I've never thought about things in that way. You're right, I can choose to be happy right now, and I am.'

How many people do you know who say that they'll be happy once they get their new car, new job or new home? But what happens when they get that new car? They love it for a while, but as soon as they get bored with it and a faster, flashier model comes out they're once again saying, 'I'll be happy once I get that new car!' What they're doing is putting happiness outside of them, in an object of some sort. But that's not where happiness lies. Happiness lies inside of us and all it takes to be happy is for us to choose to be so.

WHAT'S YOUR CHOICE?

When you're at home, do you look out of the window and see a wonderful view? Or do you see the dirty windows? If you walk into someone else's home do you notice the beautiful paintings on the walls or do you see the untidiness in the room? You need to make a choice about what you're going to focus on. It probably won't be so easy to be a happy person if you always look for the negative rather than the positive. Remember that if we continually say, 'I'll be happy when…' we're actually choosing to while away our life in a state of 'unhappiness' until we reach this destination called 'happiness'. However, once we truly own our thoughts and the way we feel, we can choose happiness in whatever we do.

Defining idea...
'Most people are as happy as they make up their minds to be.' – **ABRAHAM LINCOLN**

110. Cheap as chips

Frugal living - is it scrooge-like penny pinching or everyday money saving? Well, it's up to you to decide how far you want to go.

It's actually possible to save a lot of money around the house in very easy ways. That money soon adds up – and the more you save, the sooner you'll have financial freedom. Household cleaning is one area where savings can be made. The basic thing to remember is don't believe the hype! Instead of using the latest expensively advertised 'miracle' cleaning fluid, consider using old-fashioned, cheap and effective home-made cleaners. The three best materials to buy for a variety of cleaning jobs around the house are white vinegar, bicarbonate of soda and your favourite scented essential oil. Those, combined with hot water and a bit of good honest elbow grease, will tackle most jobs – and with no nasty chemicals so it's environmentally friendly as well as very cheap.

A teaspoon of bicarbonate of soda on a damp cloth gets rid of most of the stains that proprietary cream cleansers do. A teaspoon can also be added to a white wash to make it bright. A large box of bicarbonate of soda can be bought cheaply at the chemist's or hardware shop.

Add a few drops of essential oils, like lavender or chamomile, to water in a washed out spray bottle (ask friends to save these for you; they're very useful). This can be used lightly when wet dusting, which is good for getting rid of dust mites that can cause allergic reactions. It makes the room smell great, too! Tea tree oil can be used as an antibacterial cleaner in this way too.

Here's an idea for you...
It is worth shopping around for the cheapest electricity, gas, and other suppliers – customer loyalty doesn't necessarily pay. There are websites that allow you to compare prices, such as uSwitch.com in the UK and upmystreet.com in the USA. Make sure you find the best deals before you contact a variety of irritating sales people who might never leave you alone, ever – not even when you're dead!

White wine vinegar is a great surface cleaner for glass – TVs, windows, glass doors, mirrors, etc. Fill a washed out spray bottle with half vinegar and half water and use sparingly. A crumpled up newspaper is a great 'polishing cloth' to finish these surfaces. When you finish with it, shred it and add it to the compost heap. Vinegar is also great for getting rid of limescale (simple chemistry if you think about it; limescale is *lime*scale, so it is alkaline, and vinegar is acid).

Instead of carpet cleaner, vacuum thoroughly to raise the nap and then sprinkle baking soda on the carpet. Leave overnight, then vacuum again. This removes smoke, pet and food smells.

A great way to clean aluminium cookware and utensils is to use cream of tartar. Fill the pan you want to clean with water and add cream of tartar (two teaspoons per litre). You can put aluminium utensils inside the pan. Bring it to the boil and simmer for a while until the pan looks clean, then rinse.

I've never seen the point in spraying chemicals around the room to make it smell better. I actually think that all it does is make it smell different. Don't forget in these days of double glazing that an open window will ventilate and freshen a room. To make a natural air freshener for the kitchen, pop a few cloves and a cinnamon stick in water and simmer them until the kitchen is full of the smell – this is a good one if you are selling your house, too, because it is a 'homely' smell.

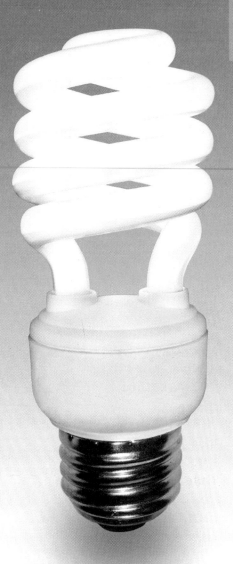

Defining idea...
'Our life is frittered away by detail... Simplify, simplify.'
– HENRY DAVID THOREAU

When utility bills arrive, it seems as though you are paying money for nothing. You know you run the washer, lights, TV, computers etc., but can it really cost that much? Well, the short answer is yes. You need to find savings.

Install energy saving light bulbs all over the house. They are more expensive, but last longer and save money in the long run. It goes without saying that you should switch off lights when you leave a room.

Make sure you switch off all of your electrical appliances at the wall before you go to bed. Apart from minimising the fire risk, lots of electrical appliances use a surprising amount of power even when they are on standby.

At the risk of sounding like your granny, I would urge you to peg washing outside to dry. It saves power if you don't use the tumble dryer, and the sunlight can help to brighten whites. Alternatively, use an indoor airer.

111. Check out your assets

controlling your money gives you control of your life. It buys your freedom. Money under control gives you a breather and can release you from a job you hate.

If you want to stop working yourself into the ground for money, the bottom line is this: don't spend it. Too often, we work to earn money to spend; we spend it and have to work again. With a financial cushion, you can choose to work part time or take a risk and start a business. You tie yourself to a stressful, unsatisfying job by continually living beyond your means. You live from pay cheque to pay cheque, saving nothing.

WHAT CAN YOU DO?
Break down how much you spend each month. You could be in for a surprise. It certainly was for me when I carried out this exercise! I found I was buying myself little 'treats' to cheer myself up because I was so tired, and I was getting down about working so hard. What I couldn't see until then was that the 'treats' I was buying were getting more expensive as my income rose. That meant I was forced to work harder to afford the treats – so I worked harder. The upward spending spiral needed to be broken, and tracking my spending was one way to do that. Today, there are still many treats and rewards in my life. They might involve giving myself time to dig a new veggie bed (therapeutic, trust me), or they might involve a splurge on a meal out. I just make sure that I no longer live beyond my means.

Here's an idea for you...
Track your spending for a week. Be really anal and write down everything you spend, even including a cup of coffee. It's tedious and seems small minded, but it gives you an idea of where your money is going – and that could be a real wake up call.

It may be a nasty shock when you identify where you spend your money, but it's better than going on complaining that you don't know where your money goes. Do you spend a lot on takeaways because you come in late and tired? Do you spend a lot on ready meals because you have no time to cook? Are there things you are spending money on that you can do without? Don't get into the mind-set that it's about denying yourself – instead, think that it's about making choices to bring you towards a positive goal, such as working fewer hours.

CREATE A FINANCIAL PLAN
Once you have a real picture of where your money goes, make a list of expenses such as your mortgage or rent, utilities, etc. Are there any ways to economise there? For instance, using energy saving bulbs and appliances can save money, as well as the environment. Then look at monthly bills such as satellite TV, club membership, etc. Is there anything you are willing to give up to move you towards being able to work fewer hours or to retire earlier?

Use any money you can gather from the savings and cut-backs you choose to make to pay off consumer debt. This is even more important than saving. Credit and store cards charge ridiculously high interest rates and should be paid off as soon as possible. Really think hard about whether it is worth buying anything on credit. That cute little piece of plastic does more than anything else to keep you on the work treadmill. Look at any debts you have closely. Prioritise them, paying off those with the highest rates of interest first. If you have credit card debt, shop around for a new card with a 0% offer on balance transfers. This can give you months of

Defining idea...
'To know when you have enough is to be rich.' – **LAO TZU**

payments that hack lumps off the debt rather than merely pay off interest charges. Pay as much as you can every month. Once you are out of debt, think about saving. It is worth talking to a financial advisor at this point to find a savings plan that fits your needs.

These financial plans may mean that you can't buy everything you want. But, think carefully: what do you want more – consumer goods or the financial freedom to work less and enjoy life more?

112. Cut the crap: decluttering for dummies

As we go through life, we all collect piles of crap that we drag along behind us like Jacob Marley's chains, but the more we have, the more there is to keep clean and tidy. Declutter and free yourself!

We've all watched the TV shows and laughed as lifestyle gurus embarrass people by laying out piles of their stuff for all the world to see. However, how would your home look in the decluttering spotlight?

Once you decide to downshift, a strange thing happens. Even if you weren't a packrat before, you can start to look at things in a new light – that bottle might make a good cloche; suddenly you have a box full in the garage. Or you can hold on to items 'just in case' they come in handy. The piles grow and the cupboards bulge. Soon you are suffocating in a pile of 'things'.

I am, by nature, Queen of the packrats. However, I married a man who is quite the reverse. While for him this is undoubtedly a cause of angst, for me it is a blessing. He marches sternly around in my wake curbing my excesses. (Believe me, the urge to keep things 'just in case' gets worse when you have outbuildings!)

Successful downshifters are resourceful people, clever with their hands and inventive. They make an art form out of reusing and recycling – but it can get out of hand. Then it's time to declutter. We downshift because we want a simpler life, yet the more stuff

Here's an idea for you...
Save photos – not objects. When you store baby toys, Cub Scout uniforms and tiny shoes, you are trying to hold on to a warm memory. However, a picture can evoke the memory as much as the item itself. If you have a photograph of the object or outfit being used, try to steel yourself to give away the real thing.

we have, the more complicated it gets. Speaking from experience, too many things crammed into a house can be oppressive.

Walk around your house – and sheds! – and take a cold hard look. If you are anything like me, there'll be stuff that you haven't used in years. Get rid of it!

Here's how to get started. Walk round with a black sack. There are probably things in every room you can throw out or send to the recyclers. You know the stuff I mean: single socks, old magazines, broken things you have been meaning to fix for months, out of date dried food packets. I guarantee that this bit is really satisfying.

The harder bit is deciding what to give away. Get two large boxes and go into the first room. (A note: do not try to do the whole house at once. Do a room at a time, and do it thoroughly.) Collect together everything that doesn't belong in the room. Dump them in one of the boxes so you can carry it round the house, putting things away in the right place.

Look hard at the things that do belong in the room -- for now. If you haven't used an item for a year, or you don't really like it anymore, put it in the second box. This is the box of goods to sell/take to the charity shop. I realised the other day that gathering dust on a shelf in the utility room were a microwave egg poacher and a microwave crisp maker. Guess what – I gave away the microwave a year ago and didn't buy a new one because I wanted to rely less on electrical appliances. Needless to say, those goods have now been given away.

Defining idea...
'In order to seek one's own direction, one must simplify the mechanics of ordinary, everyday life.' **– PLATO**

Once you have enough stuff gathered together – and it won't take long! – take it to the charity shop straight away. That way you cannot change your mind.

Watch what you bring home. There's no point in decluttering and then filling the space with more stuff. Make sure that when you buy something, you get rid of the item you are replacing. It's not rocket science, but it is important.

Get organised! Think hard about storage options. When you can't find things you need, you get frustrated, and waste time. But be careful that you aren't organising new storage instead of getting rid of things. Remember, even though you can't see the things in the cupboard, they are still there.

Try to store things where you use them. It sounds obvious, but trailing to the utility room for something you need upstairs in the bathroom is a nuisance. Store clean towels in a trunk in the bathroom; tools in boxes or on racks in the shed, etc.

113. Commuting costs

commuting has costs in terms of money time, and the environment, but perhaps most importantly in terms of personal stress. There are alternatives that offer benefits to you, and your employer.

Outside major cities, which often have well-developed mass transit systems, an average of 70% of people commute to work by car, so gridlock in urban areas is inevitable. This, of course, results in stress and frustration – before the working day even begins!

THE COSTS OF COMMUTING: **FINANCIAL**
Given that employees pay £13 billion to commute 3,000 miles per year by car in the UK alone, it's mind-boggling to imagine what the expense might be across the whole world. Even workers who use public transport can find the costs of season tickets punitive. Businesses also pay a price in terms of mileage allowances, congestion charges and lost time as employees travel a further 1,600 miles for work purposes.

THE COSTS OF COMMUTING: **ENVIRONMENTAL**
In the mid-1970s, transport accounted for one fifth of the energy consumed in the developed nations. It now uses up one third and traffic accounts for roughly 25% of carbon dioxide emissions. This pollution can lead to health problems, especially in urban areas where air quality may be poor. Traffic also creates noise pollution, which is a significant factor in stress levels for local residents.

Here's an idea for you…
Think about going part time at work if it's financially possible, and spend the released time building up freelance work or your own home business. This will initially be hard work, but it will ease the path towards downshifting in the long run. Rather than going 'cold turkey', which can be a major risk, dip your toes in the water and see if you can find alternative ways to make money. I began to write when I was still teaching full time. Then I worked as a supply teacher and a sessional lecturer while I built up my writing career. My 'commute' today is to fall out of bed, tumble down the stairs, grab a coffee – and the day begins!

Major road building programmes – supposedly to decrease road congestion – affect the environment. New schemes are threatening countless sites of special scientific interest (SSSIs).

Commuting even turns semi-rural villages into 'dormitories' because the people leave in the morning and don't return until nightfall. This has implications for vital local businesses, such as shops and post offices, which may eventually be forced to close because of the lack of day-to-day customers. Looking round our nearest village during the day, you could be forgiven for thinking that a smart bomb had eradicated the five to sixty age group entirely, leaving a population of retirees and rugrats.

THE COSTS OF COMMUTING: HEALTH
You'll be thoroughly unsurprised to hear that commuting causes stress! Sitting in heavy traffic worrying about being late for meetings makes your stomach churn and your chest tighten. You are more likely to react aggressively to any incidents that occur. Long, busy or difficult journeys can make you feel fatigued and drained even before you reach work. Train journeys can be just as stressful as driving when trains are late, delayed or crammed with commuters. Almost half of people say that rush hour commuting is the most stressful part of their day.

The air pollution caused by all those commuting cars has been implicated in the rise in cases of asthma. The pollutants are generous: they do not just fall outside the car, covering passers by in a layer of grime, they also affect the driver inside the car. Quite apart from asthma making you feel wretched, there is a monetary cost. This obviously is felt by the health services, but it also has implications for employers. The number of working days lost due to asthma doubled in the decade between 1982 and 1992.

WHAT'S THE SOLUTION?

Quite simply, less commuting. Our work culture needs to change to allow more flexible working – not just so that people commute at different times of day, because that is only shifting the problem. Greater provision for working from home would improve matters all round, and the technology is available already. Laptop computers, virtually universal availability of broadband internet access and the gradual introduction of videoconferencing is making it easier for people to spend at least some of their working life at home, leaving 'office time' for *necessary* face-to-face meetings.

These arrangements would improve life for employees. It would also have knock-on benefits for companies: a less stressed workforce means potentially fewer working days lost to sickness and lower staff turnover.

114. Live by the seasons

Animals and plants work with the rhythms of the year. We humans are programmed to do the same.

If you live in the town and work in an office the seasons can pass by almost without you noticing. The only difference is that, if you're lucky, you get to potter in the garden for half an hour after dinner in summer.

It is a very different life for those who make an effort to fall into the routine provided by nature. You will learn to enjoy the changes that each season brings, and find yourself in tune with the turning wheel of the year.

Before electricity, our forebears lived like this year in, year out. Try this: for a week go to bed within half an hour of the sun setting and rise with the sun. In summer you will pack more in; in winter you will rest. Intuitively we know this is more balanced.

When things are not growing much, because it's cold and weather conditions are poor, you can spend time making things indoors, such as crafts to sell or perhaps a new chicken coop, put together in the shed or outbuilding. You can take time to reflect upon your successes and challenges, and think about how you can change things for the better. You can even – shock, horror – spend the time just reading or dreaming by the fire – it's allowed!

Our bodies respond to the seasons. As we add more layers of clothes to our bodies with the coming of the colder weather, we can feel a sluggishness setting in as the days shorten. Some people suffer from seasonal affective disorder, an extreme version of this feeling. Getting outside and

Here's an idea for you...
Keep a journal of the jobs you do in your garden, how they go and how the garden changes with the seasons. Add sketches if you feel like it. It may not be (nor may you want it to be) *The Country Diary Of An Edwardian Lady*, but flicking back over the pages will help you get a sense of the changing seasons and your place within their rhythms.

working in the garden, perhaps digging new beds, can help to improve this condition. It increases the amount of daylight that you are exposed to and this helps to alleviate symptoms.

Conversely, as the days lengthen, and the sap is rising in nature so fast you can hear it crackle, you experience a jolt of energy. Spring is approaching like a soft green juggernaut, and the gardener must spring into action.

You plant seeds when the soil warms – I tend to test it with my hands pressed against the soil, waiting for that 'bone cold' that seeps into your body from chilled earth to pass. I know other folks who walk on soil barefoot to see if the earth is ready – again, waiting for the ground to be warm enough so the cold doesn't chill the bones in your feet. I even knew one old man who tested his beds with his bare buttocks – he grew lovely crops, but strangely enough, no one wanted to eat them.

DON'T FORCE IT!
Just because you are used to buying strawberries from the supermarket in January doesn't mean you need to try to

393

grow them then, using all manner of cunning devices and light boxes. The Victorian kitchen gardeners, who supplied the 'Big House' with pineapples for the table, spent countless man hours on producing few fruits, at a huge financial cost after laying in complex heating systems in their conservatories. They did it basically to show off how rich the lord of the manor was. In Victorian times, pineapples had a great 'wow' factor. Today, although growing pineapples under cover is possible, the rather more humble kitchen garden created by the downshifter should arguably be more concerned with establishing a good supply of seasonal fruit and vegetables, and enjoying each season as it comes.

Think about it: salad crops begin to lose their allure as the days shorten and our bodies crave warming, stodgier fare. Traditional salad crops grow less well in winter, even under cover unless you add quite a bit of heat. But the root crops that grow so well, and are ready for harvest in the winter gain in value as we think about making warming stews and soups.

The gluts of produce you harvest as the season progresses can be frozen (either as they are or rendered into sauces), bottled, pickled or preserved. There's nothing more likely to evoke the pleasures of warmer days on a dark winter's night than a pot of home-made strawberry jam with the lid popped off to release the sweet fragrance of summer.

115. Boxes of delight

Many people today order organic vegetables to be delivered on a regular basis via 'brown box' schemes.

Organic food is no longer considered 'alternative', nor is it only to be found in health food shops. Organically produced food is a growing mainstream consumer trend. Whether it is disquiet about food production as a result of the BSE crisis, GM food and animal welfare, sales of organically produced food are growing quickly. The annual market share has risen to over a billion pounds in the United Kingdom alone. Many farmers are converting to organic methods as they become economically viable. We should not forget that intensive farming methods were a response by farmers pushed into over-production to make a living, using herbicides, pesticides and fungicides to produce as many crops as possible from their land.

Organic is a legally defined term. There are very strict guidelines to adhere to if you wish to become certified as an organic producer. These are laid down by both national and international laws. It is an offence to use the word unless a product has been certified by a recognised organic agency. In the United Kingdom, The Soil Association certifies up to 70% of organic food produced.

Farms gain organic status by going through a two-year conversion period, during which no chemical fertiliser or pesticides may be used. Once the farm is certified as organic, the farmer does not use such chemicals at all.

Food produced with less than 70% organic ingredients is not legally allowed to use the word *organic* on its label. If you are converting to organic status, your labels are permitted to say 'under conversion to organic farming'.

Here's an idea for you...

If you want to learn about growing with organic principles, join the Henry Doubleday Research Association or similar organic group near you. (Check out hdra.org.uk/links/index.php for worldwide information.) The HDRA has a scheme called the Heritage Seed Library (and other organisations have similar schemes). This is a system that organises the growing, saving and distribution of heritage seeds that are no longer available for sale. You can become a seed guardian and grow seeds, especially to save them for distribution.

Organic produce does seem to go 'off' sooner than other food, but that is down to the lack of artificial preservatives. The food does taste better, though! Organic food can be more expensive, but many community organisations are able to give you information about bulk-buy schemes that can make things more affordable. Brown box schemes can be a cheaper way to buy organic food because it comes straight from the supplier to you, cutting out the middle-man.

Defining idea...
'Manifest plainness – Embrace simplicity – Reduce selfishness – Have few desires.'
– LAO TZU

To join an organic box scheme as a consumer, you pay a fixed amount to receive a regular (sometimes weekly) box of organically produced fruit and vegetables. The produce available varies with the seasons, and vegetables may include carrots, potatoes, cabbage, sweet corn, kale, chard and salad vegetables amongst others. The fruit on offer includes strawberries, raspberries, grapes, apples and pears. Some box schemes e-mail customers with a list of what is ready to pick, so you can order what you want to be delivered. The food is fresh, and you are supporting local producers. Some suppliers will also deliver meat, wine, dairy produce and dry goods.

Search online for lists of these box schemes to find one that you think will best suit your needs.

BECOMING A SUPPLIER
Brown box schemes are mushrooming (sic) wherever there are organic growers. In Victoria, British Columbia, several brown box programmes deliver by bicycles fitted with specially designed aluminium trailers – and that's about as green as you can get.

If you would like to become a brown box scheme supplier, first you must apply for certification as an organic holding. This takes time. There are many certification bodies, such as The Soil Association. Your first step is to contact the organisation and request an initial application form. Once this is filled in and submitted, the certifying body will arrange to send an inspector for an initial visit, after which he or she prepares a report for the certification committee. If your application is approved, a certificate is issued. Organic registration and certification requires a licence fee.

You must keep detailed records of your food production processes if you wish to be certified as an organic producer. You will also be subject to annual and random inspections to make sure you adhere to organic production guidelines at all times.

116. Crop rotation

No, this doesn't mean you have to spin your carrots or turn your turnips. It just means that you don't grow the same type of crop in the same place every year.

Crop rotation reduces the chance that diseases will build up in one place, giving you sickly or diseased plants, and it stops the soil from becoming impoverished. Permanent crops (such as fruit bushes, fruit trees, many herbs, rhubarb, asparagus, strawberries, artichokes etc.) do not need to be rotated and can be planted anywhere in the garden that pleases you. You do not need to move them.

Annual crops that you harvest, and then they are finished (such as carrots and other root vegetables, potatoes, peas, beans, leeks, onions, beetroot, cabbage and greens) are different. You should establish four beds to give you a rotation. This sounds like a fuss, but it's worth it. If you grew cabbages, sprouts and cauliflower (members of the *Brassica* family) in the same bed every year, you would run the risk of the ground becoming infected with club root – a disfiguring disease that makes cabbages sickly, with, quite literally, roots like a club that cannot take in nutrients properly. If you move the bed that you use each year, you reduce the risk.

Likewise, carrots and parsnips should be moved year by year because they are susceptible to root fly. Leaving them in the same bed makes it more likely that the pests will build up to epidemic levels the next year. In the same way, onions should be moved to reduce the risk of onion fly. Rotation has been used for centuries to combat these problems.

Here's an idea for you...
Use potatoes as a starter crop for any bed before you begin your rotation because the bulky leafy cover blocks the light and stops many weeds from growing. Moving potatoes from bed to bed helps to keep weeds under control.

Another important reason for crop rotation is to stop the soil from becoming impoverished by losing nutrients particularly used by a given crop. Rotation makes use of goodness in the soil left over from previous crops.

When planning your beds, it makes sense to group plants from the same family together; it also makes sense to group plants together that enjoy the same growing conditions. By grouping together plants that have the same nutritional needs, you will be able to feed the soil specifically to suit each group. Peas and beans like lime and are greedy feeders, so lime may be added to the bed. Brassicas like fairly alkaline soil, so it would make sense for them to follow the peas and beans into a bed on the next rotation.

HOW TO ORGANISE CROP ROTATION – YEAR ONE
The most commonly used system is known as the three-bed system. The confusing thing is, it uses four beds. Basically, you divide your plot into four beds. The first bed is for your root vegetables, such as carrots, parsnips, Jerusalem artichokes, beetroot, etc. I like to add a leaf mould and plenty of comfrey 'tea' to this bed before planting. Make sure, if it's a new plot, that there are not too many stones in the soil. (But don't think you will ever remove them all – they breed! I just tell myself they are good for drainage.) Too many stones, and your root veggies will fork as they hit the stone, and grow into strange shapes.

The second bed is for brassicas: cabbages, broccoli, cauliflowers, Brussels sprouts, kale, etc. It should be fed with manure and comfrey tea as above, but I like to add a little lime to the mix the autumn before planting.

The third bed is for heavy feeders, so dig in as much manure as you can over the winter. In this bed you can plant potatoes, beans, peas, celery, sweet corn, marrows, courgettes, tomatoes, leeks and cucumbers.

The fourth bed is left to lay fallow. It is not the end of the world if you do not have room to leave a bed fallow each year; it just helps to avoid the soil becoming impoverished, and it reduces the risk of soil becoming infested with diseases.

YEAR TWO AND BEYOND...
Rotate the beds so that you now grow the plants from the first bed in the second bed, the plants from the second bed in the third bed, and the plants from the third bed in what was the fallow bed, leaving what was the first bed fallow for a season. (If you do not have a fallow bed, the plants from the third bed end up in what was the first bed.) In years three and four, everything moves on a bed again in the same way. In the fifth year, everything is back where it started in year one.

117. Vegetable matters

For many people, growing vegetables to feed their family is one of the main things they want to achieve when they downshift. There are many to choose from.

Fresh, crunchy carrots, lifted from the soil; earthy new potatoes and sugar snap peas – there is nothing like growing your own vegetables. They need a minimum of cooking and few sauces because their intense flavour is unlike any vegetables bought in the supermarkets, which will have been harvested and stored for days.

If you only have a small area, concentrate on things that are expensive to buy. However, there are some vegetables that should be found in most vegetable gardens.

Cabbages – Fresh spring cabbage, bursting with sweetness; curly leaved savoy, with its rich 'green' flavour – there are cabbages for all year round. Cabbages need rich, fertile ground heavy with manure. Seeds can be sown straight into the beds, or you can sow them in plug trays and transplant them outside in about five weeks.

Broccoli – Broccoli is quick to grow, and has so much more flavour when grown at home. The purple sprouting variety is delicious and unusual, but just as easy to grow. Broccoli needs plenty of space, with plants growing up to a metre tall! Broccoli seems to grow best when the seeds are sown in place, but they can be grown as plugs and transplanted.

Here's an idea for you...
Grow asparagus in well-drained beds for a delicious treat – savoured all the more when it is so expensive in the shops! Asparagus may be grown from seeds but for a quicker start buy crowns (basically roots). Keep them weed free and they will be productive for up to 20 years. The ferny fronds that grow after you stop cutting the spears (in early summer) are lovely for floral displays.

Cauliflowers – Cauliflowers can be temperamental things, prone to branching off. Keep them well watered, though, so they grow steadily and you will be rewarded with tight curds that make the most delicious cauliflower cheese you have ever tasted. Again, these will grow from seed or transplants.

Onion family – These like rich, well-manured soil. I put in more unusual varieties, such as red onions and shallots, but a good onion and leek bed will keep you in material for stews for months! You can grow onions from seed, but I grow mine from sets, which are small onions that put on growth quickly.

Carrots – Carrots grow well in lighter soils that must be kept weed free. If you want carrots without strange forks and shapes dig over the bed and make a fine, stone-free tilth. Sow carrot seed sparsely, straight into the ground – the more you have to thin them out, the more chance there is of carrot root flies getting a whiff and colonising your beds.

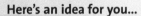

Parsnips – Parsnips also do best in a light soil, but they can be slow to germinate so don't lose heart. Don't water parsnips too heavily or they may tend to split and become soggy. The flavour improves with frost, so dig them as you need them.

Sweet corn – Sweet corn is an amazing crop to grow. It grows tall, up to 1.8 metres, and whispers as the wind blows through it. In fact, it can get a bit spooky if you have a large patch and you're a devotee of horror films! Sweet corn is wind pollinated and needs to be planted in blocks rather than rows so that the pollen can move from one plant to another.

Tomatoes – Strictly speaking, these are fruits, but they are generally eaten as a savoury so they are included here. Different varieties of tomatoes can be planted outdoors or in polytunnels and greenhouses. The seed should be sown indoors and the seedlings transplanted at about 15 cm tall. They are greedy feeders, so add organic fertiliser such as comfrey tea to your watering can. Home-grown tomatoes surpass the taste of any water blown varieties bought in the supermarket – even those bought on the vine at great expense. If you grow nothing else, poke some tomatoes in the conservatory.

Sweet peppers – Except in the warmest areas, these are best grown indoors. The soil should be rich and well manured, and the plants will need plenty of water. Green, orange and yellow peppers are just less ripe versions of red peppers. You will get six to eight peppers from most plants.

Lettuces – Lettuce grows best in light soils, with plenty of organic matter. Never allow them to dry out or they will be more likely to bolt (run to seed). Sow your lettuces in rows straight into the ground. Also, make successive sowings – i.e. sow a short row every couple of weeks to avoid a glut that needs using all at once.

118. Get fruity!

Fruit in jewel colours, ripened in the sun and brought straight to the table, what more could you ask for? Fruit is the crowning glory of any smallholding.

All too often, supermarket fruit flown in from the other side of the globe has very little taste. So what can you grow at home? Obviously this depends on your climate, but a huge range of fruits can be grown for the table wherever you live.

Apples – Apples can be grown on all manner of rootstocks, from large standard trees to small patio trees. They are easy to grow and give a good, reliable crop. If you are planting apple trees, check whether they need a pollinating partner and plant accordingly to ensure the tree sets fruit. Crab apples are great for making jelly and are full of pectin, a necessary ingredient for making jams set.

Pears – Pears need fertile soil. They can be grown as large trees or bushes. Check the rootstock to see the final size the tree will make before planning. There are self-fertile pears, but check – you may need to plant cross-pollinating varieties.

Quinces – This beautiful tree is a relative of the pear. Quinces are self-pollinating and easy to grow, and the fruits make a scrumptious jelly, or wine.

Nectarines and apricots – These trees need protection from frosts. If you live in a cold area, they may be better grown in a polytunnel or greenhouse. If the flowers appear very early, before there are pollinating insects on the wing, you have to pollinate the flowers yourself by tickling them with a soft paintbrush, transferring the pollen from one flower to another.

Peaches – Peaches
need well-drained soil. If you live in a cool climate,
they are best trained against a wall for shelter as they
are prone to frost damage. If they flower early, be
prepared to pollinate them with your paintbrush.

Cherries – You can grow dessert cherries –
sweet ones for eating – or more acidic cherries
for bottling. A mature tree can yield an amazing 35
kg of cherries!

Plums, damsons and greengages – These trees need deep, rich soil but give a great
return. A mature standard plum tree can give you 25 kg of fruit. The blossoms may
need protection from frost, but otherwise these are easy to grow and productive trees.

Strawberries – Strawberries like well-manured soil. They are easy to grow and give
a good crop, obligingly sending out runners that can be potted up to make new
plants. Once the strawberries have formed, and are ripening, protect them from
birds with fleece. I also use bottle cloches to keep slugs at bay. Straw is sometimes
put under ripening strawberries, but it can harbour slugs. Old carpet tiles are a
cheap and effective alternative.

Raspberries – Raspberries are a great fruit to plant, even if you have limited space.
They give a heavy yield, and can be trained up wires strung between posts, to make
a garden screen. After the canes have fruited they should be cut down to the
ground because the fruit is formed on year-old canes.

Here's an idea for you...
Why not grow grapes in your conservatory if you have one? Grapes can be grown
outside in warmer areas and some varieties can even be grown in cooler climes if
against a wall. If you are growing grapes inside, choose a large pot, or a
permanent indoor bed, and add plenty of sand to the soil.

Blackcurrants – Blackcurrants need rich soil. Enrich the soil with manure or compost when you plant them. They will grow in semi-shade or full sun, and prefer well-drained soil. Mature bushes can grow large, so leave about 1.5 metres around the plants. Blackcurrants fruit on year-old stems, so cut out old stems after they have fruited to encourage new fruiting growth.

White and redcurrants – White and redcurrants are variants of the same species. They fruit on old wood, so there is no need to prune. Although they do not fruit as heavily as blackcurrants, they produce enough to make a welcome addition to summer puddings and redcurrants make wonderful jelly.

Gooseberries – Gooseberries are easy to grow and give a good crop once they are mature. The bushes will crop for up to twenty years. They need well-drained soil but it must retain moisture. There are many varieties of gooseberries, including sweet red dessert berries and berries for cooking.

Blackberries – Cultivated blackberries are generally larger and sweeter than their hedgerow counterparts. They should be planted in manure-enriched soil and trained along wires fixed to a wall or strung between two posts. After they have fruited, old canes can be cut down to the ground.

Loganberries and tayberries – These hybrid berries should be treated like blackberries. They look like large, rather dark raspberries and are very sweet. They prefer slightly acidic soil and can be trained up a wall or on wires.

119. The undercover gardener

Providing plants with shelter from harsh weather allows you to extend the season and grow more tender crops. Bring on the 'polytunnel'!

Polytunnels can be moved to different parts of your land, and offer a large covered growing area at a relatively low cost – so what are you waiting for? I got a polytunnel for my fortieth birthday. For some women it's diamonds; for me, this was a long-held dream come true! If you live in a cool climate, a polytunnel allows you to grow many things you could not grow outside, such as aubergines, peppers, okra, and melons. The protection a polytunnel offers lengthens the season, and allows things to ripen, such as tomatoes, that may not ripen outside in colder regions unless the summer has been a good one.

In addition, polytunnels can provide a winter growing season. This can allow you to grow some of your favourite crops all year round. Heat loss from a polytunnel is greater than through a greenhouse, but with the correct choice of crops you will be able to grow through the winter.

Once you have decided to buy a polytunnel, you have the 'adventure' of erecting the beast to look forward to. Choose a flattish site, preferably in a sheltered area. Think about the services you might need, such as water and electricity. You can manage without electricity but having no water is much more of a problem. You will have to water daily, especially in hot weather. Soaker hoses pegged to the ground are one option. If you are not near a water supply, don't forget you can also use water butts to collect water for use in your tunnel. Incidentally, keeping water inside the tunnel is a good idea, particularly if you are watering seedlings. Water that is too cold can 'shock' your plants.

Here's an idea for you...
If you are buying a second-hand tunnel, do all you can to ensure you get to help to dismantle it. This gives you a good idea of how the pieces go back together. If you don't help to take it apart, you may find yourself with a puzzle you can't put back together!

Many suppliers now offer the option of heavier duty covers for exposed and windy areas. The first thing to do is to erect the hoops, digging them into the ground and adding cement to the holes on exposed sites. Then add 'hotspot tape' to the hoops to prolong the life of your cover. There are two ways to secure the cover to the framework. You can either bury the edges of the covering in a trench, or attach them to a wooden side rail. If you are burying the cover, make sure it is well secured in the earth. The strength of your polytunnel depends on how well you fix the cover to the ground.

There are various grades of cover for you to choose from. Go for the best you can afford. A standard polythene cover lets about 90% of the light through. Other grades are heavier; some let more light through. If you are undecided, go for standard polythene. Your cover will need to be replaced every five to seven years, and if you want to try something different at a later date, you will have the opportunity.

Enlist the help of a friend to erect your tunnel hoops – and another for adding the cover. Don't try to put the cover on when it is windy, or it may tear and you may end up

Defining idea...
'The thankful receiver bears a plentiful harvest.' – **WILLIAM BLAKE**

airborne! Adding the cover on a hot day is a good idea because the heat of the sun will soften the plastic and this will help to strain it into a tight fit.

You will also have to think about doors. Check that the door you choose is wide enough to get a wheelbarrow through, or you will find life gets rather difficult. Ventilation is another consideration – in summer, temperatures can easily exceed 100°F. Apart from leaving the doors open, you can spray water on the inside of your polytunnel to reduce the temperature. You can also provide additional shade by growing shade plants (I grow grape vines).

Once your polytunnel is erected, weed control becomes an issue. As soon as the cover is on, the weeds will shoot away. I have covered the floor of my tunnel with black weed-control membrane, because the field where it is situated is very weedy.

You can plant straight into the ground. I have planted nectarines and peaches straight into the soil, knowing they will be protected from the extremes of the weather. You can also grow plants in pots or raised beds.

120. Chicken run

Keeping hens is a delight. For very little effort, they repay you with eggs that taste better than any others you'll have eaten before, including free range.

Because you are getting the eggs fresh from the hen – and you know what she's eaten and how she lives – the golden-yolked beauties she gives you are without compare.

It is simple to get started with hens. Even a suburban garden can support a trio of hens – but don't buy a cockerel unless you want to be bombarded with complaints! Hens do not need a cockerel to lay eggs – you only need a cockerel if you want eggs to be fertile, for hatching.

Hens need secure housing. Whether in the country or in suburbia, foxes prowl daily, looking for unwary poultry. It is nice to see hens range freely, but I have seen too much carnage to allow that now, when foxes are sliding by during daylight whenever the fancy takes them. Instead, fence off an area and place the henhouse inside it. The hens have freedom, but are protected from predators. The fencing needs to be 3 m high, with around 10–15 cm of the mesh buried in the ground to foil a burrowing predator.

Here's an idea for you...
When you are clearing a bed after cropping, or establishing a new bed, give your hens access and they will clear the ground of green weeds and bugs such as slugs and wire worms. I have a simple timber frame, with chicken wire round the sides, that is the same size as my beds. I let the girls loose for a few hours and they help clear the ground while fertilising it at the same time.

The henhouse itself can be anything from a shed with a closable pop hole (hen exit) and run, to a triangular purpose-built arc. Your hens need somewhere to lay their eggs, and somewhere to roost. You need to have easy access to the eggs without disturbing the hens. Specially made hen sheds are available which have doors on the nesting boxes for egg collection.

You must provide your hens with bedding. (Ours like wood shavings best, but also lay in boxes lined with hay or shredded paper.) They need to be cleaned out regularly, and the bedding changed frequently to avoid an infestation with mites. Hens also need water on demand. We have a metal water dish but you can buy all manner of automatic troughs if you prefer.

Hens need grain, which you can buy cheaply in sacks from agricultural suppliers, or markets. This can be scattered on the ground for the hens to peck, but I prefer a metal hopper strung from the roof of the run. This is like a tube with a dish attached to the bottom. There is a gap in the tube, which you fill with grain. As the hens eat the grain, more drops from the full tube and refills the dish.

Hens also eat kitchen scraps and garden waste, and love fresh greens such as cabbage or kale. You can also offer your hens layer's meal or pellets. Hens that have access to ground in which to scratch are happy hens – they do not really need extra grit. If your hens are more confined, offer them ground shell grit. It helps if you can

Defining idea...
'To fulfill a dream, to be allowed to sweat over lonely labour, to be given a chance to create, is the meat and potatoes of life. The money is the gravy.' **– BETTE DAVIS**

move hens around to scratch at different parts of the garden from time to time because keeping them in one place for too long can lead to a build up of parasites. Hens also like an area where they can scratch in the dirt to give themselves dust baths. Apart from keeping them happy, it helps them to rid themselves of parasites.

Make sure you have everything ready for your hens before they arrive; it is easy to get carried away and have anxious hens waiting to get out of boxes as you are trying to assemble their shed.

We have had everything from recovering ex-battery hens to beautiful but tiny bantams and silkies. What you choose is up to you.

Hens – *Rhode Island Reds* are a good choice; they are a traditional breed and quite hardy. They lay beautiful brown eggs. *Light Sussex* is another hardy and attractive traditional breed. They lay large browny/buff eggs. *Marans* are beautiful, stripy birds that lay large speckled dark brown eggs (but not in huge numbers). The Light Sussex/Rhode Island Red cross is also popular. They lay well, and have the added benefit that their chicks are white if they are male, and reddish if they are female. If you are raising your own chicks from eggs, that is very useful – it can be downright impossible to sex chicks and very young hens.

Bantams – These are smaller than hens, and lay correspondingly smaller eggs – kids love them. My favourites are *Old English Game*. These look like a child's drawing of a hen, and the cockerels are hysterical – very fiery natured, but the size of a large crow!

5 ways to lose the yen to spend

'I am, therefore I spend' is the 21st century mantra. But psychologists believe that too much consumer choice is affecting our mental well being. Live free. Start here. Curb the shopping habit.

1. Limit choice. Research shows that when you make a purchase from a small number of items, you are more likely to feel good about what you've bought. Opt for small boutique shops rather than malls.

2. Stop window-shopping. Comparing costs and shopping around only makes you less happy with your final choice. Drifting around shops aimlessly makes you aware of what's out there and consequently more dissatisfied.

3. Get perspective. Experts say we are paralysed by so much choice. Very few purchases are worth sweating over. Think carefully before buying a house. Don't waste time agonising over which mobile phone. Make your choice. Move on.

4. Make Monday 'No-Spending Day'. Or any other day. But once a week try to get through the whole day without spending a penny. It's a challenge but it will teach you valuable lessons about what's important and what's not.

5. Give up comparing yourself with others. Give up being a 'maximiser' – having to have the best of everything. Learn to be a 'satisficer' – knowing what you've got is 'good enough'. Yes, you guessed it. Satisficers are a lot more content.

413

121. More honey for your money

Bees are fabulous, drowsy but industrious, they remind us of ourselves!
They also have the added benefit of providing honey and wax.

Got a problem? Had a major life event such as a birth, death or marriage? As tradition has it, you should go and tell it to the bees so it's handy if you've got some!

Before sugar cane became accessible to the developed world, honey was the sole source of sweetener. It's cheap to produce and is very saleable if you need to boost your income as a downshifter.

Before you even consider buying your own hives and colonies, join a beekeeping group and get experience. They are very friendly and will be able to steer you in the right direction when you are ready to buy your own equipment. Some groups sell off their old equipment too.

You need a bee-proof outfit, boots, a beekeeping hat with a face protector and gloves. Using a smoker before handling the hive or the bees is a sensible safety precaution – the bees don't like the smoke, but rather than making them angry it makes them react by filling their honey sacs, which in turn makes them bloated and sleepy. They are easy to remove from the frames then with a soft brush.

Here's an idea for you...
Don't forget that the wax is as valuable as the honey, so collect it. The wax is the cappings cut off the honeycombs. It can be made into wonderful fragrant polish and the best, sweetest smelling candles in the world. Melted with a gentle heat, you can add herbs, such as lavender flowers, to make the wax even more fragrant.

Your hive doesn't need to be a beautiful antique affair; bees are happy in a plainer home! It needs to have a waterproof roof, and a narrow slit for bees to enter the hive. It has a brood chamber, filled with frames for the bees to build the combs. Above the brood chamber are 'supers' – the boards removed to obtain honey. There is also a frame called a queen excluder, which comes between the brood chamber and the supers. 'Clearer boards' are used for separating bees and honey. These are placed between the brood chamber and the supers, and they have a one-way system – the bees can enter the brood chamber but can't get back into the supers. Within twenty-four hours, most of the bees will be clear of the supers – the part you remove to obtain the honey.

Put your hive or hives in a sheltered position, away from strong winds, and near to sources of nectar and pollen, such as a herb garden or patch of wildflowers. Placing a hive in your orchard or near your fruit bushes and trees has the added benefit of ensuring the bees pollinate your blossoms too.

415

relax and enjoy life

WHO'S IN THE HIVE?

In a colony of bees in a hive, there will probably be between forty and sixty thousand bees. There is, as every child can tell you, only one queen. She lays the eggs to maintain the colony. There are also a few hundred drones. These are male bees and exist to fertilise the queen. The thousands of worker bees collect the pollen and nectar. They are undeveloped female bees. When they are newly hatched, they feed the queen and the grubs, and help foraging bees unload their booty. After about fourteen to twenty-one days, they begin to work outside the hive, carrying water, pollen and nectar. They also clean the hive, removing dead bees, debris and faeces.

THE BEEKEEPING YEAR

In early spring, the queen bee starts to lay eggs. You should feed her with sugar syrup as natural food supplies will be low. Nectar and pollen plants are scarce, but you can think about planting food plants with catkins and early flowers especially for your bees to visit at this time of year. In late spring bees start to fly on warm and sunny days. They collect nectar and pollen from blossoms such as hawthorn, apple and plum trees.

By early summer, pollen and nectar supplies are high, and the queen is laying many eggs. By late summer, honey is ready to harvest. Remember to leave at least 16 kg of honey in the hive for the winter. You can remove between 9 and 18 kg per hive if you harvest your honey once a year. After the harvest, the bees will clean the nest, and you should start feeding sugar syrup or candy (icing sugar and water) for the bees to build up winter reserves.

122. Hitting the bottle

Ruby red raspberry jelly, glowing blackberry jam, squash and red onion chutney and peaches poached in brandy - preserves are the jewels of the downshifter's winter store cupboard.

With a few jars and a sturdy pan, you can bottle the essence of summer. Opening a jar and breathing in the fragrances transports you back to warmer days – and reminds you why you slowed down in the first place.

Bottling fruit – You can bottle fruit the innocent way – or the boozy way. Fresh fruit can be bottled in sugar syrup. Add about 225 g of sugar to 600 ml of water and stir it over a medium heat until the sugar dissolves. Bring the solution to the boil. Pack clean, trimmed fruit into a wet sterilised jar (boil them in water to sterilise them) and pour the syrup over the fruit. Tap the jar on the table to allow air bubbles to rise to the surface, and seal the lid. Keep the bottled fruit in the fridge.

Boozy bottled fruit lasts longer, and makes a lovely dessert with ice cream and meringues. Pack fruit such as raspberries, strawberries or currants tightly into a sterilised jar, and pour in cheap generic alcohol until the fruit is submerged. (Gin or vodka works very well, with the added bonus that the colour of the fruit totally infuses the alcohol; peaches go well with brandy.) Seal the lid, and this lasts for years, with the pungency of the fruit essence growing stronger over time.

Jam – Cook your fruit in a large, heavy-bottomed pan. With raspberries and strawberries, as well as other soft fruits, simmer the fruit until it looks pulpy and mushy. Add sugar (special jam sugar can be bought from the supermarket). The

Here's an idea for you...
Make herb vinegars and oils with the bounty from your herb garden. Simply add sprigs of washed herbs to sterilised bottles and pour in oil (olive oil works well) or white wine vinegar. The bottles look pretty stood in the window and the warmth of the sun helps the flavours to infuse. Use the oils and vinegars in salads and cooking.

amount you add depends on the type and amount of fruit you are using. Keep the jam simmering, but do not let it boil because it burns easily and tastes dreadful. To test for 'setting point' you can use a thermometer, or drop a blob of jam on a cold saucer – if the blob forms a skin you can wrinkle and push with your forefinger, it has reached setting point. If not, return the jam to the heat for a little longer.

When the jam reaches setting point, leave it to stand for 15 minutes. Then pour it into warm, sterilised jars. Cover the top of the jam with circles of waxed paper and seal the top with a lid or cellophane. It's worth decorating the jars if you are thinking about selling your jam. You should label the jam with the date it was made, and the ingredients.

Jelly can be made in the same way as jam, but the fruit pulp is sieved out, which seems a bit of a waste!

Chutney – Chutney is just savoury jam. I take my chosen vegetables (whatever is bountiful in the garden at the time, which makes for some odd mixtures but experimenting will help you find the tastes and textures you like) and simmer them in cider vinegar until the vegetables are tender when poked with a knife. Add soft brown sugar and simmer the mixture for about an hour until it thickens. The amount of sugar and vinegar you need depends on the type and quantity of vegetables you are using. Ladle the hot chutney into sterilised jars, then seal and label them.

Defining idea...
'I feel a recipe is only a theme, which an intelligent cook can play each time with a variation.' – MADAME BENOIT

Pickles – You can pickle some vegetables, such as onions or cabbage, without cooking them. Others, such as beetroot, need to be boiled before pickling to give them a palatable texture.

Prepare your vinegar – the pickling medium – well before you are ready to pickle your vegetables. I add my chosen spices to warmed vinegar, which I then put back into the jar for up to a month so the flavours infuse well. Slice and cook your chosen vegetables, and pack them into sterilised jars. Fill the jar with vinegar until the vegetables are submerged, and add a little more. Seal the lid. The vinegar is highly acidic and bacteria will not grow in such inhospitable conditions.

Fruit curds – Curds are easy to make and are a great way of using up excess eggs. They can be made with any citrus fruits, including oranges, limes, mandarins, kumquats, etc.

Grate the rind of three or four large fruits (obviously more if using smaller fruits). Squeeze the fruit and collect the juice. Put 120 g butter, 900 g sugar, the juice and grated rind into a pan. Heat the mixture until the butter melts and the sugar dissolves. Beat four eggs in a ceramic or metal bowl. Place the bowl in a pan containing boiling water to a depth of about 4 cm. Add the juice mixture to the eggs and mix well. When the mixture thickens, remove it from the heat and put it in sterilised jars. Keep curd in the fridge because it doesn't last too long.

419

123. Free and easy

Propagation is easy and the equipment you need is cheap and readily available. Go ahead, get new plants for free.

Vegetative propagation – making new plants from parts of growing plants (for example, taking cuttings) – is an easy way of freely obtaining new plants. This type of propagation gives you clones; plants identical to the parent plant. New plants grown from seeds are more variable.

TAKING CUTTINGS

This simple technique allows you to create new plants to replace plants that are becoming woody and past their best. It is a good way to produce young plants to make a hedge of lavender, box, or rosemary cheaply. You can take cuttings without harming the parent plant as long as you are careful and many cuttings can be taken from a single plant.

Don't worry if you do not have a greenhouse – cuttings can be grown easily on windowsills. All you need is the correct temperature and light levels for cuttings to grow successfully.

You can take cuttings for most plants, including perennials (and the tender perennials we grow as bedding plants). When you take cuttings, try to take them in the morning before the sun has much heat in it, so the plants are turgid and full of water. A wilting plant will not allow you to take successful cuttings.

Here's an idea for you...
Make new plants from conservatory and house plants, such as African violets
(Saintpaulia) and Cape primrose *(Streptocarpus)*. Take whole-leaf cuttings from
African violet, planting the stem in gritty soil. They root quickly. With *Streptocarpus*
you take slices of the long leaves, cut widthways. Insert the cut edges into gritty
compost, and tiny plantlets appear along the veins of the cut edges. These soon
grow into strong young plants and can be sold along with herbs, etc. at local sales
or markets to raise money.

As you collect the cuttings, put them in water or a plastic bag to conserve
moisture. Take them inside as soon as possible and insert them in cuttings
compost, several cuttings round the edge of the pot. Be careful not to allow them
to touch. You can insert the bottom of the cuttings in rooting hormone (available
from garden centres) first if you prefer, but many cuttings will root even without
the hormone.

After you've put the cuttings in the compost, water them well but use a fine rose
or a spray bottle because you do not want them to become waterlogged, or for the
water spray to dislodge them.

Once the cuttings have rooted you need to harden them off. That means you need
to get the plants accustomed to being outside in cooler conditions. Firstly, pot the
cuttings up. Remove them gently from the pot and tease the roots out so you have
separate plants. Pot them in plant pots filled with multi-purpose compost. If you
have a cold frame, the cuttings can be put inside to shelter them from the worst of
the weather as they become established.

SAVING SEED
You can save the seeds from 'dry seeded' plants such as beans, peas, poppies and
brassicas very easily. Wait for the seeds to mature on the plant if possible, then snip
the heads over a paper bag (not plastic because any moisture will be trapped and
cause the seeds to rot).

Defining idea...
'You aren't wealthy until you have something money can't buy.' **– GARTH BROOKS**

If you fear a long bout of rain as the seed pods or heads are coming to maturity, snip them a little early and hang them up in a dry, well-ventilated place. Once they are dry, again store them in paper.

Seeds from pulpy fruits, such as tomatoes, have to be dealt with differently. You can squash tomato pulp on kitchen tissue and wait for it to dry out before collecting the seeds in a labelled paper envelope – the labelling is important so you know what variety you have saved, and the date you saved it.

You can also pulp tomatoes and mix the pulp in a jar with a little water. Leave it to ferment, then scrape off the mouldy layer that forms. Drain and rinse the seeds with cold water and dry them quickly before storing them in paper.

Keep your seeds dry and cool to preserve them for as long as possible. Never keep seeds in a greenhouse or polytunnel because the heat will damage them.

The best thing I ever did, seed wise, was to join the HDRA (Henry Doubleday Research Association) seed library. Apart from helping to conserve old heritage varieties with your membership dues, joining gives you access to the seed handout once a year when saved seed is distributed. I have some excellent heritage varieties that cannot be bought in the shops from this scheme, and now save my own seed. You can, of course, swap seeds with other gardeners and become a 'seed guardian' where you grow heritage varieties for the purpose of saving pure-bred seeds for the library.

124. Home grown herbs

Herbs can be used to flavour food, make houses fragrant, dye cloth and 'doctor' animals, and humans! Every garden should have some.

It's little wonder aromatic herbs have been grown since humans first planted seeds – there are few pleasures more satisfying than a walk in the herb garden on a warm day. Besides the flavours and heady perfume, a herb garden also supplies you with a natural pharmacy. As with any self-administered remedy, though, take advice from a qualified practitioner as necessary.

Herbs generally like warmth and a sheltered spot. They also like well-drained soil, so prepare your soil by digging in plenty of grit to make it free draining (particularly if you are gardening on a heavy or clay soil).

There are perennial herbs – those that come back year after year – and annual herbs, which need sowing every year. Biennials are herbs that are sown one year and grow to maturity the next year before dying off and needing to be re-sown with new seeds. Read on to find out what you should grow, and why.

PERENNIALS
Mint is the thug of the herb garden. Be careful about where you put it because you will never be rid of it. For this reason, many people like to grow it in containers. Bees and butterflies love this herb when it is in flower. Mint is a good culinary herb – lovely on tiny potatoes fresh from the garden – and makes a soothing tea, which is especially good for upset or unsettled stomachs and pregnancy sickness.

Here's an idea for you...
Make your own teas and tisanes. Use a small bunch of fresh herbs (about 25 g) or a heaped teaspoon of dried herbs, and put them in a small teapot kept especially for the purpose. Add boiling water and leave the herbs to steep. Strain them carefully to avoid getting 'salad teeth'. An old-fashioned tea strainer works well. Alternatively, you can buy a 'tea ball' – a small, spherical metal strainer on a chain – that you fill with herbs and dangle in a cup of hot water.

Rosemary bushes grow best in light soils, but having dug lots of grit into my heavy clay soil they grow prolifically here. Rosemary leaves, rubbed from a fresh sprig, make a fabulous flavouring for tiny roast potatoes and Mediterranean roast vegetables. In addition, rosemary makes a good astringent – just make strong tea and wipe the liquid across your skin to tighten pores. Rosemary also makes a rinse for putting glints and highlights into dark hair, and is good for dandruff sufferers.

Sage is a downy leaved plant that grows easily. However, it can become 'leggy', with long woody stems. Rather than cutting back hard, and potentially damaging the plant, I tend to take cuttings yearly. Sage is great for sauces and stuffings and the tea is also good for throat infections, or used cold as a mouthwash. Strong tea, used cold, soothes insect bites and stings.

424

Defining idea...
'Like people, plants respond to extra attention.' – H. PETER LOEWER, plantsman

Thyme grows easily on light soils, but heavy soils need grit dug in. Bees love the flowers in summer. Thyme is a great culinary herb, and is also a fine tonic for the digestive system – not just for humans but also livestock. Thyme tea with honey also promotes sound sleep.

ANNUALS AND BIENNIALS

Basil is a delicious culinary herb. It is perhaps grown best in containers inside to protect it from the weather. Apart from the green variety, you can now buy seeds of purple and ragged edged basil for variety. Home grown, organic basil makes the most wonderful pesto. Basil also has mild antiseptic properties.

Borage is a beautiful plant that I would not be without – not least of all because the flowers look so great in a jug of Pimms! They are also delightful when crystallised in sugar for dessert decorations. The tiny blue star-like flowers are irresistible to bees and other pollinating insects, so include a few borage plants in your fruit garden. It self-seeds easily, so once introduced will be there to stay.

Angelica is an architectural plant said to be an aid to fertility – so go steady! However, it also has culinary uses. The stem can be candied in sugar – it is the source of the tiny expensive pots of green sweetmeat sold by confectioners for decorating cakes and desserts.

Parsley is ubiquitous as a culinary herb, but also has great stomach soothing properties. Tea made from this plant will help to soothe cystitis. Chewing a sprig freshens spicy breath, too. Parsley is also good for livestock, and can increase milk yields.

125. Self-sufficient in suburbia

Is it really possible to create a downshifted utopia without moving to the country? The simple answer is yes. It's all a matter of scale.

Obviously, a large garden is better than a small one if you want to feed yourself, but you can even grow food in an apartment without a garden if you use containers.

Starting off with a 'garden farm' could save you lots of grief – and money – later on if you decide that living off the land is not for you. It's a lot harder to decide that you've made a mistake after you've hauled your family miles out into the country, changed the kids' schools and left your old life behind. Garden farming gives you a taster of the delicious food you can produce but with a dose of reality thrown in, in the form of digging in all weathers and arranging for someone to 'hen sit' if you go away for the weekend.

Cottage gardeners in centuries past had riotously attractive gardens that mixed flowers, herbs and ornamentals with fruit and vegetables. As a garden farmer you can do that too. Many fruit and vegetables are attractive in their own right, such as brightly coloured ruby chard, purple orache and plump terracotta pumpkins. Rhubarb is a great foliage plant, as is curly kale. The best part is you can eat it all! The key to a productive garden in a small space is cunning. Use all of your surfaces. On fences and walls, grow climbing fruits, such as loganberries and tayberries, espalier apples and peaches. Grow food vertically, such as peas, beans and raspberries, to maximise space. Use willow wigwams to give you extra room. I plant

Here's an idea for you...
When you are planning what to grow, think about what your family likes to eat, and what is expensive. If you have a very small garden, avoid space-greedy plants such as cabbages, sprouts and main crop potatoes, but grow tiny earlies and specialities such as delicious pink fir apples in tubs. Concentrate on expensive delicacies such as asparagus, fruits and sugar snap peas. Be adventurous. Try rare varieties, such as those available from the Henry Doubleday Research Association seed bank.

a mixture of sweet peas and beans together – it looks pretty, and attracts pollinating insects too.

Plan your layout carefully, making sure to leave space for a compost heap and a greenhouse or small polytunnel – invaluable for starting off seedlings and overwintering tender plants. The position of your beds needs to be thought through. I prefer to garden in raised beds, which can be made cheaply and easily from planking, and even painted if you like. Don't feel that you have to plant in neat, well-spaced out rows either.

When I lived in London, I intercropped food in my small urban garden, which meant I planted fast growers such as lettuce in between rows of slower growers, so the space wasn't 'wasted'. I have also experimented with block planting rather than rows because it takes up less space, potentially. Grown either way, my crops have been fine and the productivity levels have not been noticeably different either way.

You will have to be careful that your small area does not become 'over-farmed' and worn out. It is even more important for you than for the larger scale smallholder to feed your soil to keep it rich in nutrients. Add lots of well-rotted compost and manure, and make liquid compost by dangling a hessian bag of horse muck into a water butt and leaving it to steep. Water your plants freely with this. I also keep a patch of the herb comfrey (which the bees love) for making liquid feed. Regularly

Defining idea…

'A garden is never so good as it will be next year.' – **THOMAS COOPER, journalist**

cut back the leafy parts of the plant and put them in an old bucket or tub. I weight mine down with a large heavy slab so the juice squeezes out as the leaves rot down. My dad makes his in an old tea urn so he can turn on a tap and the treacly goodness trickles out, ready to be added to water in a can.

You also have to be careful to think about crop rotation. It sounds like something only a large-scale farmer would worry about, but in a small space it is even more important. Basically, you should plan your beds so that you do not grow the same type of crop in the same bed season after season. A particular crop needs a particular type of nutrient, and leaching them from the same soil year after year will impoverish your soil. Not using crop rotation will also make the risk of disease more likely as soil becomes infested with pests or spores from diseased plants. It makes sense to change the bed you use on a yearly rotational basis to avoid these problems.

126. A lot of scope for growth

Allotments are of vital importance, giving many urban dwellers and those with tiny gardens an opportunity to become at least partially self-sufficient.

Following World War II, many thousands of acres of land – including parks – were put down to allotments. Sadly today many are disappearing under housing and road schemes.

I'm biased. I grew up on an allotment. No, my parents didn't dump me there to go feral! Rather, they were the proud owners of two and a half allotments that were brimming with produce and won prizes.

The pleasure of working in the fresh air and the satisfaction of harvesting food you have planted and cared for is almost primal. If you don't have a large garden, an allotment is the ideal solution.

Basically, an allotment is a rented strip of land for the cultivation of crops. Patchworks can be seen along railway embankments all round the country. They appear in unlikely places, tucked in among houses and poked in behind school playing fields. Allotments are administered by local councils, and if you want one you have to put your name on a waiting list for a plot. There are generally rules about what you can and cannot do on your plot. You will be given a list when you take over your allotment.

Here's an idea for you...
Many plots on offer will be choked with weeds. Divide the allotment into 'bite-sized chunks' and beg old carpets from friends and family. They will think you are mad, but the carpets can be laid on weedy areas to block the light and kill off weeds. This makes it easier to dig over and remove roots when the time comes to cultivate the area.

Allotments are no longer purely the province of the grey gardening brigade, although they are certainly still well represented. Huge ranges of people are now taking on allotment gardens to provide healthy food for their families. Many allotment holders have children who are given their own plot to grow child-friendly favourites such as pumpkins for Hallowe'en and huge nodding sunflowers. These are the gardeners of tomorrow.

It's so exciting when you get your letter telling you that you have reached the top of the waiting list and a plot is available. Don't get carried away, though. There are a few points you need to consider before you sign for the plot.

Think about site security. Vandalism and theft are heartbreaking realities on the allotments. It is truly awful to arrive at the plot to find your greenhouse smashed and your plants uprooted. Therefore, if possible, take a site that is fenced. If it is also surrounded by houses, that is a great help. Something else that deters the yobs is if the site is active, with people working their plots for much of the time.

Think about access to the site. Will you be able to walk there, or will you rely on a car? If so, what parking is available? If you have to walk miles with tools and compost – and even heavy crops – you will soon get fed up.

Is there a supply of water near your plot? You can (and should) add water butts to your plot, but a source of water nearby will help to get you started. It's also the allotment equivalent of the office water cooler, where you get to meet old hands and learn about what does and does not grow well on the site.

If you have a choice of plots, don't take on a larger size than you can handle. It is easy in a fit of enthusiasm to take on a huge plot and find you cannot cultivate it all. A word of warning – don't try to cultivate the whole plot at once; get an area up and running – planted and productive – before you move on to the next area. Otherwise, you may get discouraged and give up as you are not seeing any benefits. A few strawberries or fresh carrots will keep your spirits up and get you motivated.

It is worth adding a small secure shed to your plot to hold your tools because it gets annoying to have to carry your tools backwards and forwards. Adding a small primus stove and a kettle to your shed means you have somewhere to ruminate and survey the land, too! Sheds can be bought cheaply second-hand.

A second-hand greenhouse would also make an invaluable addition to the allotment. This extends the growing season and gives you a place to start off seedlings. Again, these can be bought cheaply. If possible, buy a second-hand greenhouse that you have to take apart because you will be able to make notes about how to put it back together again.

Defining idea...
'Happiness is not in the mere possession of money; it lies in the joy of achievement, in the thrill of creative effort.' **– FRANKLIN D. ROOSEVELT**

431

127. Self-contained

Even a tiny garden, or an apartment with a yard, can be used to grow edible produce if you know what containers to use.

Containers are a convenient way to grow many tender and specialised plants. If you have limited space, container growing is a must. No space is too small to grow food. It can be grown wherever sunlight penetrates. You can grow plants in pots on windowsills, in conservatories, on balconies, in windowed stairwells and in roof gardens. If you live in an urban area this is even more important, because you need to build yourself a green oasis of calm that you can slip into to slough off the stresses of the day along with the grey grime of city living.

You have to be inventive and adaptable to make the most of your limited area. Use all of your vertical spaces, by fixing trellises for growing peas and beans – they don't need much floor space. Use hanging baskets for herbs and tumbling cherry tomatoes. And build window boxes for herbs and salad plants.

The great thing about container gardening is that you can start small, adding to your collection whenever you are ready. Try to grow a small amount of a wide variety of crops until you find what works, and what your family enjoys.

CONTAINERS
You can use anything that will contain compost. Old plastic catering-size food containers are ideal and available very cheaply – look in classified ads for details. Avoid non-food containers in case they have been filled with anything toxic.

Here's an idea for you...
Make your own 'growbags'. Even though the commercial varieties are cheap, they are of variable quality and may not be organic. Fill strong rubble sacks (from a builders' merchant) with your own home-made compost, worm casts, rotted manure and leaf mould mixed with a little soil. Seal the end with duct tape – it's waterproof and strong. Lay the 'growbag' on its side in its final position and use a craft knife to make a slit or window in the side. Then plant your tomatoes, cucumbers or whatever you fancy.

Recycled sinks – not just the expensive antique variety, gorgeous though they are – together with old dustbins and tyre piles can make fabulous yard containers. They are big enough for you to grow fruit trees. Basically, anything that is big enough for the plant you want to grow is fine. Look at growth charts to work this out. Use your imagination – family and friends will likely have containers they are finished with that will be useful too.

Wooden troughs are easy to build from rough wood and can be painted to add rustic charm. These can contain anything from salads to climbers such as peas and beans. Recycled plastic containers can be bought cheaply from gardening centres and they are light enough for use on a balcony or in a roof garden. Baskets lined with polythene are also useful and light, and they are decorative too. If you use clay or pottery pots, make sure they are frost resistant if you intend leaving them outside during the winter.

Be sure to clean containers thoroughly to make sure you do not transfer any diseases from year to year.

COMPOST
If it is humanly possible, have a compost bin. These are often available at a subsidised rate from your local council, so check it out. Worms are also a great

Defining idea...
'There are no gardening mistakes, only experiments.'
– JANET KILBURN PHILLIPS, gardener

addition to your compost making efforts. You can buy special kits or alternatively you can buy brandling worms (Eisenia foetida) from a fishing supplies store and add them to a container yourself. You can use any container with a tap at the bottom – adapting old wine-making equipment works well. The tap allows you to drain the liquid (essentially, worm pee) from the bottom of the container. This makes a great feeder to spray on plant leaves. Dilute 1:20 with water and put it in a spray mister.

The container needs a shelf inside for the worms – a piece of wire mesh works well. The worms have to be kept out of liquid they produce or they will drown. Add about 1.5 to 2 kg (dry weight) of shredded newspaper to the bin after it has been moistened with water. Then add the worms. Give them kitchen waste to feed on and remember they aren't keen on citrus or spicy foods. Add shredded newspaper as necessary to stop the container becoming anaerobic and smelly. Keep a lid on the top to exclude flies.

The worm bin should be totally emptied twice a year, after leaving it for a fortnight without adding any new material. The worms will wriggle to the top, and are easily removed to a temporary pot whilst you remove the rich matter left in the bin. You then start again with fresh newspaper.

128. Food for free

canny people can live off the land. They hunt all over for the bounties of nature — the ancient ancestors of the cultivated plants we eat today.

Hedgerows, meadows and streams even today yield a wide variety of food and useful plants for the informed collector – just make sure you know what you are picking!

Marsh samphire, blewits, ramsons, pepper dulse – the sensual indulgence of these foods can be heard as you breathe their names. I have been a fan of wild food since I nibbled shiny red 'bread and butter' – or hawthorn berries, to you – on the Sussex Downs as a child, their sweet-potato flavour bridging the gap from the early afternoon until dinnertime.

Obviously, you have to be careful that the food you gather is the food you think it is – and not just with gathered fungi. Studying field guides and attending the proliferation of courses run by local wildlife organisations are great ways to avoid mistakes. You also have to be careful that the food you gather is not near to a road, and thus tainted with lead from traffic. Ensure, too, it comes from an area untouched by agricultural chemicals. You should never uproot the plants, and only take small quantities of leaves, etc. from any one specimen.

Even bearing these warnings in mind, the fun that can be had – and the flavours to be discovered – make a foray for wild food a rewarding and pleasurable activity.

Here's an idea for you...
If you are a little worried about collecting wild food, grow some on your own patch. I love wild strawberries, with their tiny sweet fruits. I have grown a patch from seed and they now merrily romp in the shade of my willows. I also grow wild rocket because I like to gather it in large quantities. And I grow violets and primroses specially (I don't gather wild ones, which is undesirable and prohibited) so I can crystallise them for sweets.

Coming home with a basket of wild food ready for the kitchen makes me feel in touch with my pagan forebears who stepped on the earth lightly, and were rewarded for their stewardship with an overflowing wild store cupboard.

IN THE WOODS
Sweet chestnuts, with their spiky, silky cases, are a great source of protein – and can be gathered in parks as well as woodlands. Take them home and roast them – roast chestnuts are a delicious winter tradition. They are also lovely candied (poached in sugar syrup) or made into a purée, which is a tasty and protein-rich pie filling when mixed with onion and mushrooms.

Fungi may be gathered and eaten, so long as you are very careful about identification. There are over 100 types of edible mushroom in the UK, including chanterelles, blewits, oyster mushrooms and ceps. There are also a few poisonous varieties; some fatally so, such as the amanitas. Although I have been on organized fungus forays and enjoyed the delicious 'fry up' at the end, I only gather the mushrooms *Agaricus campestris* – field mushrooms – that grow in my fields as a result of all the horse dung that accumulates there.

Defining idea...
'On the motionless branches of some trees, autumn berries hung like clusters of coral beads, as in those fabled orchards where the fruits were jewels...' – **CHARLES DICKENS**

AT THE BEACH

Many types of seaweed are edible, including carragheen, dulse, kelp and filmy green sea lettuce. Perhaps the most famous is laver, the type eaten as a delicacy in parts of south-western Wales and Japan. In Wales it is made into a purée and sold in cakes called laverbread, which are often fried.

IN THE HEDGEROWS

Hazelnuts fresh from the hedgerow are a delight. Careful as you pick them, though, because they grow in small clusters and are easily shaken to the ground, to be lost for ever in the inevitable tangle of briar and nettles growing below. Wild rowan berries (*Sorbus aucuparia*) can be gathered to make into tart jelly, as can vitamin C laden rose hips.

IN THE MEADOWS

My absolute favourite 'meadow food' is wood sorrel (*Oxalis acetosella*), with its shamrock-shaped, emerald green leaves. It tastes sharp and fresh in a salad, and has been eaten in this way (and in sauces) for centuries. Apparently, the food police decree that you should not consume too much because it contains oxalates (salts that it is not good to consume in large quantities) but a little of what you fancy, as they say, does you good.

Fat hen (*Chenopodium album*) is another great wild vegetable – and not just for the name. It is one of the first plants to colonise ground disturbed by road building, new housing estates, etc. It has been used as a food since Neolithic times and is largely eaten in the same way as spinach. It is loaded with iron, having more than Popeye's favourite.

129. Find your balance

How's your work-life balance? Perhaps you need to explore the benefits of setting clear priorities in your working and personal lives and then to sticking to them no matter what. It might be time to get to grips with the merits of living a portfolio life.

Wandering around a graveyard, you're unlikely to come across a tombstone with an epitaph that reads: 'I wish I'd spent more time in the office.' OK, so it's a bit of a glib, overused line, but the fact is that in any sane, balanced life, we'd want to spread our energies between income generation and the other things that matter to us.

The concept of work–life balance started to emerge in the 1980s, I suspect in part as a reaction to the macho, lunch-is-for-wimps, work culture that all too many companies seemed to be promoting at the time. In *The Age of Unreason*, management guru Charles Handy used the term 'portfolio living' as a way of describing how the different bits of our life fit together to form a balanced whole.

What are these different bits? Handy identified five elements in the typical portfolio, namely:

- **Wage (or salary) work** – i.e. money paid for time given.

- **Fee work** – i.e. money paid for results delivered.

Here's an idea for you...

If you decide to put a work portfolio in place, it would make sense to review it periodically to see how it's working for you. For each element in your portfolio, make a note under the following three headings.

- Amount of income generated

- Time commitment (number of days)

- Degree of work satisfaction (give the work a rating out of 5 where 5 = extremely satisfying and 1 = not satisfying at all)

If you're generating high income from something and getting high satisfaction as well, you're onto a winner. On the other hand, something which generates little income and low satisfaction should be on its way out of your portfolio.

- **Homework** – that whole catalogue of tasks that go on in the home – cooking, cleaning, ironing, home repairs, looking after children, etc.

- **Gift work** – e.g. work done for free outside the home, for charities, local groups, neighbours, local schools, etc.

- **Study work** – e.g. training for a sport or a skill, learning a new language, pursuing a qualification.

More pragmatically, Handy pointed out the dangers in depending on a single source of income (i.e. the day job) and contrasted this with the benefits of having a work portfolio in which we would maintain a number of different income streams. Some of us might also have other income sources, perhaps access to a pension, or some income from letting property. The key point is that having multiple sources of income gives us a financial resilience that a single source can't.

439

Defining idea...

'Few would these days put all their money into one asset, yet that is what a lot of us have been doing with our lives. That one asset, that one job, has had to work overtime for we have looked to it for so many things at once – for interest or satisfaction in the work itself, for interesting people and good company, for security and money, for the chance of development and reality.'
– CHARLES HANDY, *The Age of Unreason*

How can we put together a portfolio? At the heart of the portfolio philosophy is the recognition that most skills are saleable if you want to sell them. If you love designing houses, or gardening, or cooking, or car maintenance, or photography, there is a market out there somewhere that you could tap into.

Likewise, any area of specialist knowledge can be turned into a money earner, through lecturing or giving talks, or perhaps as a basis for buying and selling stuff. I have a friend who makes a tidy sum buying up old hi-fi equipment, repairing it where needed and then selling it on eBay.

Any one of us can use our own particular portfolio to build the life we want. Of course, circumstances and needs change – and one of the major strengths of the portfolio approach is that it enables us to respond to change.

440

130. Car-boots in cyberspace

Selling your unwanted stuff no longer needs to involve car-boot sales, use the internet and you can get more customers and better prices.
Read on

As I write, eBay has almost 15 million British users buying and selling some 10 million items every month. More than 68,000 people earn their primary or secondary income from trading on ebay.co.uk. eBay doesn't have this lucrative second-hand market to itself any more. Amazon has started its own Marketplace offering private sellers' goods, but at fixed prices. Both eBay and Amazon Marketplace offer you an opportunity to get your hands on a potentially tidy source of income.

There are two routes into online selling. You might just want to declutter your home a bit and raise a few bob. In which case, perhaps you could start by checking out your CD and DVD collections, old paperbacks, traces of abandoned hobbies, old hi-fi/kitchen/ gardening equipment – in fact anything that you no longer have a need for. The glory of offloading your second-hand goods and chattels is that any income you make is almost certainly a tax-free zone. Everything you make you can keep.

Alternatively, you might want to consider setting up a fully fledged online business. For many people who have taken this route, their business is based around a hobby or passion, something they know a thing or two about. Six-figure incomes can be achieved from a spare bedroom kitted out with a PC, an internet connection and a digital camera.

Here's an idea for you...
internet auctions are also creating entirely new businesses. Here's one to try: set up a drop-off service where busy people and computerphobes can leave their unwanted items. Then auction them on eBay for a cut of the proceeds. It's a sort of online version of a local auction house, but one with global reach and where the saleroom never closes. A chap called Randy Adams set up just such a business in the San Francisco area. His first AuctionDrop store opened in March 2003 and by the end of December he had sold $1.6m of goods.

Whichever route you might consider, you'll want to make sure you get the best possible price for anything you're selling. Here are a few tips based on some research in the US, which revealed that the price of an item sold on eBay depends on factors that have nothing to do with its book value.

Ordinarily, in an open auction, similar items fetch similar prices. With eBay, however, different rules seem to apply. For example, items sold at a weekend commanded a price around 2 per cent higher than the same item sold on a weekday. The research suggests that bidders have more time to consider and make their purchases at weekends, and may therefore decide to pay more.

An even larger mark-up emerged with adverts for items that were accompanied by pictures. Items with pictures typically sell for around 11 per cent more than similar items without pictures.

The researchers also found that the seller's eBay 'reputation score' had an effect. Every time buyers make a purchase, they are invited to rate the transaction as a positive or negative experience. The more positives a seller can boast, the more likely this is to result in the buyer paying a premium price. High-rated sellers typically achieved around 7 per cent better prices than low-rated ones.

Defining idea...

'I think this is one of the most misunderstood things about E-commerce. There aren't going to be a few winners. There are going to be tens of thousands of winners. This is a big, huge complicated space, E-commerce.' **– JEFF BEZOS, Amazon.com founder**

Armed with this inside dope, and fuelled by the contents of your attic, cupboards and shelves, you have everything you need to join the eBay gang. As well as the fiscal benefits, it's just fascinating to watch the tactics adopted by bidders, particularly as the end of the auction approaches – at a weekend, and with a photo, of course.

SOME TIPS FOR EBAY SELLERS

Give a complete description

To avoid questions later, try to anticipate questions people may have about the item. Be sure to specify who will pay for shipping. Don't forget to mention the location of the item and whether you'll post internationally.

Provide terms for sale

To make sure you get paid for the items you sell, include the payment method and postage terms in your listing. Accepting more secure forms of payment (such as credit cards) gives you more ability to verify the buyer. You may want to insure the item before posting.

Keep your auction going

Many eBay bidders wait until the very last minute to place a bid. That means you may be missing out on additional bids if you end your auction early.

Source: http://pages.ebay.co.uk/help/sellerguide/selling-tips.html

131. The write stuff

Many of us dream of writing for a living or as a way of leaving our mark on the world. But the blank page can stop creativity in its tracks.

The blank page is a monster, far worse than any Hollywood nightmare. The blank page wages a war of fear and ridicule. It taunts you, it tells you it will never be filled, that anything you write will be a mere shadow of what's gone before. But be brave, take the plunge, and remember that this villain can be vanquished with a simple stroke of your pen.

FIRST STEPS
A common mistake when facing up to this immense white expanse is to believe that you can decorate it with a masterpiece straight away. The blank page wants you to think like this, as it's the first step to obliterating your confidence and self-respect. If you try to go for the big one first time, if you think you can wipe the smug expression from that blank with an instant work of sheer genius, then chances are after a few lines you will surrender and spend your days as a remorseful prisoner of war.

A LITTLE AT A TIME
Most successful writers will tell you that a conflict with the blank page must be a war of attrition, not a full-on nuclear strike. The only path to victory is to gradually convert that white expanse into a page of words, your words. They don't have to be a masterpiece. In fact, they don't even have to be a story, or a poem, or a screenplay, they just have to make sense to you. Begin with random words and convert them into sentences – let them lead you. Before you know it, the blank page has shrunk,

Here's an idea for you...
Do this every day. Take a blank sheet of paper, and just write for a set time at a set time. With each passing day your sketches should become more solid and less hesitant, as your confidence builds. Pick random subjects to write about and make sure you include the details, however small. When you feel up to it, start to put the bits and pieces you have been writing into a short story or a poem. You should find that the details you thought were unnecessary enable you to paint a vivid picture of something you've always taken for granted..

its taunts are fainter, mere whispers, and then it's gone. Don't think about what you're writing – nobody but you is ever going to see it – just keep that pen moving or those keys tapping until your old adversary has vanished. Those stuttered fragments will become paragraphs, then pages, and after a while you'll wonder why on earth that innocuous white sheet of processed wood was giving you the cold sweats.

GET OFF RUNNING
OK, it's easy for me to say 'just write', but if you are still sitting facing the first page of your notepad or that virgin screen, then it may not seem so simple. The first thing to do is to get rid of the idea that you are about to start writing a finished piece. Don't try and carve out a first line of absolute genius, or write the beginnings of an epic tale you've had in your head for years, as you'll be putting yourself under an unhealthy amount of pressure.
Instead, start writing a few words about the last relative that visited, your most memorable holiday, the state of your neighbour's garden, the last great argument you had.

445

Defining idea...
'Writing is easy; all you have to do is sit staring at a blank sheet of paper until the drops of blood form on your forehead.' – **GENE FOWLER, Writer and Director**

Take practically any topic you like – if your mind is still blank, make a note of any sounds you can hear or sights from your window, or just open a dictionary at a random page and pick the first recognisable word. And once you've got that subject just start writing. Don't stop, don't edit, just gear yourself towards writing as much as possible in four or five minutes. Once you've started charging forwards, you'll find the words come more and more easily.

132. Finding inspiration

You may think your muse has passed you by but it might be that she's the kind of girl who whispers rather than shouts. Ideas are everywhere, you just need to learn how to spot them.

So, you've cleared your desk, opened your notebook or a blank document on your computer, and are ready to write. But suddenly your mind is devoid of inspiration and you begin to panic. What on earth are you going to write about? While there is more to being a writer than just a good idea, without an inspirational seed for your novel, screenplay or poem you are like a knight in armour with no monster to slay and no sweetheart to rescue.

BUSES
For many of us, ideas are a lot like buses. You wait ages for one to come along and when it finally does it breaks down. Then, when you're walking home in the rain, three more turn up and everybody else jumps on board. Of course you may be one of the lucky ones, and already be nurturing the seed of an idea. But for the majority of writers, it's a difficult truth that it takes more than motivation alone to produce a masterpiece.

DON'T IGNORE IT
If you have been inspired, don't ignore it. A great many writers turn away the ideas that flit around in the back of their head, begging to be put on paper. Why? Because the idea may not fit in with the self-image they want to nurture, or because they would like to write something more 'literary'. If you do this, you may

447

Here's an idea for you...
Stuck for something to write about? Open your eyes and look around you. There is material everywhere. Read old diaries or browse through your notebooks. Read newspapers and magazines for fascinating stories. Sit in a café and gaze out of the window. Listen to conversations, invent stories for the people who walk past and write them down. It may take a while, but if you pay attention to the world around you, then inspiration will come. The trick is not to go looking for the idea of a lifetime. Sit back, relax, soak up your surroundings, listen to the scraps of thought that flutter through your brain and before you know it you'll be running round the block screaming 'Eureka!'.

be passing up a good thing. Don't ignore that persistent tug; take the bull by the horns and see where it leads.

The ideas that flutter in the half-light of our conscious mind are those that make us think, that make us laugh, or cry, or scream. Otherwise you would have forgotten them long ago. These ideas may be nothing more than a scene, a single character, perhaps something as small as a phrase. Or they might be an entire plot line, an epic journey that you have been mentally planning for years. But whether large or small, these threads are important to you, and because of this you have the ability to weave them into a work of art.

The writers I have known who have passed up these faint cries for attention have often gone on to pen strained and sterile work because the ideas they eventually work with don't engage them. Chances are, the ideas you may already possess, even if they are barely visible, have a personal significance. If you give them a chance, you will be able to draw on a wealth of personal emotion and experience in order to produce a literary work that truly connects with its readers.

BUT...

But what happens if you are champing at the bit and raring to go, but have nothing to write about? Don't worry. Ideas are the product of your experience, bits of your life, inspiration from books, films, plays, all mingled together in a turbulent alchemical mix. This bubbling cauldron of images, words, sounds, smells and thoughts is constantly generating tendrils and strands that appear as random ideas or dreams. Occasionally these strike a chord in our mind and germinate to become inspiration. This isn't always a flash of pure genius, so learn to watch out for the little things, the tentative thoughts, the shy visions – chances are the smallest of seeds will grow into an idea if properly nurtured.

What this means is that although you may not have an idea per se, you do have a vast wealth of experience to draw upon. This bank of material is unique – the people you have loved, the places you have visited, the games you have played – nobody else has lived the same life. Start to peel back the years and look at the vast web of activity that is your life, and the ideas will begin to roll in.

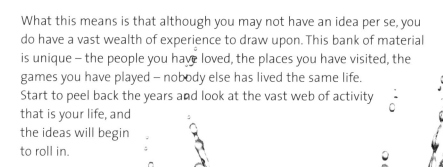

133. Four wheels bad

A great way to slow down is to ditch your motor, it'll lead to reduced costs, decreased stress and an eco-friendly virtuous glow.

Cameron Diaz, Leonardo DiCaprio and Thandie Newton all have one thing in common, apart from being famous: they ditched their petrol-guzzling celebmobiles in favour of a low carbon hybrid car, in their case, the Toyota Prius. Other stars, including George Clooney, are going all electric with models such as the Tesla Roadster.

While Hollywood celebs seem to be embracing the new breed of eco cars, the rest of us are rather trailing behind. A hybrid or electric car may be too expensive or not suit our day-to-day needs for various reasons, but there are still things we can look out for when buying a new car.

The best route is to choose the smallest and most fuel-efficient vehicle possible. This will also save money in road tax and other running costs. Look for one with the lowest CO_2 emissions of its class and which meets the new Euro IV standard.

Many new car makers are giving plenty of useful information to help you make your choice, such as eco labels that shows its CO_2 figure and estimated annual running costs, and possibly even its life cycle assessment, which examines the whole impact of the vehicle from factory to final disposal.

Here's an idea for you...
If you live in a town or city, joining a car club is a brilliant way of cutting down on petrol emissions and will save you loads in running costs as well. You only hire the car when you need it, but this can be by the hour, week, month or longer. Membership gives you access to a pool of cars near your home, which you can book in advance or on the day, and covers road tax, insurance, servicing, maintenance and valeting. Most car clubs are run on very simple lines – you can log in online (or by phone) and reserve your car on the spot. A PIN number enables you to drive the car away.

Driving more environmentally friendly vehicles can help reduce emissions, improve people's health and save money.

Manufacturers now produce low-carbon electric, hybrid and dual-fuel vehicles. Some of these low carbon vehicles also have financial benefits such as lower tax, discounts on city congestion charge, cheaper fuel options and lower running and maintenance costs.

Electric vehicles produce no emissions – CO_2 or toxic emissions – but need to be recharged often and can't travel long distances. But they are great in cities, on set routes or for short trips.

Hybrid vehicles switch between petrol (or diesel) and electricity. Because they use far less petrol than traditional vehicles, they produce much lower CO_2 and other emissions. Most big car manufacturers are planning to introduce a hybrid model in the next few years.

LPG vehicles run mainly on LPG (liquid petroleum gas), which

451

Defining idea...
'Environmentally friendly cars will soon ... become a necessity.'
– FUJIO CHO, Toyota Motors

produces much lower emissions – about 10% to 15% less CO_2, 75% less carbon monoxide and 85% less hydrocarbons – and is much cheaper than unleaded petrol.

These aren't the only options. More vehicles are being produced that emit less CO_2 and other pollutants. Specialist magazines, websites and Government bodies will have useful comparison data.

ECO-DRIVING

The way you drive your car also has an impact on the environment. But if you're eco-savvy, emissions and fuel consumption can be reduced by up to 25%.

- Drive off straight away rather than leaving the engine to warm up.
- When the engine is cold, journeys of less than 2 miles pollute by up to 60% more per mile than a hot engine.
- Use higher gears as soon as traffic conditions allow. Minimum emissions happen between 40–60 miles per hour and increase when you drive faster.
- Regular maintenance will reduce emissions.
- Restarting the engine uses less energy than ten seconds of idling, so switch off if in a long queue.
- Hard acceleration and sharp breaking use more fuel as well as being more dangerous.
- Plan ahead: choose quiet routes, combine trips and car share.
- Don't carry unnecessary weight on the roof or in the boot.
- Make sure your tyres are inflated to the right pressure and reduce greenhouse gas emissions by 5%.
- Cut back on onboard electrical devices and air conditioning to reduce fuel consumption.

134. Is there anybody out there?

Feeling green but lonely? Don't fret, there are sure to be loads of like-minded people in your neighbourhood, all you have to do is find them!

Warning: turning eco is highly addictive. Once the green bug bites, you'll want to get into the whole environmental thing in more depth, meeting other like-minded eco 'worriers', finding out more information and discovering how your local community is helping to change things.

The first thing you could do is nip down to your local library or log onto your local council's website and find out if there are any environmental groups in your neighbourhood. These could be anything from local conservation volunteers or hardline campaigners – it's up to you how far you want to go.

For instance, if you're just dipping your toe in the eco water, you could get in touch with an organisation such as British Trust for Conservation Volunteers, (www2.btcv.org.uk), which runs regular one-day conservation tasks all over the UK, during the week and at weekends.

There is sure to be a branch near you, and you can join in every once in a while or every week – the choice is yours. There's no need to book in advance – just turn up at the meeting point on the day.

Here's an idea for you...
Find out if your neighbourhood runs a local skill-swapping service, and if it doesn't, then start one yourself! Babysitting, plumbing, typing, web design, hire of tools and equipment, gardening or dog walking: you name it, your neighbourhood is sure to offer it in some shape or form. Sometimes called LETS – Local Exchange Trading Systems or Schemes – these community-based networks allow people to exchange all kinds of goods and services with one another, without spending a penny. You can set up a system of community credits, bypassing the need for direct exchanges. People earn credits by providing a service, and can then spend the credits on whatever is offered by others on the scheme. That way, you bypass the whole consumer system.

Tasks vary from tree planting to dry stone walling, footpath construction to creating wildlife habitats. You don't need to be an eco expert either – project leaders will show you the ropes and you're free to work at your own pace.

You'll make new friends, get some fresh air, exercise and help your local environment.

You could also find out if there are groups such as the Crags network – Carbon Rationing Action Groups, which has members in many towns and villages. The aim of each group is to cap carbon use and pay for excess emissions into a fund for energy-saving causes.

Normally, groups focus on just one or two measures – for example, heating, electricity, car and plane travel. The groups help members calculate their individual carbon footprints, and agree a target, perhaps 4500 kg of CO_2 per person.

Apart from helping you get your carbon footprint down, it's a marvellous way of meeting new people and widening your knowledge of the whole climate change topic. Often groups invite expert guests along to talk about their specialist field. In

Defining idea...
'If we do not change our direction, we are likely to end up where we are headed.'
– CHINESE PROVERB

a similar scheme, whole towns and communities are swapping to Fairtrade goods. You can start your own local scheme, and there is help and advice available at www.fairtrade.org.uk.

Not everybody wants to belong to a group or organisation, and there are many other less formal ways of tapping into your local community. Why not arrange a swap party, for instance, with people you work with, your children's friends' parents, neighbours or community groups? Swap parties are the eco-friendly way to get new books, clothes and CDs without contributing to a consumer drive. The idea is that everyone brings things along to the party that they don't want anymore – computer software, homemade produce, tools, old school textbooks, bottles of wine – it could be absolutely anything. Anything left over can be sold (with the money going to an environmental cause) or donated to charity.

You can do the swap thing online, too, through networks such as Freecycle and Swapexchange (www.swapxchange.org), who have local groups all over the world. Here you can swap your junk, and also find about car sharing schemes, trade swaps and even accommodation exchanges.

It doesn't have to be tangible items that you exchange. Many local communities operate local community trading groups where members exchange their goods and services with each other without payment.

135. An awfully green adventure

Swap theme parks for green parks and clothes shopping for bird spotting with a low cost, low carbon day out for the whole family.

How come days out with the kids always seem to involve long, hot journeys in cars which mysteriously end up full of fast food cartons, sweet wrappers and empty plastic water bottles?

But it doesn't have to be that way. For a start, you could go by train or bus, far more eco friendly forms of transport than a car. You'll probably get to see more of the countryside, and as you can usually get family travel discounts it can end up being cheaper, too. You could even just walk or cycle somewhere local. Even the smallest or quietest neighbourhood has its eco secrets to reveal, whether it's an ancient pond full of fascinating creatures or a patch of long grass where you can hunt for mini beasts.

Of course there are endless alternative technology centres, biodomes, wildlife centres and the like to visit, but you could also create your own agenda. It's good for children to learn that a great day out doesn't have to involve huge sums of money, and in fact some of the nicest places are absolutely free!

SEA-LIFE SPOTTING
The coast is an ideal place to appreciate the pleasures of the natural world. You'll be able to spot wildlife such as gulls, ducks, otters, seals, dolphins, porpoises and even whales, although you may have to join a boat trip for some of them.

Here's an idea for you...
Leave the car behind and have a day out by public transport and foot. Plan a trip with points of interest along the way – a hill for kite flying, a park or woodland, a ruin, a waterfall or a beach. Canals, old railway lines, waterside walks and nature trails are good venues in both town and country. Get the kids to note down features such as plants and animals, colourful rocks, churches and farms. Keep any walking doable for their age, and build in escape routes in case you need to bail out. Allow time for breaks, take a picnic or include a visit to a family-friendly pub or café.

Remember to take a good pair of binoculars. You can also take part in an organised beach clean-up, helping to tackle the growing problem of litter.

SPONSORED EVENTS
Get some fresh air and exercise and raise some cash for your favourite eco charity with a sponsored walk, cycle or swim. Ask friends and relatives for donations, and pick a route that is easy for the whole family. You could plan your own event, or join one of the many up and down the country. When you've finished you'll all have a real sense of achievement.

WIND FARMS
Some wind farms are open to the public and have visitor centres and viewing platforms. But even if they aren't, they are often sited near common ground and it is fascinating to go up close to these huge, white windmills and get a feeling for how much energy they produce.

Defining idea...
'Money is not required to buy one necessity of the soul.'
– HENRY DAVID THOREAU, American writer and philosopher

CONSERVATION

Many conservation bodies such as the BTCV (www2.btcv.org.uk) run one-day conservation tasks all over the UK. Tasks vary from tree planting to dry stone walling, footpath construction to creating wildlife habitats. It's the ideal way to make friends, get some fresh air, exercise and help your local environment.

NATURE TRAIL

Younger children enjoy having a simple task, so set them a list of ten things you're likely to come across on a local walk. Include easy-to-spot wildflowers, leaf skeletons, empty snail shells or round pebbles. You don't have to take what you find, you can just tick them off a list or snap them on a camera.

Or go on a mini beast safari. Find a patch of long grass and a couple of nets. Carefully sweep the nets through the grass a few times and then examine what you have caught before releasing them. Expect to find ladybirds, moths, dragonflies, butterflies, grasshoppers and caterpillars.

ORGANIC FARMS

Take the kids to see where food really comes from with a trip to a working organic farm. They'll be able to watch (and maybe even help with) cows being milked, eggs collected and crops planted or harvested. Younger children may be able to feed piglets, goats and lambs. Or visit a 'pick your own' farm.

Downshift and live your dream life

You've thoroughly relaxed the pace of your life and now you're revved up by your vision of how your life could be. You've glimpsed the future and it could be fabulous. The dream life beckons.

If you think you are ready for the ultimate in slowing down – downshifting – then we have the ideas to inspire you.

QUIZ: **All change – are you ready?**

1 You are preparing to downsize by working either part-time or changing profession to one that pays less. You...

- a. have already started cutting back on spending
- b. are spending as usual. You feel that you won't have the same expenses when you're not working in your present role so that will compensate for a drop in pay.

2 You have experience of working from home or spending long periods of time on your own with only children for company.

- a. Yes. For years, you've been pushing to work as much from home as possible.
- b. Not really. But you can't see that it's tougher than working as you are at the moment.

3 You have road-tested your dream life.

- a. Yes, you have lived in your chosen location, perhaps even renting a property in the area and trying your new life on for size as far as possible for a few weeks.
- b. No, that sort of experimentation is impossible right now, but every change has its drawbacks. It's just a matter of overcoming them as you meet them.

4 You are the sort of the person who likes their own company.

     a. Absolutely. Your idea of heaven is long walks on your own and whole days when you hardly speak to another soul.

     b. Not really. One of the reasons you want to downsize is so that you can reconnect with a community and get involved at a local level.

Mostly a)s

You have not only thought long and hard about your dream – you've put some part of it into action. Read *idea 139* for some more inspiration. Good luck.

Mostly b)s

You are still at the 'pre-contemplation' stage of planning your dream life. Jumping in too soon (that is, now) may lead to dissatisfaction which could be avoided with a little more preparation. Downsizing can be lonely, expensive to begin with and disorientating. Read *idea 136* for some ideas on changing your world from tomorrow and *idea 143* to get you focused.

136. The low-impact consumer

A new kind of consumer has been born, and the pared-down approach means spending less and getting things free.

The eco movement has spawned a whole new vocabulary, and one of the new buzzwords is 'freegan' (free + vegan). Dining on food leftovers from dustbins may have once been the preserve of tramps, but for some it is now more of a lifestyle choice. Greener-than-thou freegans veer away from consumerism and instead scavenge around to meet their needs, including finding food thrown out by shops and restaurants.

And why not? Supermarkets simply dump 5% of their food, most of it completely fit for consumption, as a faster, cheaper option to giving it away. The freegan movement is especially popular in America, particularly New York, where people regularly go through the bins together on 'trash tours', but is becoming more widespread elsewhere. If you fancy trying your hand as a freegan, stick to a few basic rules:

- Wear gloves when you scavenge, and use a torch at night.
- Don't ignore signs that say 'No Trespassing'.
- Leave the bin in the same condition as you found it.
- Examine use-by dates, and stick to packaged or bagged goods if you're not sure about something.
- Wash all the items you find before eating.
- Small to medium shops usually provide richer pickings than large supermarkets who tend to lock bins up.

Here's an idea for you...

Feeling bold – and hungry? Then try being a 'freegan' for a week, and discover first hand how much commercial food waste goes on. (A freegan could be described as a scavenger with a conscience, someone who survives on other people's leftovers!) Once you get going on your foraging mission you'll be astonished at how much food is dumped behind shops, markets and restaurants at the end of each day, much of it fit for purpose but all destined for the local landfill site. If you're squeamish you don't have to eat what you salvage – although you certainly could – but it'll give you a snapshot of how much food is routinely thrown out by our health and safety-obsessed society.

Skips: Skips outside houses or other buildings undergoing renovation may just seem full of junk, but to the dedicated low-impact consumer they are a treasure chest for 'skipping' or 'dumpster diving'. You can usually assume that anything in a skip isn't wanted, but if you're not sure ask the property owner before carting it away.

Precycling: You can cut down on waste by 'precycling', preventing waste before it happens: bringing your own packaging, buying in bulk, avoiding junk mail and disposables, extending the life of what you've got and not buying what you don't need. Ardent precyclers carry their own little kit: a washable container, a set of cutlery, a cloth napkin or handkerchief, a bottle of water and a reusable shopping bag.

relax and enjoy life

Freecycling: If you don't want it, pass it on. There are several free goods swapping web-based organisations, notably Freecycle (www.freecycle.org), made up of many local groups across the world. Freecycle groups match people who have things they want to get rid of with people who can use them, keeping usable items out of landfills, reducing consumerism and lessening the impact on the earth.

Wild foraging: Instead of buying industrially grown, pesticide sprayed foods shipped half way around the world, get back to your roots and find and harvest food growing wild in your own community.

Free events: Make the most of free-for-all events where you can exchange goods instead of discarding them, share skills, give presents, eat food, dance, listen to music, sing and generally have fun.

Car-sharing: Whether it's called 'lift-sharing', 'ride-sharing' or 'car-sharing', it pretty much comes down to the same thing – sharing a car for a journey rather than driving alone. The environmental benefits are obvious, as are the financial ones. The Internet is good place to start to find out about local schemes, or your council may have information.

Allotments and community gardens: Once you've paid the rental for your patch, everything you grow in your allotment is your own, meaning you can have a year-round supply of fresh fruit and veg completely free.

Bicycle collectives: Find out about groups that facilitate community sharing of bicycles, restore found and broken bikes, and teach people how to do their own bike repairs.

137. Walk, don't run, out of the day job

Here we'll focus on the key financial issues involved in kissing goodbye to the corporate life in order to do your own thing.

Except for an élite few, those of us in a salaried job are unlikely to see our pay increase by 25 per cent this year. It's not the way things happen. Pay scales, salary review processes and the like are not the backdrop against which dramatic pay rises tend to happen.

This can make heading for the open road of self-employment – where there's no inherent cap on earning potential – seem like an attractive alternative. As organisations continue to downsize, outsource and generally give growing numbers of staff the boot, there are increasing opportunities for us to trade the company car for the mixed joys of working for ourselves.

Look, it's not my job to give you career advice or tell you whether this would be a good move for you personally, but you do need to be aware of the financial implications of going self-employed...and it's not all good news.

A move from salaried work to fee-earning work carries with it greater autonomy and the promise of increased income, but without the security provided by an employer's remuneration and benefits package.

Here's an idea for you...
When you set up on your own, there will be nobody to insist that you put in place a new pension plan, increase your life assurance cover and so on. It becomes your call, and your call alone. Don't forget these, and check what insurance is compulsory. Some public liability insurance will probably be required if the people need to visit your premises. You may also need it if you visit the premises of your clients/customers, say to service equipment.

When you stop working for a company, they stop paying you a salary. Alright, that may hardly qualify as a revelation, but have you thought about the whole raft of benefits that disappear along with your final pay cheque? The company pension goes, your death-in-service benefit goes, and you are no longer covered by group insurance schemes for public liability (the 'health and safety' insurance that protects you and visitors to your company in the event of accidents).

You'll also be saying goodbye to the world where the monthly salary cheque is for a predictable amount and hits your bank account on a predictable date. In its place will be...well, who knows what? Chances are that your income stream will flow in fits and starts, at least initially. Do you have a financial cushion in place to underwrite your living expenses until your business picks up momentum?

According to a report by NatWest Bank, around 400,000 new businesses are launched each year in the UK. You've doubtless heard some of the horror stories about the number of new businesses that fold within a few years, sometimes just a few months. The stories are pretty much true. On average, 20 per cent of new businesses crumple within 12 months, with over 50 per cent disappearing within three years.

Defining idea...
'Your career is literally your business. You own it as a sole proprietor. You have one employee: yourself. You are in competition with millions of similar businesses: millions of other employees all over the world. You need to accept ownership of your career, your skills and the timing of your moves. It is your responsibility to protect this personal business of yours from harm and to position it to benefit from the changes in the environment. Nobody else can do that for you.'
– ANDY GROVE, *Only the Paranoid Survive*

There are a number of finance-related reasons why your new business might go to the wall:

- Overestimating sales and underestimating how long it takes to achieve them

- Underestimating costs

- Failing to control costs ruthlessly

- Losing control over cash, i.e. carrying too much stock, allowing customers too long to pay, paying suppliers too promptly

- Underpricing

Look, there are financial upsides to being self-employed, not least of all because the tax regime is still a very favourable one. And if you make a roaring success of your business idea, you definitely have a big opportunity to put your corporate salary in the fiscal shade. The point I'm trying to get over is that the financial dice aren't entirely loaded in favour of self-employment. Please don't underestimate the benefits of salaried work in a rose-tinted rush to be your own boss. There may be gold in them thar hills but it will still need some digging out.

138. It's a team game

It's probably easier to live life to the full if we have people around us who support and encourage us.

We all know that teamwork is critical and yet for many of us it's a challenge. We often end up in competition with people rather than working with them.

THE FIRST TEAM

The first team that we become aware of in life is, of course, the family. When I was growing up, I don't think I ever realised this or thought of it in that way. Did my family work as a team? Only very rarely. I had an older brother and sister who were six and seven years older than me respectively and I must have been a complete nuisance to them virtually all the time. I wanted to be part of whatever they wanted to do, and they must have spent more time thinking up ways to get me out of the way than actually having fun. Dad was an amazing man and I totally adored him and can still clearly remember one thing that we occasionally used to do together where I felt important and part of his 'team'. He had a passion for fast cars, and the older he got the faster they got. He used to take them for test drives, which included timing how fast they could go from 0 to 80 miles per hour. I was in charge of the stopwatch and, boy, did I feel proud. However, did we ever sit down as a family and think about how we could all effectively work and play together? Did we ever ask ourselves what our different strengths were and what we could bring to the family unit? Sadly, never. Even sadder is the fact that I didn't recognise how incredibly powerful this could be until after my own children had grown up and so I missed the opportunity to do it with them as well.

Here's an idea for you...

Get your family together and draw up a vision for your ideal family – how it would be, how it would feel and what it would be doing. Discuss the strengths that each person might bring to this vision, the role each person would choose to play and the behaviour they may want to demonstrate. Now see how committed and determined each person is to creating that ideal. This process could be equally powerful at work with your team.

A DIFFERENT APPROACH

One of the things I discovered about myself in my period of huge growth following my many mistakes was that I didn't feel it was OK to ask for help. I thought that if I couldn't do it all for myself then I wasn't good enough. The other thing I discovered was that I was even less comfortable if I was in a position where I had to work with someone else. I really didn't like it if they wanted to do something differently to me. I wanted them to do it the same way as I would have done.

Defining idea...

'The way a team plays as a whole determines its success. You may have the greatest bunch of individual stars in the world, but if they don't play together, the club won't be worth a dime.' **– BABE RUTH**

So, what's teamwork about? It's about knowing what you want to achieve, having a clear vision and then agreeing who has what strengths and abilities to bring to the party. Then each individual might think of all the ways that they could both do their bit and encourage and support everybody else to do theirs. Communication is critical to teamwork – ensuring that everyone knows how their bit is going so that any decisions that need to be made can be made with absolute certainty that all the necessary information is available. In my experience working in business, this is where it goes wrong nearly every time. Individuals can get so carried away with their part of the job that they forget what impact their decision could have on someone else's area, which can cause chaos and upset.

139. A dose of reality

You've decided to downshift. You've brimming with enthusiasm, but who's that in the corner with a face like thunder? Make sure the family shares your dreams before you go too far!

It's all very well daydreaming about your downshifted Shangri-la but without your family's agreement and support you may as well stop now because it won't come to pass.

Downshifting is a major, life-changing event. If you have a partner and/or children, they must share your dream or you are doomed to fail. Major lifestyle changes are stressful, and you will need support. If your partner is coerced into moving to a smallholding in the country and his or her natural habitat is a swanky wine bar or Harvey Nicks, you will both regret it.

With your partner on board, you're more than half way there because you will have someone to share the challenges – and there *will* be challenges – as well as the triumphs. If he or she is ambivalent, you have a serious PR job on your hands. It may help if you point out the reasons you need to downshift. Talk about the way in which your day-to-day work adversely dominates your life. The technology that makes your work easier can make your life harder, for example: you are available almost twenty-four hours a day, via e-mail, mobile phone and instant messaging. It's hard to leave the office behind when you take the technology home.

Here's an idea for you...
Before you sit down to have 'the talk' with your partner, prepare as though you are
going to a business meeting – think things through carefully, do your homework
and prepare your arguments. Talk reasonably about your ideas – hard when you are
feeling passionate, but necessary! Calculate the minimum you will need to live on
in your new life, and explain how you will meet those costs. Explore different ways
of earning an income, perhaps by working as a freelance. You need a safety net, and
you need savings. Ideally, you should set aside enough money to keep you for six
months before you begin.

Talk about what work is doing to the pair of you. Are you healthy? Or are you
victims to one illness after another? Do you feel constantly tired? That may mean
you are overworking, or it may mean you are becoming depressed by the
circumstances of your life. Do you drink too much? Alcohol is often used as a quick
fix to relax after a 'hard day', and that easily turns into a habit. Do you regularly
skip meals because you are too busy? Or do you 'comfort eat' to crush down the
feelings of stress and powerlessness that modern working conditions create?

You may have found that your personal relationships have all become work
centred, so even social occasions are bogged down by discussions about office
matters. Your partner may feel that your work dominates your life to the point at
which downshifting becomes not just desirable, but necessary. Make no mistake, if
you downshift – particularly to live on a smallholding – you will still be incredibly
busy. The work is hard, takes many hours and like any other form of work it
expands to fit the time available. But although you will not have more time, the
time you do have can be much more flexible. You will be able to spend more time
working side by side with your partner, working towards a common goal, which
can be very cementing for your relationship. You will also be able to be flexible
about childcare, sharing the labour more equally, and spending more time with
your children.

Defining idea...
'Change. It has the power to uplift, to heal, to stimulate, surprise, open new doors,
bring fresh experience and create excitement in life. Certainly it is worth the risk.'
– LEO BUSCAGLIA, Lecturer and counsellor

I have found that when I spend more time with my hands in the soil, it's like I am
literally *grounding* myself. I become less short-tempered and more nurturing.
Without going 'New Age' on you now – just when you were listening – I've
discovered that I need that contact with the natural world to function properly. The
irony is, after making the momentous decision to give up work outside the home
and write full time, I have found myself busier than ever. It is too easy to get into a
spiral: if I take on that contract, I can buy a greenhouse; if I take on that project, I
can buy more goats; if I write that book, it will pay for that building work. I end up
working longer hours than I did before I left the rat race. Guard against losing sight
of your aims and being seduced back onto the treadmill.

140. Happy homebody

Is commuting getting you down? Do workplace politics leave you cold? Consider working from home and leave all that stress behind you.

Take my commute, for example. I travel all the way down the stairs, turn left, make a cup of coffee, sit down and the day begins. Bliss, in my view! But is working from home right for you?

Ask yourself, what do you like about the work you are doing now? If you are thinking about downshifting to the country, and moving towards self-sufficiency, constant crowds are probably not your 'thing'. But if you enjoy office banter, revel in 'teambuilding' exercises, delight in office politics, and crave the next instalment of gossip around the water cooler, working from home may not be for you.

However, you may prefer to have more chances to order your own day. Working at home gives you the opportunity to organise your work so that if you need to go to a meeting at school, or visit a nearly empty open garden, you can. That doesn't mean homeworking is all about slacking – you still need to get the work done, but you can do it at a time that suits you and your family.

(Incidentally, don't get into a work ethic kick – working at home just as you did in the office. Taking time to eat lunch in the garden, or a bath in the afternoon recharges your batteries and makes you more productive.)

Here's an idea for you.....
Put out feelers and start developing a support network. Whatever type of work you do, there's sure to be an online community set up to support it, for instance. I belong to several writing communities, and have made good friends who are able to provide sound advice as well as companionship. It is also worth looking for local face-to-face groups in your nearest town. Your local government offices or library may well hold details of these community-based groups.

It's not just small children who benefit from more time with you. Teenagers like having easy access to a parent, too – and not just for handouts! Being available at incidental times of the day gives you the opportunity for many more of the 'casual' chats teenagers have with you in passing – when they tell you about the stuff that really matters in their lives.

ARE YOU LONESOME...?
Working at home can be isolating. Before you decide to work at home, check that you will enjoy the peace and calm. If you feel lonely and crave company, homeworking may not be for you. If you are happy with your own company, go for it. I find that my writing demands quite a high degree of concentration, so I like to minimise distractions – and working at home during the quiet of the day helps me. If I want company, I go out – it's as simple as that.

The main disadvantage of homeworking is the likelihood of distraction. Beware the household tasks that suddenly shout at you as you gaze round the room; shoo away the cats that flop down thunderously on a keyboard, or decide to play football with your equipment; ignore dogs that noisily demand walks – but most of all, let your friends and family know that sometimes you must not be disturbed.

Defining idea...
'**Normal** is getting dressed in clothes that you buy for work and driving through traffic in a car that you are still paying for in order to get to the job that you need so you can pay for the clothes, cars and the house that you leave empty all day in order to afford to live in it.' – **ELLEN GOODMAN, columnist**

I'm not sure whether some people don't actually believe that you are working because you are at home, but the interruptions are regular. You have to decide which ones are acceptable or welcome – good friends who ring up and ask if they can call in for coffee and won't be offended by a refusal – and which you have to discourage.

I have a writer friend who actually takes her car down the street in the morning so people don't know she is at home. It sounds extreme but it works for her. You must develop your own strategies.

476

141. Getting down to business

Have you always fancied being your own boss and starting your own business? Think carefully about the pros and cons to save you from exchanging one sort of stressful life for another.

You may have decided to combine a downshifted lifestyle with starting your own small business to help you to take control of your life. Make sure you are being realistic.

New start-ups can be exciting, and the thought of being your own boss is attractive. However, think whether you really want to exchange one life-consuming job for another – even if you like The Boss better! It is possible to combine a business start-up with downshifting, but be cautious.

When I got married we were poor students and needed to do things on the cheap. I bought some netting and hand edged it, and made my own veil, stitching freshwater pearls and coral beads all over it. I ended up being commissioned by people via family and friends to make others. I phoned the offices of various wedding magazines and told them about my unique work. Photos of my creations appeared in all of the glossies. Voila – I was the proud owner of an organically developed business, growing out of a niche in a specialised market.

That is the key to combining a business with downshifting. Make sure the business grows out of an interest you have, such as craft working, writing, growing and selling vegetables or whatever it is you enjoy – and are good at. Make sure the

Here's an idea for you...
Ignore the scammers and pyramid sellers and search online yourself for ideas
about the types of business that might suit you. The Work at Home Moms site
(wahm.com) is interesting, and not just for mothers. Entrepreneur.com is another
source of low-cost ideas for business start-ups. Remember to keep your BS
detector on full alert and be careful if you sign up for any newsletters – they
might sell your e-mail address to other companies and leave you with thousands
of extra junk mails.

business fits into your life, rather than taking it over. If you do decide to start a
business as a part of your downshifted lifestyle, think small. If you do not want to
think small, you are probably not looking for a simplified life, and you'll probably
never be able to truly downshift.

By all means go for a big start-up, supported by venture capital, if that is your
dream. However, if you do, forget about spending more quality time with your
family or growing your own fruit and vegetables because you simply won't have
time.

WHAT CAN I DO?
You can possibly cash in on the e-commerce revolution working from home,
depending on what it is you have to sell. For example, eBay is not just used by
people supplementing their income and decluttering their houses; there are also
people on the site who run full-scale shops. Many of these are people working
from home and selling goods they have made themselves, such as candles, woven
willow goods, soaps and bath bombs. Others specialise in a particular line of used
goods – kitchenalia, toys and models, clothes or books. Others sell specialised
goods for a niche market, such as gothic clothing, metaphysical goods, or craft
materials.

Defining idea...
'Opportunity is missed by most because it is dressed in overalls and looks like work.'
– THOMAS ALVA EDISON

It costs little to set up an e-shop and you can also sign up to online banking facilities such as Bidpay and Paypal. These charge a fee per transaction, but it means you can accept immediate payment for items rather than waiting for a cheque to clear.

You can also sell goods at markets or even from your home. I know one woman who runs a very successful business from an outbuilding on her smallholding, buying, selling and renting out baby and toddler equipment. I know a farmer's wife who runs a dress exchange in a similar way, keeping a whole area supplied with posh frocks. I also have a friend who sells New Age supplies, such as oils, crystals and books, from a room in her house, mail order only. She targets appropriate publications for advertising and takes stalls at New Age fairs to promote her business.

I know other folks who sell services, such as accounting, tutoring, pet sitting and photography. There are as many 'work at home' jobs as there are downshifters. You just have to find the one that is right for you.

142. Release your creative self

No time for that novel you've always wanted to write? Want to take time to look at the scenery - and paint it? Slowing down gives you the chance to get your creative juices flowing.

We all have the capacity for creativity. It may be expressed in many ways – whether that's music, garden design or weaving – but we all need time to connect with our creativity to feel whole.

One of the best things about slowing down for me has been reconnecting with my creative self. That sounds pompous, but it really is as important as that. Unless you are very lucky, your creative skills are unlikely to be used in your everyday working life. You become creatively constipated and your ideas will not flow; you will be unable to think freely and laterally. It takes creative thinking to come at a problem from a fresh direction to find a solution.

You may find time to have a creative hobby, such as scrap booking or painting; but if you downshift, creativity becomes part of your everyday life. The problems you are faced with every day – and let's not gloss this over; they will be many and various – force the creativity cells to spark up and fly. Let's face it, if you have moved to a smallholding in the country and decided to be as self-sufficient as possible, you are not going to want to (or be able to) throw money at problems, or call in immediate specialist help.

Here's an idea for you...
Don't get bogged down by some outdated, teacher-engendered view of yourself as 'not artistic'. Allow yourself to explore a variety of different types of creative activity. Book yourself on some taster courses at the local college or community centre, or look at books in the library to find something that inspires you. Remember, it doesn't have to be traditional art: it could be weaving, cooking, web design, graphics, garden design – whatever takes your fancy. Don't forget to look online for inspiration too.

As a smallholder, you have to use your innate cunning to solve problems, and that involves creativity. Problem with slugs? The downshifter's answer is more likely to be crushed eggshells and cloches cut from plastic bottles than expensive electrified copper-gizmos. Want to build raised beds? The downshifter is likely to use old boards or planings from the sawmills as bed edgings rather than expensive (and not aesthetically pleasing) plastic edging from the garden centre.

Creativity is the downshifter's best friend. Apart from the problem-solving aspect, creativity can make us more at home inside ourselves. That doesn't mean we all have to rush off on some dippy-hippie body painting retreat – although, actually, that sounds like fun – but it does mean that downshifting gives you the space to think about what you would like to try. There is nobody looking over your shoulder telling you what you can't do, so silence your internal critic and have a go!

Until we moved to our smallholding, I'd never had a go at weaving willow structures, although I'd always fancied it, and admired willow tunnels at open organic gardens. I'd always thought 'I could do that' – but never had. Now I have made both living willow and dry woven structures, including edging for beds, and a living willow igloo. I have planted hundreds of willow whips of different colours, from yellow to purple, and increase my stock each year. If I was not a writer, I think I would probably be happy running courses in creating willow structures and art.

Defining idea...

'Creativity is a type of learning process where the teacher and pupil are located in the same individual.' – **ARTHUR KOESTLER**

In the renovations we have carried out since we moved here, we have converted the dingy, corridor-like kitchen into a fabulous art and craft studio, where the whole family keeps ongoing projects and craft resources. If the resources are out, on display in baskets and tubs, they inspire you as you pass by, and even just looking at them gives me great pleasure and enriches my life.

We stripped the plaster off the walls (three layers, including the original horse hair, beetle wings and lime!). The mess was horrific, but after many days scrubbing we had sparkly sandstone walls, which I have pointed myself. I filled larger gaps with small fossils. Now, I wouldn't like to do it for a living – it was a labour of love – but without moving to this type of country ramshackle property, it would never have occurred to me to have a go. That's at the heart of downshifting; the way we are constantly prodded by our situation to explore new activities. Have a go – you never know what skills you will discover!

143. Should I stay or should I go? Moving to the country...

The countryside has a culture all of its own and life moves at a different pace. This can be wonderful - if you adjust.

Moving from urban areas to the country should be approached as though you are emigrating. Plan to expect a shock to your system. The countryside has a special energy all of its own, but sometimes you have to look quite hard to see it! Rather than the bright, brash energy of city life, the energy of the countryside throbs along unobtrusively under the surface. 'Incomers' (namely, anyone who has not lived in the area all their lives, and cannot trace their family back to antecedents such as Great Aunt Betsy who was a maid up at the Big House) can find this all a bit baffling and frustrating. They react to the inevitable delays and seeming lack of any sense of urgency with frustration.

Get used to things moving more slowly in a small village. Queues form as people talk about their kids, bunions, the weather – whatever. This can be annoying when you are rushing to send a package to the city people you freelance for, because they are still moving on 'townie time' and don't appreciate the delays. But isn't this different rhythm one of the reasons you moved to the country?

If you are to enjoy rural life, you must do your homework about where you live, who else lives there and what they are like. It is important to scope out the neighbours, especially if you are fairly remote. It is very handy to know there is a friendly face – and, more importantly, willing hands – if you have an emergency. Our neighbours stepped in to take our daughter down to the village to school, for

Here's an idea for you...
If your downshifted home is next to or near farmland, make friends with the farmer sooner rather than later. If you have a relatively small acreage of land, you may find it hard to keep the grass cut, for example, and the local farmer may well be able to help you out for a small fee. It also helps to know when 'things' are going on – the awful stench of silage may only be around for a couple of days a year but you'll definitely want to avoid it coinciding with a garden reception for your daughter's wedding!

example, when I broke my leg (during a drunken moonlit hedgehog rescue – enough said!).

There are many places to meet locals, including of course the pub, the shops and the local school (if you have children!). There will also be many and varied local events for you to join in with.

When you first arrive, try to be unobtrusive. You only have yourself to blame when people laugh scornfully if you roar into town in your newly purchased 4 x 4 and designer country casuals. Instead, ease in gently. It's hard when folks peer at you and you feel like the new kid in school, but try to think before you speak, too. It's very easy to come across as brash and patronising if you join a group and immediately

Defining idea...
'The best things that can come out of a garden are gifts for other people.'
– JAMIE JOBB, author

try to make a mark. Sit back instead; listen and take the measure of the place.

You will find many new friends, often in the strangest places. I have some really unusual pals these days, but have learned some very valuable lessons about what will grow locally, raising various types of stock and what works *here*. You don't have to accept everything as though it was handed down on tablets of stone (keep your bullshit detector set to maximum sensitivity – country folks can have a weird sense of humour!) but people who have lived in an area for many years have information and wisdom you will find nowhere else. I even know how to skin, stuff and mount a weasel these days – and they don't teach you *that* in most cities!

How do you know when you stop being an incomer? Actually, it's unlikely that you ever will, especially to the old die-hards. But you'll know you've been *accepted* when you find bunches of surplus carrots, baskets of blackberries and dahlias wrapped stylishly in newspaper on your step – they had too many; they were passing: see?

10 ways to become richer by going slower

Prepare yourself for the downshifted life by learning to live on less.

1. Cut up store cards – they're a grossly expensive form of credit and getting rid of them will mean less time trailing around shops.

2. Run through some possible financial futures and what you might do if circumstances change – rates go up, redundancy threatens. 'Scenario planning' can help you feel in control. This might slow down your rate of purchasing.

3. Shred a credit card or two. With less credit, you'll feel freer.

4. Don't save – if you have any debt. The interest you earn on your savings will never be as high as the interest you lose on an equal amount of unpaid debt.

5. Set a budget for Christmas and make it a challenge to find delightful gifts within your budget. This means shopping earlier which will, yes, slow you down.

6. Review everything you spend on – cable TV, mobile phone, utility bills – and find six ways to save money. For instance, subscriptions to magazines are cheaper than news-stand purchases. It takes time but ultimately it will save you time and money.

7. Join the library – another nice, slow place to hang out.

8. Pay bills by direct debit, including credit card minimum payments. Less hassle, thus giving you time.

9. Go to matinees at the cinema – they're often cheaper and quieter – or use the special 'buy one cinema ticket get one free' offer currently operated through one mobile phone network every Wednesday.

10. Bike or walk rather than driving four days out of seven. Slower. Better for your health. Cheaper. What's not to love? At least use public transport four days out of seven if at all possible. It usually gives your brain some space from stressing even if it does take longer.

144. LETS make a difference

LETS is a system of local community-based mutual aid networks. It is ideal for downshifters who have limited financial resources.

People in LETS (local exchange trading system or scheme) barter goods and services with each another. There is no money involved! The LETS movement started in Canada, but now extends around the world. A number of likeminded people form a group, putting together a list of the skills and goods wanted and offered by the members of the group. This list is sent out to members regularly, and the fun begins!

The knowledge and skills of the people who live in an area make up its real wealth. LETS keeps this wealth working in the community. People who have developed a wide range of skills and abilities are highly valued members of the LETS community – and these are people who may not have wealth or high-powered jobs in wider society. Elderly people, with a lifetime of knowledge and experience, are highly valuable to LETS groups. People who work full time caring for their children may have skills and experience that are poorly valued by society at large; however, their talents are recognised and further developed within the LETS community.

LETS groups can build members' self-esteem by empowering people and helping them to make their life more comfortable and debt free. Because they can get local goods and services through LETS, they spend less money and disposable income increases. LETS groups are different to conventional society, where the labours of some are valued more than others. Members set a value on their own labour and goods, and equality is maintained.

Here's an idea for you...
If you think you haven't got much to offer a LETS group, think again. Start by making a list of all the things you love doing. This may be massage, gardening, cooking, childcare, craft work, anything! Then look at the items cluttering up your house that you don't want or need and list them. Then make a list of the goods or services you'd like to have access to, but don't, because you can't afford them or can't justify spending money on them. Once you have your lists, you're ready to trade!

People feel less isolated if they are part of LETS. As part of an interdependent community, members have a reason to contact new people without 'cold calling', as it were. Elderly people, supporting parents, and single-income families with a stay-at-home parent can easily build new contacts and make friendships through a LETS introduction.

LETS members pay a small registration fee and are given a registration number. This number is needed for trading to begin. Members' lists of the goods and services they have to offer, and what they want to acquire, are published on a trading sheet. There is usually a charge (in LETS credits) per line for the listing – this pays the person who compiles the sheet. Regularly check your list to make sure it is up to date.

Many groups have regular meetings, which have a social aspect as well as an opportunity to trade. They tend to have a 'bring and share' meal, and trade goods, gardening equipment, plants and seeds as well as services. Groups also hold LETS Project Days. These are days of activity as a group, organized to carry out a specific task. This can either be something for the benefit of your LETS group, such as setting up a website, producing literature or group promotion, or it can be for the benefit of an individual LETS member, perhaps someone moving house, renovating a house or a gardening project. All participants earn LETS points for their efforts.

Most groups elect a LETS Committee at an Annual General Meeting. These maintain LETS accounts and update trading sheets.

Defining idea...
'Money was invented so we could know exactly how much we owe.'
– CULLEN HIGHTOWER, US salesman and writer

When a member finds someone offering a skill they need, or an item, they contact the person offering it and agree a price. The 'purchaser' pays for the service with a LETS cheque. Cheque books are issued to members and cheques are written out and given to the member who provides the goods or services. These are then sent to the group treasurer, who adjusts the members' accounts with debits or credits. The payments in your account may be used with any group member – it doesn't have to be a one-to-one trade between you and the person you traded with.

LETS is a great way to improve the quality of your life and the quality of the lives of others. The system rejects the consumerism that drives society today, where people are judged by what they have more than by what they do and are. And with LETS you can't get into consumer debt – part of what the downshifting ethos rejects. LETS also encourages you to become part of your community, which is crucial to becoming a successful and happy downshifter.

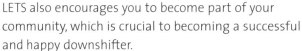

145. Look before you leap

If you are wondering how to get started with downshifting, becoming self-sufficient or productive gardening, you need to do your research.

There are many organisations, books, websites and courses out there designed to help you. Here's the pick of the bunch.

BOOKS – I always start with books. Apart from being a writer, I'm a voracious reader. If you are like me, you'll like to pore over them, and dream your dreams – and never more so than with downshifting. Relevant books vary from extensive manuals to pamphlets, but they have all been really useful to me. You will find most of these books at the library, or you may prefer to buy them (many turn up in second-hand bookshops).

You won't get far on a book list about downshifting without bumping into John Seymour's ***Complete Guide to Self-Sufficiency*** (ISBN: 0-751-36442-8) in one imprint or another. This weighty tome covers everything from allotment gardening to scything and thatching. It has such a wealth of information that I would recommend it above most others.

Home Farm by Paul Heiney (ISBN: 0-751-30461-1) is another favourite of mine. It has lots of well-organised information and is easy to dip into at the level you want – be it garden farm, home farm or smallholding. The pictures – many of the author and his family – are great for fuelling dreams of what might be.

Henry Doubleday Research Association, ***Encyclopaedia of Organic Gardening*** (ISBN: 0-751-33381-6) is a 'must have' for me – and anyone who wants to garden organically. It is packed with useful, hands-on information and I return to it often. If organic gardening is of interest to you, you should join the HDRA or similar

Here's an idea for you...
Join a local allotment, community gardening or smallholding association. Apart from
the material benefits, such as cheap seeds, tools, etc., there is a wealth of knowledge
among members. You could even set up a 'lend and exchange' group, with seed
swapping and larger tool loans, on a co-operative basis with fellow members.

organisation. Apart from being a source of invaluable advice, you can also join the
Heritage Seed Library and gain access to many heritage varieties of delicious
vegetables that you just cannot buy. You can also very cheaply buy pamphlets that
tell you everything you need to know to get started as an organic gardener.

Cottage Economy by William Corbett (ISBN: 0-953-83250-3) is a classic. The book
was written in the 19th century with a view to improving the health of country
labourers, but don't let that put you off. It has lots of useful – and cheap – ideas,
and Corbett was a grumpy old bugger, so it makes for quite an amusing read!

Food For Free by Richard Mabey (ISBN: 0-00219060-5), together with its companion
Plants With a Purpose, enriched the childhood of my sister and I as we gathered all
manner of wild foods and lugged them home, much to my mother's horror. It's
invaluable.

I could go on, as a book addict. But you get the idea. Read the books, dipping in and
out to get an idea of what is – or can be – involved in becoming more self-sufficient
at the level that suits you and your family.

Defining idea...
Learning is not compulsory... neither is survival.'
– W. EDWARDS DEMING, Management guru

MAGAZINES – without doubt, the number one 'must have' magazine for downshifting gardeners is ***Kitchen Garden Magazine***. I've subscribed since I read the first issue and still wait eagerly for the magazine to arrive each month. It's full of 'readers' gardens' and allotments. As well as expert advice on growing, it has contributions from Sue Hammon, a chicken expert. Sue runs the Wernlas Collection, a supplier of rare breed chickens. Her columns have been invaluable to me as I have set up new trios of hens and bantams, etc.

A new magazine, ***Grow Your Own***, published by Matthew Tudor, is also proving useful. **Country Smallholding** is an interesting buy, with real life stories, and *Smallholder* magazine has some useful articles.

I have a set (bought second-hand) of a part-work I remember my parents collecting week by week in the 1970s. It's called ***Grow Your Own*** and it's well worth looking out for because it is full of practical, inexpensive ideas for growing food in the garden.

WEBSITES AND FORUMS – useful sites I know include **rivercottage.net, countrysmallholding.com, smallholder.co.uk**, and **thekitchengarden.co.uk**. They are all packed with great ideas. You could, of course, do worse than join my own forum ('Downshifting to the good life' on yahoo groups) and chat with others following the downshifting dream.

COURSES – many courses are available at agricultural colleges. Search for colleges near to you on the internet. You can also search for specific local courses in green woodworking, willow weaving, organic gardening and the like.

146. Downshifting with children

Many people who decide to downshift have kids. In fact, your kids may well be the reason you decide to downshift. What's the downshifting experience like for them - rural heaven or pastoral purgatory?

With its generally lower levels of pollution, lower crime levels, and space and freedom to be outdoors, the countryside is an attractive option to some parents who see their children becoming prisoners in their own urban homes.

The strong sense of community in rural areas supports family life. When everyone knows everyone else (and not only their names but also their lineage and, I suspect, blood group and sexual preferences!) you feel safer about letting your children out of your sight. It's not because bad things don't happen in the countryside; they do – paedophiles can be found anywhere and children will get into dangerous situations whether they are playing on urban building sites or around farm machinery. The difference is that in a small village people know the children and are more likely to keep an eye on them and let you know what's going on.

If you have very young children (under five), downshifting is great. Your children will still have access to toddler groups and playgroups, as in the city. However, the trendy baby-gymnastics, violin-playing, 'make a baby genius' groups, beloved of the professional classes in the city, are in very short supply – which I see as a good thing!

Here's an idea for you...
Involve your children in the decision to downshift – and how far you take it. Draw
up a list of pros and cons together, and discuss them fully. Air any qualms openly.
Talk to other families who have downshifted to get views from other children of a
comparable age to your own. (You can contact other families via downshifting
forums, smallholding groups, etc.)

Downshifting gives you the time to enjoy your children. When you are out at work
full time, you may see your child for just a few rushed moments in the morning on
the way to the child minder, and then for half an hour before bed at night. Do you
really want such a limited input in your child's life? Downshifting gives you the
opportunity to organise your time so you can go pond dipping on a bright spring
day, and work alongside tiny pairs of hands in the garden. That's priceless! Even if
you enjoy your work, it can't be compared with the pleasure you get from spending
unrestricted time with your children.

For children starting school, having downshifted parents is still a boon. You are
there to drop them off; you are there at home time. Whether your children are six
or sixteen, they still need adult ears to listen carefully to the story of their day. The
cup of coffee I have at 4 p.m. with my sixteen-year-old daughter keeps me in touch
with the vagaries of teenage girl angst. You are still busy as a downshifted parent,
but you are always available. Whether you are in a field spreading compost, or
working from a study at home, your children know they can get hold of you when
the inevitable crises loom.

495

Defining idea…

'Learn wisdom from the ways of a seedling. A seedling which is never hardened off through stressful situations will never become a strong productive plant.'
– STEPHEN SIGMUND, journalist and strategic communications specialist

School-aged children in the country probably get more freedom than their urban counterparts. Where traffic is less of a worry, it is easier for older schoolchildren to cycle to their friends' houses and there's more space for ballgames and den building. There is also likely to be a variety of clubs for children of this age group, run by the school, church and community centre.

Teenage children can find downshifting more of a challenge. If you are moving somewhere very remote, be aware of the strain this will put on your teenager. You will have thought about their journey to school, no doubt, but don't forget the difficulties he or she may face socially – and be prepared to do lots of chauffeuring.

147. Buying a smallholding

You have been growing vegetables and fruit for some time; you may even have some chickens. If you do decide to go the whole hog and buy a smallholding, what should you look for?

In the 1970s, there was a boom of urbanites moving to the country. In those days, derelict cottages with vast tracts of land could be bought for a song, and the new age of 'back to the land' pioneers began. Some early downshifters thrived, but for others it was a Utopian dream and they were ill-prepared for the reality. Lack of experience and the enormity of what they had taken on overwhelmed them. Many gave up and trudged back to town.

How can *you* avoid this? Firstly, be prepared and go into it with your eyes wide open. Scour the downshifting websites and visit smallholdings and open farms to get a feel for the life. Then you need to find the right smallholding for *you*. Check out different regions; drive around and take trips to find the areas you prefer.

Think about the type of smallholding you want to run. If you want to keep animals, uneven or steep fields are fine, especially for goats and sheep. If you mainly want to cultivate crops – especially in sufficient quantities to sell – you will need flatter land that's easier to work.

When you find a property, go several times and preferably in different weather. A smallholding on a summer's day may appear delightful, but it could be a much bleaker place in gales and driving rain! Walk round the land as well as looking at

Here's an idea for you...
Take a holiday in winter on a working farm in an area you favour. The trip won't give you a definitive experience, but it will give you an important taste of winter in the country. The days will be short and probably bitterly cold. Spend the majority of your time outside to see how it feels. Remember that livestock needs feeding and tending even in deep snow and high winds, and chores still need to be done. Look on this as an initiation!

the house and any buildings. Look at water supplies and fencing. Even if the fencing is falling down, it needn't put you off – but it does need to be factored in to the value you put on the smallholding, and what you are willing to pay. Get an idea of what it will cost to put anything right.

If you like the place and put in an offer, pay for a detailed survey. You may find many faults. Many old rural properties have been bodged together during the course of many years – even centuries – which is part of their charm. However, rubble walls will have been built before damp-proof courses arrived and attractive old beams may be full of rot. The survey results needn't put you off; they will just give you an idea of what you are getting into and what remedial costs may be required.

Defining idea...
'The trouble with the rat race is that even if you win, you're still a rat.'
– LILY TOMLIN, comedian and actress

Check the utilities connected to the house. Water is, of course, imperative – but does the property have mains water, or is it served by a well, bore hole or spring? In remote areas, mains water may not be available. Wells can dry up in hot weather. Be prepared to have any water tested for purity if necessary. If your water is not mains supplied, you will need to have it checked regularly anyway to avoid stomach upsets.

Whilst thinking about water, check for flooding hazards. What is the level of the land surrounding the house? Check that run-off rainwater will not flood the house from roadways or banks, for example, and don't overlook any watermarks on outside walls.

You should also consider what sort of heating and lighting is available. Many properties in rural areas are without gas because of the cost of piping in a supply. We have no gas supply, but we have oil fired central heating and wonderful open fires. If you consider relying on solid fuel for all your heating and cooking needs, be realistic because quite a lot of maintenance is involved. How much time do you want to spend chopping wood? Small amounts are fine (as the saying goes, it keeps you warm twice – once in the chopping and once in the burning), but large amounts take an inordinate amount of time. It's exhausting, too – and that's without hauling the unchopped wood.

It is also worth thinking about solar or wind power. Generous grants may be available for installation costs. We are currently adding both types of power not just because they are green energy sources, but also to give us an alternative source of energy to compensate for our tenuous connection to the national grid.

148. Get down and dirty

If you are trying to buy a smallholding check out the soil before you purchase the property – both the depth and type. Without good, hearty soil, your vegetables and fruit will never thrive.

Save yourself heartache later on. Grill the vendor about the land, and take good notice of what is growing already (even if it is just weeds). Ask permission to take samples. Don't be afraid to be cheeky. Turning over a hand trowel of soil (or, better still, a spadeful) will show how deep the soil is. If the soil depth is very shallow, you may have problems, so it is worth checking. But beyond the depth of the topsoil, how do you check what *type* of soil you are dealing with? Quite simply, test it. You need to know about your topsoil before you can think about what you can grow.

There are five main types of soil: sandy, clay, loam, chalky and peat. Sandy soil is light and easy to dig. If you pick up a handful, it will feel loose and a little gritty. In windy areas, this type of soil can even blow away! Water runs through sandy soil quickly, and nutrients can be leached out of the soil as the water drains away. All is not lost, however – a sandy soil can be improved by the addition of lots of organic matter such as compost, and well-rotted manure to make it more water retentive and bulky.

A clay soil is heavy, and can be hard to dig. When you try to dig a clay soil, it sticks to your spade, and your feet. A handful of clay soil will stick together if you add water. It will roll into a ball between your thumb and fingers. In dry spells, clay cracks and can become iron hard and inhospitable to plants; in wet spells,

Here's an idea for you...
Place a small amount of soil, about 5 cm, in a jar. Add water to fill the jar and shake it. Leave it to settle overnight. Any gravel and coarse particles such as grit and sand will settle on the bottom. Lighter, smaller particles will form a layer on top of this and any organic matter will float on the surface. If the gravel and sand layers are the biggest, you have sandy soil. The gritty layer above this shows you how much loam is present. If the clay layer – the tiny particles – is the thickest layer, you have a clay soil.

puddles may lay on the ground for days, drowning growth. Clay soil has very small particles, and the best way to improve this type of soil is to dig in plenty of organic material such as leaf mould and well-rotted compost, together with manure.

You can also help matters by digging in the autumn, leaving the large clods exposed to the cold weather and frost. This will help to break them down into a fine tilth. We have managed to create a rich, very productive soil here on clay using these methods. Be careful, though, not to tread on clay-based beds if you can avoid it. If the soil is compressed, the aeration is lost.

Loamy soil is dark and crumbly, and full of organic material. When you rub a handful between your fingers, it will feel smooth. Loam is great for growing most plants.

Chalky soil is pale, even to the point of looking grey. Again, water drains away quickly and you will need to dig in plenty of water retaining organic matter in the form of manure, compost and leaf mould.

Peat-based soil is confined to a few areas, but it is very fertile and water retentive, as the soil is made up from decomposed plants. However, it can be very acidic.

ALKALINE, NEUTRAL OR ACID?

The pH level of the soil can affect what will grow there. Most vegetables prefer a slightly acidic soil, with a pH of between 5 and 7 (neutral being 7). Potatoes, marrows and tomatoes like their soil slightly more acidic, at around 5 to 5.5. Brassicas prefer a slightly alkaline soil, with a pH of around 7.5.

So, it's time to get out the test tubes and indulge your mad scientist fantasies! You can buy simple pH testing kits from garden centres (both online and 'real'). You take soil samples from different parts of your garden or land and add different solutions to determine the pH balance of your soil. You match the solution colour to a supplied chart and the colour shows you the pH level of your soil samples.

If your soil is overly acidic, you can dig in lime to correct this. I tend to dig it in after I dig over ground to leave it to overwinter. The rain washes it through the soil, ready for spring planting. This only needs to be done every two or three years. If it is too acidic or alkaline, most plants cannot easily absorb the minerals and nutrients in the soil and they will be stunted.

149. Downshifting to another country

A restaurant in Spain or a guesthouse in Greece? Downshifting to warmer climes may be your ultimate dream, but it could go sour if you don't plan the move properly.

Think carefully about what problems you could face in not just changing your lifestyle, but changing countries too. People downshift to other countries for a variety of reasons. They may want to experience a different lifestyle, perhaps having had a taster while on holiday. Property may well be cheaper, offering the chance of a more relaxed lifestyle.

For many years, Spain has been a retirement destination for northern Europeans. More recently growing numbers of people are moving there to live and work, perhaps to less highly paid, but less stressful jobs.

Before you take the plunge, however, it is well worth taking a long hard look at the area you wish to move to, and your own motivation. Do your homework and you are much less likely to find yourself on the next plane home, sadder but wiser.

PROPERTY

With property prices continuing to rise sharply, buying an affordable family home with a decent garden can seem like an impossible dream for many young people wanting to settle and have children. Going on holiday has allowed people to see the standard of living and the cost of housing in other countries. It often seems so much cheaper, and the way of life can feel much more relaxed. Of course, it would do, to you ... you're on holiday!

Here's an idea for you...
Language teachers are in demand, so consider taking a course to teach your native tongue to your hosts. Teaching English as a foreign language (TEFL) is one such course. Then advertise. Even notices in shop windows can bear fruit. Work can then be done to supplement your income, even if you are planning to grow your own food.

Search around on property websites and specialist magazines to get a handle on the cost of property in the area you favour. It helps to have an idea of what you can expect for your money before you start looking seriously through agents.

Make sure you can afford to take holidays to your target areas to check out the services available. It can be very isolating moving to a new country, especially if you are not fluent in the language, so make sure you know how and where to seek information to make your projected move as smooth as possible. Are there any extremes of weather conditions? How hot does it really get? What's it like in winter – many areas surrounding resorts can bubble with activity in summer but a lot might shut down out of season. Once you start viewing properties, make sure you see your potential new home in winter or bad weather as well as on a hot summer's day.

LANGUAGE
It goes without saying that you need to learn the language of the country you have chosen – otherwise you will miss out on many aspects of life, including companionship. Children will learn quickly to communicate – perhaps because they are less self-conscious as well as being more linguistically adaptable. It can actually be more difficult to make sure they retain their native tongue, especially as they are totally immersed in the foreign language at school.

Help yourself by learning the basics of the language at least before you go. Sign up for evening classes. Watch and listen to the appropriate satellite TV channels and

Defining idea...
'Live as if you were to die tomorrow. Learn as if you were to live for ever.'
– MAHATMA GANDHI

radio stations. Watch your DVDs in the appropriate language (you have many options with modern DVDs) with subtitles in your native language at first.

Once you get to your destination, listen and interact as much as possible. The local market and shops are great places for meeting and talking with people. You learn a lot by jumping in at the deep end!

WORK
Be very clear about what you will be able to do to earn money. Make sure you know what permits or licences are needed before you can work or run a business, as well as the tax and insurance benefits you can expect. If you are working for yourself, the same applies. Be sure to do your homework before you depart to save extra stress when you arrive. It's amazing to watch TV programmes about people with no catering experience who decide to buy a bar abroad and then can't understand why it doesn't work out.

Similarly, if you are intending to live self-sufficiently, make sure you research what will and will not grow on your new property. Remember, orange or olive groves look idyllic but they are arid places – so, if you are not prepared to spend time and money on irrigation, your garden may well not be very productive.

505

Index